LIFE IN A JUNGLE

MY AUTOBIOGRAPHY

BRUCE GROBBELAAR

WITH RAGNHILD LUND ANSNES

deCoubertin
BOOKS

First published as a hardback by deCoubertin Books Ltd in 2018.

First Edition

deCoubertin Books, 46B Jamaica Street, Baltic Triangle, Liverpool, L1 0AF.

www.decoubertin.co.uk

ISBN: 978-1-909245-57-0

A CIP catalogue record for this book is available from the British Library.

Cover design and typeset by Leslie Priestley.

Printed and bound by Jellyfish.

To my parents,

Beryl Eunice and Hendrik Gabriel Grobbelaar

and my stepfather

Denys Davis, the gentle giant.

They all had a part of my upbringing

but only my mother had

sole guidance to whom I am today.

Contents

1

Pegged to the Ground

AT THE RAYLTON SPORTS CLUB AMONG THE ELEGANT, TREE-LINED Avenues of Rhodesia's capital, Salisbury, I found myself tied between two poles at the back of my dad's goal. It was Saturday afternoon, the focal point of the week. My mother was playing hockey on an adjacent field and my dad was keeping goal in the football match. I could only run three metres back and forth – so most of the time I would sit and study his movements in front of the goal. I was a child of two goalies: my dad minded the goal when playing football and was a cricket wicketkeeper too; meanwhile my mother was a hockey keeper. In other words, I was literally born to be a goalkeeper.

Life consists of many challenges and my family took on a big one when I was just two months old, moving from Durban in South Africa to Salisbury, the capital of Rhodesia. My father had been a driver of double-decker buses in South Africa and moved north to Rhodesia when a position on the railways became available. It was December 1957 and we all held South African passports, which presented some hurdles to pass before Rhodesian citizenship was granted the following year. Although I'd live in South Africa again on several different occasions, Rhodesia, later to be named Zimbabwe, became and remained my country.

My father, Hendrik Gabriel Grobbelaar, was the youngest of eleven brothers. He was a very handsome man. His eyes were hazel, which is the same colour as a lion's – half-brown and half-green, or like the colour of the grass in springtime in the savannah. He had a full head of dark hair. My dad was just a very free-living man, a Casanova who enjoyed his women, smokes and alcohol. He was always well dressed in trousers and a shirt. The only time I saw him in shorts was in sports outfits, either playing tennis, football or cricket. He was an accomplished sportsman and also played baseball and lawn bowls.

My mother, Beryl Eunice, was a stunning lady of five foot six. She made her dark hair wavy, had a straight nose, really pretty teeth and dark-brown eyes; that's where I got my eyes. She was the eldest of three girls. She dressed very elegantly and I remember the smart skirts she used to wear for her work as the accountant for a shoe store. She was very good at her job and later she opened up two shoe shops of her own in Bulawayo.

My family was vast. I had more than 70 first cousins whose roots stretched across southern Africa's colonial past. Many had fought on opposing sides in the Boer War, six decades before my birth. My father was born in the Transvaal and was a proud Boer. My mother descended from a Welsh Fusilier stationed in Cape Town Castle with his wife, my great-grandmother, during the Boer War. She was originally from the island of St Helena. She had given birth to my grandfather, Edward Ernest Banning, in Cape Town Castle and because it was designated 'home soil' it would give me and my siblings a claim on British citizenship.

Having left for Rhodesia, we lived in Sinoia (now Chinhoyi) for three months before moving on to Salisbury, the capital city now known as Harare. Including my grandparents, we lived in two garden apartments on Baker Avenue, which is today Nelson Mandela Avenue. I was the middle child so I found out early that I had to fend for myself. My mother had become a parent aged 28 and she bonded tightly with her first born, my sister Jacqueline Bridget. I came along two years later, then eight years after me my brother Mark Edward arrived – and he was my mother's little baby throughout our childhoods. Mum, of course, would only address us by our first and middle names when we were in trouble. I can still hear her now: 'Come here, Jacqueline Bridget…' It became a feature of our childhoods.

My first language was Afrikaans, and I spoke nothing else until I was seven. In the house we only spoke Afrikaans, as my Afrikaner father didn't allow us to speak English. That was his rule. My mother on the other hand was English-speaking, so when we started at school, the rule changed and she allowed us to speak English at home. After that, I didn't speak Afrikaans too often. I still remember it, even though I am a little rusty.

When I was six, we moved to another apartment. The same smells were always there: the vendors cooking mieles, or corn porridge, on the side of the roads on a fire drum in the dark or being boiled in big pots. That smell and the one of wood fires always take me right back to Rhodesia and my first years.

I loved the hustle and bustle of the place. The Avenues, the suburb of Salisbury where we lived, was a very Americanised place. The streets were one-way and avenues went across the other way in a grid system like in New York. So all the streets go east to west and the avenues go north to south. The city is absolutely beautiful in spring, because of the jacaranda trees. October, the height of spring in the southern hemisphere, has always been the best month to see Salisbury, as the avenues going to the city centre are covered in purple flowers.

Just to the south of the city was the Chitungwiza township. West was Arcadia, the industrial area of the city and the main black area. Due north was Mount Pleasant and to the east, the Borrowdale horse racing course. The nicest houses were in the northeast. We were living just outside the city on the south side. That was until my father developed Buerger's disease, an inflammation of the arteries and veins attributed to smoking. The pain, caused by a limited bloody supply to his legs, was troubling him, so he went to South Africa to have an operation when I was seven. My mother decided we were all returning to South Africa with him and we settled in Benoni, an old gold-mining town outside of Johannesburg, renowned for its lakes and horse stables.

I was enrolled at Rynfield Junior English School and it meant I was able to play football. In Benoni there was a junior Afrikaans school and a junior English school, and despite only speaking Afrikaans up to that point, I started going to the English school, which would prove vital for my football career. Had I gone to the Afrikaans school, I'd have played rugby instead.

We were in Benoni for about eighteen months and our neighbourhood was a real blue-collar place, with bungalow houses. Behind our backyard there was a big field we had to cross on our way to school. The only problem was that field was full of blue crane birds, and if the blue crane was bigger than you, it would chase you across the field and attempt to peck at you. The only ways to prevent an attack were by either carrying a broomstick or growing up fast.

AFTER MY FATHER'S OPERATION AND RECUPERATION WE RETURNED to Rhodesia. The Raylton Sports Club became the centre of our social lives.

In the club you could play tennis, snooker, football, baseball, lawn bowls and hockey. It became the routine for the whole family during the week: work or school followed by an evening at the sports club. We'd be there at weekends too, only breaking away on a Sunday for dinner at three o'clock in the afternoon. Even now, when I think of my mum, I think of her dressed in white, because white was the colour of her sports outfits. She looked like a doctor. She was very busy and worked hard – and then she relaxed at the sports club, as she was just as sporty as my dad. Having the club just round the corner from our home made it easy for my parents to enjoy their sports.

On a Saturday, the games would be competitive, and the different sports took place simultaneously. My dad would play football and my mum hockey. The substitutes on my mum's hockey team took care of my sister, Jacqueline, on the sidelines, while I was pegged to the ground behind my dad when I was very young. He was my hero as a goalkeeper. I watched him over and over again, studying him. I watched other Rhodesian goalkeepers play, those competing against my father, but none of them appeared to be as good as him. It was only when my father introduced me to a film about Lev Yashin, the great Soviet Union goalkeeper, that I realised my father was not, in fact, the greatest goalkeeper in the world.

WE HAD A HOUSEBOY CALLED LUMICK. HE AND HIS FAMILY LIVED IN a small house at the back of the garden, called a *kia*. It was more of a concrete hut with a corrugated roof. When it rained the metal made a tremendous noise.

Lumick had two sons called Fanwere and Gordon. After school I used to go and eat food with them, and this way I learned a lot about the culture of the Rhodesian black man. Lumick cooked for our family because my mother was at work all the time. He would be given instructions what to buy, and routinely African boys made a stew. So stew it was. He would do a fish stew, beef stew, or a pork stew, with onions and garlic. Later, my stepfather taught Lumick how to make goulash. Whenever I went to Lumick's *kia* at lunchtime, it was half a loaf of bread for us each and one bottle of Coca-Cola, and that's what we ate – bread and coke. For dinner, he would say, 'Oh, we've got something special for dinner.' Another stew? 'Yes...'

We considered Lumick almost as part of our family. When we left for that spell

4

in Benoni he had wept at our departure and we were all equally as sad. He had, of course, been unable to join us because of South Africa's stringent apartheid laws.

Rhodesia wasn't quite an apartheid state, but there was racial segregation and we were taught at school that there was a fundamental difference between white and black people, that we were superior. Integration was not encouraged.

Perhaps the situation in Rhodesia had more in common with the American Deep South than what was going on across the border in South Africa: Africans were not welcomed in white bars or restaurants. In cinemas a black man could show a white man to a seat but not sit in it himself. The rules on public transport followed a similar pattern. In Rhodesia, white and black men could sit on the same buses but the white man would be at the front and the black man at the back. In South Africa, there were white buses and there were black buses. In Rhodesia there were much higher standards in white schools than black ones, meaning that social and economic divisions were reinforced over time. But if black parents had enough money to send one of their children to a good school, it was possible to get in – unlike in South Africa, where the divide influenced every part of life.

I had no choice in where I was born and brought up and knew no better. It was accepted as normal. The sight of Lumick and his children walking around with no possessions wasn't a shock because I knew nothing else. It was only later, through travel and experience, that I learned that this was all wrong.

'PACK YOUR STUFF, WE'RE LEAVING!'

One day out of the blue, our mother told us the news that would change our family forever. With no warning whatsoever, my father had decided he wanted a new life, and he left us. He had met someone else. I was ten, my baby brother Mark was two and my sister twelve.

As much as this was a massive shock to us, I knew my mother and father weren't getting on. He used to have wild parties with the hockey and football groups at the sports club. They fought. He drank and smoked, even though he was told not to by doctors because of his Buerger's disease. One day I heard my mother say, 'If you want this woman, you go...'

After my parents split all of a sudden I was transformed into a father figure for my brother. I had to look after him. I changed his nappies. They were the old-style towelling nappies, which you have to fold and put a pin into on either side to keep everything in place.

My mum was the only one who got divorced in her family so it wasn't an easy time for her. She grew up as a Catholic and it was compromising for her in the first place when she chose to marry my father, a Dutch Reform Afrikaner. Trying to find a place where they could marry had been a challenge. It proved easier for her to convert to Anglicanism and so they got married as Anglicans.

Finding out my mother was so strong at such a young age opened my eyes. Other women had always flocked around my dad, and he stepped over the line. Not just drinking beer. He smoked marijuana and there could have been other things my mother didn't like. Seeing my mother go through such a hard time, how she had to struggle to get a new home to live in, was my life's first real disappointment. But she was very determined, wanting to carry on with the same enthusiasm as before. Three children had to be fed, clothed and put through school. She knuckled down and became our hero.

We went to Dave Crommer's home. He was a friend from the sports club and taught me how to play cricket. He was much older than my mother and I knew him as 'Uncle'. He gave my mother two bedrooms of his house so we could get by – my father's departure had left her high and dry and unable to afford the flat we had lived in. Dave was a widower, so he took my mother in. He had played cricket for Rhodesia as a spin bowler – and he asked me what position I played. I told him I was a wicketkeeper, and a batsman. He guided me and my cricketing improved a lot. Dave was a fantastic person. His kindness showed me that not every man was like my dad.

Gradually, my mother was able to put away money through her bookkeeping job. Getting a new flat was a sign she was back on her feet again. It was a white concrete duplex in The Avenues: 99 Livingstone Avenue. Downstairs there was a lounge on the left, and a balcony overlooking the street straight in front of you. Upstairs, there was a main bedroom and three smaller bedrooms, and then a shower and bathroom. My mum decorated the place and she had a lot of plants, which brightened it up and made it feel homely.

The flat was only 200 metres from my primary school, the David Livingstone School. It's a black area now but back then it was a middle-to-poor all-white area.

Unfortunately for Lumick, our houseboy, there was no longer any accommodation for him because the block of flats had no outside space. He ended up living a few blocks away with a friend, cycling to work every day.

There were plenty of kids around and we played on the streets. We went in the drainpipes under the roads. There were rats, snakes and other creatures. Some street kids of my age used to sleep down there, unless it rained, when the pipes would rapidly fill up with water.

I only had one pair of shoes when I went to junior school so when I came home, Lumick used to take my shoes off me: 'Right, outside, barefoot!' This was to save them for school or any special occasion like when we went into town. It meant playing football in bare feet, going to the sports ground barefoot, riding your bike barefoot. Though eventually, when I started playing proper games, my mother bought me a pair of hand-me-down football boots. And so, my childhood was largely spent barefoot.

My parents still went to the same sports club, still drank in the same bar – but on opposite sides of the room. The Raylton Sports Club was now a ten-minute bicycle ride away. The journey involved navigating your way through streets where dogs would chase the bikes. You had to pick your route carefully. Once, a Doberman bit me and it got a good whack with a baseball bat when its teeth sank into my legs.

Until I was allowed to drink at eighteen, I used to wait outside the bar of the sports club and play in the swimming pool area, hoping my dad would come out and talk to me, since he never visited us in our new home. Yet my old man never came. Later, when I was old enough to enter the bar, conversations would be brief. I was desperate to see more of him, I missed him, like anybody would miss their dad. But he wouldn't stick around long and, soon enough, he'd return to his game of snooker or shoot off to work.

Despite my wanting him in my life, I was also angry that he'd left us. He had been my role model and hero. He had let us down. My younger brother was too young to appreciate the impact but my sister and I felt a void. We reacted by rebelling.

2

Running Away from Home

WHEN I WAS THIRTEEN, MY MOTHER GOT A NEW BOYFRIEND AND I didn't like him. They were in the same circle of friends in the sports club. He was a recluse, sat by himself; and my mother, being my mother, would go and speak to him because she was the caring type. He had dark hair, rimmed glasses, medium build; he was an average sportsman and dressed like an office worker. I was angry because she was going out with a man that I didn't want her to be with; meanwhile my father had married a new woman, Rene, and had started a second family, settling in a little farming community in the Eastern Highlands, towards the border with Mozambique.

All these years later I realise that my mother was in a bad place at the time. She had three kids. My sister was fifteen and about to get pregnant. I was thirteen and for the first time dealing with the flood of hormones that hits teenage boys go through. I, of course, didn't see that. Instead, I thought to myself, *Hey, I'm out of here*.

At eleven-thirty on a Friday night, I came back from the sports club and decided to write a note, placing it on my mother's bed while she was sleeping. I climbed down the drainpipe, went out on the main road and hitchhiked from there, catching a bus that black people used, then a taxi, eventually taking me the 230 kilometres to Inyazura where my father lived.

The greeting there was not the one I expected. Rene, my father's new wife, answered the door at 3:30am. 'There is your bed,' she said. A few hours later, my father came into the room, shouting: 'Get up!' Outside, he tied me to a tree, beating my backside with six strokes using a hose, saying words that I'll never forget: 'Don't ever do that to your mother again! Your mother brought you into this world. I helped, but your mother is the one you don't disrespect ever again.' And I haven't. Those words are still with me now.

It wasn't the first time I endured corporal punishment at the hands of my father. Beatings were his way, though only if we were really naughty. We were brought up with the cane or the strap. 'Go into my cupboard and pick the belt you're going to get hit with,' he'd warn. 'You're going to be hit on your behind four times.' Things that would qualify for a beating included lying and not being home for curfew. As soon as those street lights went on you had ten minutes to get back, otherwise you'd be picking a belt. It might shock some parents today but that's how we grew up. My father came from a background where such punishment was routine. His family had been miners and manual labourers.

At school, the rules were the same. If you didn't do your homework, you'd get summoned to the headmaster's office where the girls would get a smack on their hands and the boys on their backside, only ten times harder.

Humiliation was another tactic. You would be called up in assembly on Monday morning in front of the school. The headmaster would stand there and say, 'Right, after assembly I'd like to see Mr Bruce Grobbelaar at my office.' There, the punishments would go up incrementally from two strikes of the cane to six. Once you were on six, you were always on six – whatever the offence. The cane would leave welts and if my mother ever saw a welt and find I'd misbehaved and been punished by the headmaster, I'd get punished by her as well. 'Right, take the belt!' and she would hit me straight on the welt, as a punishment for being punished. A double whammy!

Academically, my skills suited the sporting path I took. As a goalkeeper you need to be good at geometry – measuring distances and angles. You've got to get the distances right. Luckily, I was always good at maths. Maths was my favourite subject together with geography and history. You've got to know what happened in the past to make the world like it is today. You need to know your own family history, because that's what shapes you.

My mother was from a nomadic family. Her father had fought in the Second World War and my great-grandfather was, of course, in the Fusiliers during the Boer War and had been stationed in Cape Town, where my grandfather was born. Grandfather played the saxophone and the trombone, and when the Boswell Wilkie Circus used to go on tour, he would travel with them, playing in the band.

My grandmother and her daughters went with him, my mother being the eldest of three sisters. My mother's family travelled around and if they liked somewhere, they would stay. I was a bit like that: a football gypsy. Though the game would dictate where I settled for long periods of time, I wasn't afraid of moving.

For me, school became really fun when I played sport. I played rugby, athletics, basketball and I swam. But football always had priority – even over school work. When I signed up with Salisbury Callies when I was fourteen, I sometimes had to skip school to play for them as I occasionally had to travel quite far to get to away games. Luckily I was being paid to play at that stage, so it made being called into the office to get a smack on the backside for missing lessons a little more bearable.

MORE PAIN WAS WAITING. AFTER I RAN AWAY, MY MOTHER TOLD HER new boyfriend he was not the one for her. They had been seeing each other for six months. So this person who I didn't like disappeared. No longer on the scene. I thought nothing of it until years later when my mother told me what had actually happened. Devastated by her rejection, he had ended up shooting himself a couple of weeks later. It was so hard on my mother having to live with that.

Meanwhile, my dad still worked on the railways. He was hard-working and had been a good sportsman, but his health problems were starting to curtail him.

Nevertheless, his passion for football remained. I remember him encouraging me to go and watch a game that involved the local police in Yasura. I remember it because next to the field was bushland. When a lion appeared, everyone ran away and jumped on the bus carrying the away team. Some perched on the roof. The lion was tamed by a marksman with a tranquilliser and after that, the game recommenced.

Following my surprise arrival on my dad's doorstep after running away from home, I had a few days' holiday with him and he then put me in a boarding school in Umtali, now called Mutare, right on the border with Mozambique.

After six weeks at the school, I turned yellow. It was jaundice. I was sent back to stay with my father and stepmother. Though jaundice isn't contagious, unfortunately my father didn't have such medical understanding – so I was left to sleep on the porch. My whole body was in pain. The doctor came and gave me an injection and told me to drink lots of fluids – so I got orange juice. I was off school for about three weeks, and when I got better, my father put me on the train back home to my mother in Salisbury, where my mother's friend Denys Davies picked me up. He took me to the hospital, got me checked over and made sure I was OK and then drove me home, where my mother was waiting. Did I disappoint her? Yes, I probably did. When you're thirteen and you leave a message explaining that you've run away to live with your father, it must hurt. Yet she forgave me, as good parents do.

I went back to my old school and it was the same old routine. Riding my bicycle for five miles to training and another five miles back. Jacqueline, my fifteen-year-old sister, became a parent in the same period and soon after would marry her boyfriend, Joe Roy, a singer in a rock band. He developed a liking for the Mormon faith – he was what we called a 'Bush Mormon', which meant he smoked, drank and swore and went to church when he felt guilty. He was a long-haired hippie-type and played the guitar, singing with his sister Bunny in the bars around Salisbury like Le Coq d'Or and La Boheme. He was not the sort of character my strait-laced family would have approved of, but what did they know? Today, nearly fifty years on, he is still happily married to my sister, and his rock'n'roll days are long behind him. Now he is a bishop in the Mormon Church.

Back then, with a pregnant daughter, a tearaway son and a toddler, it meant lots of pressure and lots of stress on my mother. Being a single parent in Rhodesia was no easy thing, but she took it in her stride. She carried on with her life and her friendship with Denys became something more. Denys Davies looked a little bit like Bob Paisley in appearance, with light-brown hair going grey, combed to one side. He loved working on trucks and was a mechanic, with a son and two daughters from his previous marriage, and he proved to be one of the nicest blokes you could ever meet. It was only after my mum got together with Denys that everything calmed down. He was a huge stabilising influence on me. Finally my anger faded. I had to be the man of the house before he joined us, and that was hard.

One day, returning from a cricket game for a team called Mount Pleasant, dressed in my whites, I found an empty house. I went to the back of the garden to ask Lumick where my family was. 'Don't worry; they'll be home soon. Go and get changed into these clothes,' he said. He presented me with a nice shirt, shorts, long socks and shoes.

'What do you mean? These are good clothes.'

'Yes; your mother told me to put you in these clothes.'

'Where are we going?'

'Don't worry, your mother is coming.'

Next minute, my sister walked through the door with Gillian, Denys's daughter and her best friend school, and they were dressed up all nicely. 'Sorry you missed it, Bruce.'

'What do you mean, missed it?'

'Oh,' Gill says, 'your mother just married my father!'

In walked my mother. 'Hello, Mum.'

She turns around and says with a smile, 'Meet your new dad!'

'Oh, nice; you didn't even tell me.'

Denys said: 'Why would we want to tell you? We knew that you had to go and play cricket, so we let you go and play. How did you do?'

'We won.'

'Well done!'

We jumped into the car and went to Raylton Sports Club to have a few drinks and celebrate. I had just turned fourteen when Denys and Mum got married. While I was out playing cricket all their other kids had been present, not that I minded. I thought it was quite funny and had to laugh, because I was happy from winning the cricket game and when I came back I had got a new dad.

I GREW UP HAVING A LOT OF FREEDOM AND RESPONSIBILITY. I WAS also very fit. I'd ride my bike five miles to school, five miles back, then another ten miles in total there and back if the day involved a sports match.

Sports consumed me. I loved my sport and I excelled in everything. I was obsessed with sports because they gave me freedom while keeping me off the streets. If you didn't have much, stealing and doing drugs was common. Some friends in my neighbourhood started smoking, drinking and taking marijuana; *dagga* – that's the local slang for it. I got offered all sorts of drugs growing up. I never took it except when I was in the army, just to keep me awake. Some friends I've known for a long, long time are not very well now because they went down the wrong track when we were teenagers.

Mum was the backbone of our family. She kept us together and sane. We could have gone off the rails otherwise, and done stupid things like a lot of kids in the neighbourhood. Luckily, we led normal lives and I only ever wanted to go to the sports clubs.

I was never given anything easy in sport and standards were generally high. Alwyn Pichanick, who later became Zimbabwe Cricket's honorary life president, was the selector for the junior national cricket team. He said to me, 'Young man, we're going to go and play in Northern Transvaal; I'm going to take you. You are my wicketkeeper, but I'm going to ask you if you can come down as the thirteenth man, because I want to give this other youngster a chance as a wicketkeeper.' His name was David Houghton.

David would go on to captain Zimbabwe at Test level and have a top-class coaching career in England. But back then he was a round-faced, chubby little lad; one of those when you see the kid you think, *oh, he can't run*; but he ended up playing both goalkeeper and wicketkeeper and he was good at both. We were going down by train from Salisbury, all the way to Pretoria. The journey took two nights. That was the really exciting part. Especially since the junior hockey girls were on the train as well. However, they put the dining compartment in between ours and their cars, so you couldn't get to them – unless you got on top of the roof...

Pichanick was a legend. He was the boss and saw something in David Houghton and let him have the game instead of me. So when we went down there we had three games; David played two of them behind the stumps and I played one, just to try and even it out.

My passion earned me a place in the national team in three different sports at a young age. In rugby I was the youngest fly-half at the high school. Aged fourteen I was playing against sixteen- and seventeen-year-olds. They knew I played cricket for my country, so they knew I could play baseball as well. I loved the game and it gave me the opportunity to travel all over southern Africa; I represented both my province and then Rhodesia in a mini-series against South Africa. I was that annoying kid in your class who could play any ball game better than everyone else. Later, I was offered a baseball scholarship in the United States at North Adams College in Massachusetts, but that was after I had left the army and committed my future to the third sport at which I represented Rhodesia – football.

IN THE EVENINGS I USED TO SNEAK INTO THE PLAYING FIELDS OF MY old primary school, David Livingstone, and play football there as they had proper goals. One day I was messing about with two of my buddies, a little chap called

John Voight and another youngster called Mark Chapman. On the far side of the field, across the road, there was a car.

We'd been playing for an hour and this car hadn't moved. We had a break to get some water and when we started playing again, we saw a man in a white shirt and black pants climb through the fence of the school grounds and walk the length of the football pitch. When he reached us he said, 'Excuse me, young man, can I have a word?' I thought we were going to get into trouble; I thought he might be a teacher telling us we couldn't play on the school fields. But he said, 'Listen, young man, I would like you to come and play for Salisbury Callies.'

He turned out to be Dave Russell, the Scotsman who coached Salisbury Callies under-14s. Salisbury Callies were the only white professional club in the Rhodesia National League, the best quality league in the country at the time. They were all white and virtually all Scottish, but their participation against black and Coloured teams was demonstrative of how racial barriers were starting to break down in this period. ('Coloured' is a name used to denote those of mixed race in southern Africa; it's a distinct ethnic grouping and the ancestry is linked to mixed marriages between Khoisan women and European settlers in the seventeenth century.) They had won everything in sight when competing in the white leagues so they decided to challenge themselves and enter the black domain.

I was fourteen years of age and I said, 'I don't think my mother will allow that.'

'Well, where do you live? I'll come and ask your mother now.'

'Just down the road – Livingstone Avenue, number ninety-nine; I'll meet you there.'

So I jumped on my bike, the two other guys jumped on theirs, we rode through the school grounds, out of the front gate, down the road, and sure enough he's parked at 99 Livingstone Avenue. I took him up and said, 'Mum, this gentleman wants to speak to you, please.'

'I'd like for your son to come and play for Salisbury Callies.'

'Is that the soccer team?' she replied.

'Yes, I've been watching your son and I think that he is pretty good.'

'I cannot afford the fees for him to go to Salisbury Callies. He plays soccer for Raylton and we don't pay there.'

'No, don't worry about his fees; I'll pay his fees. I want him to come and play for Salisbury Callies.'

Only when the club promised to pay the affiliation fee and travel expenses to matches plus two dollars for every victory and one for a draw did she agree. My eyes bulged: this was quite a lot of money for a fourteen-year-old.

That's how I started my route to professional football. When I got to my first training session, there was a familiar round face as the goalkeeper playing for the under-16s: David Houghton, my cricketing mate. The same guy that I went down to Pretoria to play Rhodesian cricket with, the boy who was given a chance by Alwyn Pichanick to play two out of the three games instead of me, was a goalkeeper for Salisbury Callies too.

We trained the Tuesday and the Thursday, and then on the Sunday morning when the game was going to be played, Dave Russell said, 'David, you're sitting out now. Bruce Grobbelaar, you're going to go in goal.'

That was a pivotal moment for both of our careers: David became the Rhodesian wicketkeeper and I became a goalkeeper for Salisbury Callies. It shows how fortune can play a part in the paths we take.

Fortune made me go down the football path rather than the cricket path. I could have made a career out of cricket too, but then I would never have seen all these beautiful places that I've been to with football in the world. With cricket I'd have been stuck going to India, Pakistan, Bangladesh, Sri Lanka, Australia, New Zealand. That's it. With football I've gone everywhere; all these magical islands – Cayman Islands, St Kitts, Trinidad and Tobago, Mauritius, Madagascar. I've been all over. So would I change it? No.

Ten months after being taken from the wicket and put in goal, aged just fourteen years and eleven months, I would make my first-team debut for Salisbury Callies. For the junior teams at Callies, you'd get attendances ranging from 40 to 200 depending on the age group: the higher the age group, the more interest. The under-14s would kick off in the morning, then the under-16s at midday and the under-18s at around 2pm, all using the same pitch in the stadium. By the time the first team kicked off in late afternoon, more than 2,000 would be in attendance.

3
The Witch Doctor

CHOOSING TO PLAY FOR A WHITE TEAM IN AN OTHERWISE BLACK league took me out of my adolescent comfort zone. For the first time, I left the relative privilege of suburban Salisbury and entered the black townships with my new team. For a fourteen-year-old boy it was quite an experience to go into the townships and play in front of 30,000 people. It exposed me to a lot of Rhodesia's underlying racial tensions and the challenges facing the country after decolonisation.

The Bush War that I later had to fight in had its origins in this period, if not before.

In Salisbury we knew there were lots of problems on the farms, but we thought Rhodesia's civil problems were mainly limited to rural areas. Going into townships in the cities I became more aware of racial tensions. Extra police appeared when we played the black teams. The big problems were between the Coloured teams – the mixed-race teams – and the black teams. There was a Coloured team in our league called Arcadia and whenever we played them it was war. Whenever the black teams played them it was even worse. The football matches had the potential to break down racial barriers, but they also had the potential to reinforce them. If we played an away match at a black township and won we'd need a police escort out of the place.

It was a complex issue to understand because it wasn't just a simple case of black/white tensions: each tribe had different feelings and attitudes. I was intrigued by the differences and I did my best to learn as much as I could about how black Africans thought and how their emotions worked. It was important to pick up bits of their languages in order to communicate. This experience later helped me in the military, when I was sent out to protect farms in the countryside. Playing football for Salisbury also made me grow up a lot quicker than a normal teenager. We had turned the whole structure of African football on its head through the desire for competition, so there was a natural expectation to do well wherever we went.

My introduction to Dave Russell, who had scouted me, had a profound effect on the rest of my life. Dave was also the coach of Salisbury, who were managed at the time by Dick Blackley. Dave was a handsome Scottish man with a full head of dark hair swept back off his face like a mod. Dick was also Scottish, though he was balding on the sides. From the under-16 team, Dave and Dick promoted seven players at the same time to the first team and, to this day, we are all still friends. The success of the team helped. For two seasons in a row with the under-16s, we reached the final of the prestigious Castle Cup, winning it once.

Salisbury were run as professionally as any club in the lower levels of professional football in England, with a clubhouse that players, management and supporters gravitated towards before and after matches. I felt right at home there and was making good progress as a young goalkeeper. Then, in August 1972, I was unexpectedly called up to play in the first team. I wasn't yet fifteen years old and I was all too aware of the scale of expectation. Jeepers, I was shitting myself. I made a terrible mistake, allowing a backpass from the centre-half, Sandy Crockett, to roll through my legs and into the goal. We lost 3–1 and when I came off the field I could hear the crowd shouting, 'Hey, Grobbelaar! Get that green shirt off your back! Hey, Grobbelaar, you little shit! What are you doing here?' This was coming from my own fans! They were an unforgiving bunch, but, as I'd learn, a lot of supporters are. Experience and maturity would in time make me deaf to their taunts.

I didn't play in the first team again for another four months after my horrific debut, but I had plenty to keep me busy. I was also playing for the under-16s and the under-18s, as well as the second team. Sometimes it would involve three games in one day.

Then, a break came my way. Callies' first-choice goalkeeper, Walter Lowrie, a former professional with Hibernian in Scotland, picked up an injury, and I suddenly found myself plunged back into the first team at the most crucial stage of the season, when we were in the quarter-finals of the BAT Trophy. I played for one of Callies' junior teams in the morning and in the afternoon found myself with my adult teammates on the way to Bulawayo to face Matabeleland Highlanders. In Bulawayo, the bus was stoned on the approach to the stadium. The atmosphere inside was very hostile – 45,000 black faces staring right at us. It started to rain and I can remember Dick Blackley, playing on a racial stereotype, saying, 'Right, lads, you know these Africans, they can't play in the rain. Remember when you're back home in Scotland you get the rain like this; this is where we're going to beat them.' Turning to me, he said, 'Young man, have you got gloves?'

'Yes, I've got my gloves on.'

'Right, you just go and do your bit; don't worry about a thing.'

I had more confidence than on my ill-fated debut and I pulled off some impressive saves. Even those hostile faces were moved to praise me 'This is not a white man! This is a black man in a white man's skin. This is a Jungleman!' some of the supporters muttered. That was the first time I heard the nickname which to this day is how I am known all across Africa.

We beat Highlanders 3–1, but the praise from sections of the crowd at my individual performance didn't prevent a farewell that we wouldn't forget: rocks hitting the bus on the journey home to Salisbury, which were even bigger than usual because we'd knocked the Highlanders out of the cup. I was selected for the semi-final as well, and by beating Salisbury Sables we reached the final.

Preparation for this key game was not without its problems. During this period my mother had decided she was moving to Bulawayo with my stepfather, Denys. Remember, I come from nomadic stock, and my family were not afraid to move if the circumstances seemed right. But I dug in my heels. I was already a precocious fifteen-year-old, but I was also now suddenly playing football at a high level. A row ensued.

'Hey, I'm playing for Salisbury Callies. I can't move!'

'No, no, you're coming down to Bulawayo.'

'Listen, Mum, I'll find some digs...'

I ended up staying for the final but shortly before that game was to be played Walter Lowrie declared himself fit and I was cast aside. Along with my teammate Graham Shearer, who had also been left out, we tried to make our case to Dick Blackley, but the manager was having none of it. 'Nah, you guys won't even be needing your kits, you guys won't be even changing; you'll be sitting in the stands.' You can only imagine how unfair it felt, that I'd helped the team reach the final only to get knocked back when it really mattered.

The game was played in the Rufaro Stadium in front of a 50,000 mostly black crowd, against Mashonaland United. Graham and I, affronted at our omission, were shouting and cheering for the opposition. When Mashonaland striker Gibson Homela, a former international, scored from a shot from near the halfway line and my replacement missed it, I could not contain my delight. Mashonaland won 2–0. Callies and I had reached the end of the line.

The following day, I took the train to Bulawayo to join my mother and Denys. I enrolled at Hamilton High School, but my real motivation was to join Matabeleland Highlanders, the team in black and white stripes, that I had made life so difficult for in the cup quarter-final. Highlanders were a predominantly black team consisting of Ndebele tribesmen, but I wouldn't be the only white player. They had a Scottish centre-half called Martin Kennedy, who laughed when I told him I'd signed on for Callies for just $10. He told me to go big when I negotiated my contract. His fellow centre-back Boetie Van As smoked and drank like a trooper. He liked kicking opponents.

First Highlanders had to negotiate my exit from Callies. I didn't know this at the time, but they eventually settled on a loan fee of $3,500. That was a lot of money in Rhodesia in the 1970s.

I started school at Hamilton and finally a phone call came from the manager of Matabeleland Highlanders, a chap called Silus Ndlovu, who was the postmaster at Mpopoma.

'Young Bruce, would you like to come and play for my team?'

'Yeah.'

'Meet me down in the industrial estate at half-past five.' So my stepfather Denys took me down there as it was in a very dodgy area, a bit like Brixton or Toxteth used to be; places you wouldn't want to go to as a white guy. I walked over to Ndlovu's car and he said, 'How much money do you want to play for my team?' I bore in mind Martin Kennedy's advice, also that I had previously only been on a retainer of $10 for the year, and $2 for a win and $1 for a draw. So I went big.

'How about $50?'

He started laughing.

'Why are you laughing?'

'Oh, I thought you were going to ask for $500.'

'Give us $450 and call it quits,' I quickly replied. He went in the boot and pulled out a brown paper envelope, put his hand in and counted out $50, put it in his shirt pocket and I got $450 as a signing-on fee. That was my first brown envelope. It would not be the last.

My signing fee also included one sheep, one cow and one goat. Ndlovu asked, 'How do you want the animals? Do you want them as livestock or do you want them taken to the cold-storage commission, the abattoir?'

We had the cow and the sheep slaughtered and we ate the meat. But we kept the goat – a mistake. It was kept in the garden, where it ate all the flowers. My mother reacted by sending it to the cold-storage commission. The next week the goat was in the freezer.

I was fifteen, about to turn sixteen, and with my signing-on fee I used $400 to pay for a car and gave $50 to my mother. I was still at school. Life was good. The move to Bulawayo had paid off for my mother and Denys. She now owned a couple of shoe shops, one for men in the African part of town and one for women in the European part. Denys was a diesel mechanic working for Rhodesian Railways.

*

HIGHLANDERS' TRAINING SESSIONS AND MATCHES WERE HELD IN the townships, though white people were not permitted to enter the townships by the Bulawayo authorities at certain times. A curfew existed. During hours of darkness on Tuesdays, Thursdays and Fridays, it meant going there illegally, riding to a stream and crossing the border with my bike.

I'd been training for a week at the Barbourfields Stadium when a policeman stopped me at the stream and said, 'Excuse me, young man, where do you think you're going?'

'I'm going to training.'

'You can't go in there.'

'Why not?'

'Because it's too dangerous for a young, white boy to go there.'

'Well, I've been doing it for over a week, where were you then?'

'What have you been doing?'

'I'm going to go training.'

So he followed me in his police car. As I rode over the bridge, all these black youngsters were running after my bike with big smiles shouting, 'Hello, Jungleman!' The policeman turned his car round and drove back.

Three hours before games, we'd meet at the Mpopoma post office. From there, we'd travel to a house in the black township and be taken to a garden where we'd take all of our clothes off and stand in a circle. The garden was very open so neighbours and passers-by could see. From the house, a black man would appear dressed with feathers in his hair and the skin of half a leopard over his shoulders. He'd have a skirt with beads and bells, which jingled against his thighs.

The witch doctor would hold a bucket in one hand and a goat's tail in the other. Dipping the goat's tail into the bucket, he'd throw water on each player. At the bottom of the bucket would be cow dung and grass. The water would cover every inch of your body, including your eyes. At the end of the process he'd say, 'Right, go and pick up your kit.' Inside the house, the kit would be laid out with what looked like a half-rolled-up cigarette near the socks. The witch doctor would say, 'Place them in your socks… don't lose it, I want it back at the end of the game.'

Victories would be celebrated with the witch doctor at the stadium. He'd become a hero. The stadium would cheer for him and he'd appear on the field at the end of the match. If we lost, he wouldn't be involved and instead, the players bore the brunt of the supporters' frustrations. That was how match-day preparation was in Rhodesia. Especially the big games.

My teammates in Liverpool thought I was full of rubbish when I told them about this. They wouldn't believe me. For away games, we'd travel on the bus and other players would smoke ganja on the back row. They reasoned they couldn't play without it. I'd sit near the front because I didn't like the smell. The witch doctor would also be at the front. He would be first off the bus too. He'd inspect the dressing room. If he had a bad feeling, he'd come back and instruct us to get changed on the bus instead. Other teams had witch doctors, of course, and they'd lay curses.

It meant that everyone was suspicious. I did not believe it but it was a culture that could help you psychologically to gain an advantage over the opposition. Much later, when I was a manager in South Africa, I used to put crayfish tails on the door handles of the dressing room. The likes of Bloemfontein Celtic came in and looked at it and said, 'No, we're not going in that dressing room.' They went back on the bus, got dressed and we beat them 1–0.

On another occasion, one of my assistants advised me to burn some cardboard boxes in the middle of the floor in the dressing room; to then mix the ash with Vaseline and spread the mixture across the front of the door and across the handle.

Our opponents arrived the next morning and the sight spooked them. They got changed elsewhere and, again, we won. I wasn't even sure what the act was meant to signify, but you can play with minds and gain an advantage.

Not even the witch doctors could stop the supporter violence in African football. The violence was completely different to whatever we experienced in the UK. It was really bad. Different tribes would do untold things to each other. Knives, spears and machetes were used. Violence wasn't so much about football and more about territory and mentality. There are stories about fans having rubber tyres placed around their neck and being set alight.

As a goalkeeper, you'd be aware of what was going on in the stands behind you. They would throw rocks and other sharp items at one another. When I played for the all-white side Salisbury Callies and we beat the Matabeleland Highlanders 3–1 in the cup, the atmosphere was really bad. Our fans in the stands were beaten and they had to come and take refuge in our dressing room because it was the safest place. Our bus was stoned and all the windows were smashed. Since we had no windows we crouched down behind the steelwork of the bus as we drove away.

There were times when we'd won a game and one of the players would go out for a drink and he would get beaten up, especially if he went to the wrong club or the wrong bar. It was not like this every week, and not every game had trouble, but we knew when it was going to happen.

The violence and the corruption in African football made me start thinking about playing professionally on a different continent. They had no qualms about paying the referee for influencing the game, and I've said it for years and years that referees have been bribed countless times. Later, much later, they accused myself and Hans Segers of match-fixing, but goalkeepers are easy targets. The accusers and conspiracy theorists should be looking in another direction. Look towards the referees.

I was still at school during my season with Highlanders, and although it was unusual for a schoolboy to be a professional footballer it was not unknown. Certainly it did my chances with the students at Hamilton High's neighbouring girls' school no harm and the girls would come and watch our soccer games. My status as a wage-earning schoolboy brought me a string of girlfriends, some of whom I'd take out to the Marisha cocktail bar, which was owned by the Highlanders club chairman.

After years of poor reports and threats of expulsion at my school in Salisbury,

I knuckled down and worked hard at Hamilton High. I would graduate with good passes in English, mathematics, science, Afrikaans, geography, woodwork and technical drawing, and was confident in my own abilities to continue my education, but the teachers thought otherwise. At report time I came 27th out of 30, despite being older than most of my classmates, and the card was full of the same old comments, telling me to work harder, concentrate better and make a greater effort. Not until the sports section was there anything complimentary, but even that was a double-edged sword. The headmaster's comments cut to the heart of how I was seen: 'I have admired his goalkeeping,' he wrote. 'However, he is wasting his time in the classroom.'

I took the remarks to heart. If this was the best sort of report that I could muster when I was on my best behaviour and working hard, what would it be like if I lapsed into my old carefree ways again? To me, there was only one way forward and that was to leave school and concentrate on making football my career. Not only was I playing for men's teams, but I was making a name for myself too as a young prodigy: I had just come second in the national Castle Soccer Star of the Year awards, coming second only to George Shaya. The Dynamos forward was a legend of the Rhodesian game and eleven years my senior, so it was certainly no disgrace for a sixteen-year-old novice to come runner-up to such a figure.

Surprisingly I met no resistance from my mother, who thought that concentrating my energies on making the grade as a professional footballer would help make me become my own man.

My contract still belonged to Salisbury Callies, however, although the loan at Matabeleland was nearly over. At the end of the season I found out I was being sold to Chibuku in a deal worth $3,500, a record fee for a teenager. Callies had done very well out of me indeed and used the funds to pay for a cocktail bar at the club. I would have been happy to stay at Matabeleland but they had spent all of their money on the loan fee a few months earlier. It was my first experience of the realities of life as a professional. It is different now because the players have power, but back then we were meat.

Chibuku were another black team owned by a brewery in Salisbury. The company's motto was 'Chibuku shake shake' – the idea being that you shook the carton it was sold in to make the yeast rise to the top of the drink. It was a foul-tasting beer, but very popular.

The contract meant I would work for Chibuku as a junior draftsman with the stainless-steel company that produced the vats for the beer to be put in. Part of my training involved acting as production manager for the brewery and I noticed that if part of a twelve-pint carton of Shake-Shake was damaged then the whole lot was thrown away. With beer at ten cents a pint, this seemed unnecessarily wasteful, so I began loading up the bad cartons into the back of my car and selling them in the township for eight cents per pint. This was a shrewd move for everyone: I put the money in the club's drinks kitty and in Seke township I became popular as the footballer with cheap beer.

The manager was called Jack Meagher, an Englishman who had joined the club from Wankie, a team based around the largest coal mine in the southern hemisphere. He brought with him another goalkeeper, named Posani Sibanda, whom he had rescued from a car-washing job. I suppose his logic was to corner the market in talented young goalkeepers and his instincts were confirmed when we were both called up to play for Rhodesia on a national-team tour of the country designed to build up teamwork and morale.

For Chibuku, however, it was problematic to have two ambitious and talented young goalkeepers vying for one place in the team. Sibanda was a good goalkeeper and was popular with the manager and the local black community, but I felt he was too fond of the Shake-Shake – to the detriment of his performances. Meagher, however, was undeterred.

The first few weeks were confusing. I played the first game, we drew 1–1. Then Meagher dropped me, and played Sibanda. We lost 2–1. Next weekend I thought I was going to play, but no, I was replaced by Sibanda again. They drew 0–0. Next game Meagher played me and we won 1–0. He dropped me for the next game, and gave Sibanda another game. I wasn't happy.

'Hold on a minute – he loses and you play him? I draw and you drop me?'

'What are you going to do about it, you little shit?'

'You can stick this team right up where the sun don't shine. I am leaving!'

Whereon my manager replied: 'Hey, I've got your contract for two years, and you will never play football again in your life!'

'We'll see about that.'

I did believe him, but while Rhodesia was a member of FIFA at that time, South Africa wasn't. South Africa was banned by the world governing body because of its apartheid laws, but football was still played there beyond FIFA's jurisdiction. If I played in South Africa it didn't matter what Meagher said.

So I drove to Bulawayo and went into my mother's shoe shop. She greeted my arrival with shock and horror. 'What are you doing here?'

'I'm going to go to South Africa,' I told her.

'What are you going to do there?'

'I'm going to play professional football down there. Jack Meagher's talk about never playing anywhere in your life goes out the window because I'm going somewhere outside of the FIFA system.'

My mother was shaking her head. 'No, no, we're going to the barracks!'

A year's military service was compulsory at the time and if I'd gone to South Africa and stayed there, then I could have been called into the army any time I returned to Rhodesia. Her logic was that it was best to get it over and done with. So that's just what I did.

She took me to the Brady Barracks in the middle of Bulawayo. We spoke to the officer in charge. 'My name is Grobbelaar, when am I going to be called up?' He looked at the ledger and said, 'In six months' time. The newest intake is about to start tomorrow.'

'Is there any reason I couldn't go with them?' I asked.

'No reason,' he replied.

The next day, 7 July 1975, I enrolled with C Company, 147 intake. Bruce Grobbelaar was a soldier.

4

The Stick Leader

I STILL REMEMBER THE FIRST TIME I HAD TO KILL SOMEONE. I CAN see his eyes. We'd been in the bush for about three months. I was a tracker and the corporal and leader of my 'stick' – a group of four soldiers, teamed up that way because it was easy to pick us up in a helicopter. We were dropped off in the bush and had to go and follow the enemy, the freedom fighters. You search in there to pick up the spore, and you follow it and find their bombshell. Instead of following four, five or six sets of footprints, it could come down to two, where two have gone one way and four have gone the other way. Now you've got to pick up what that really means. Do you follow these tracks, or do you follow the main pack? This day we followed the main pack.

You had to be careful when the tracks splintered, as they could come around and try to ambush you, and this is what happened on this occasion. When we rounded the rocks he stepped out with his rifle, wearing camouflage. I looked at him, my pulse pounding in my ears, and the first thing I had to do was just pull the trigger, then drop, because there were others hiding in the bush. I felt nothing but relief that I shot him before he shot me. But if he had been in normal clothes rather than camouflaged ones, it probably would have been different. From my right my best army friend, Stewart 'Stooge' Ayre, hit someone, and then he turned and there was one behind me too, and he killed him as well. Stooge saved me on several occasions, not just this one, so I owe my life to him.

It all happened so quickly as the group of the enemy made for the sanctuary of the Limpopo River, firing at us as they went. Stooge and I were badly shaken afterwards, but our machine-gunner, Doe Herbst, was a farmer who had already experienced a lot of trouble from the war. Both his family and his farm had suffered, so he was full of fearless revenge. He was a big man, who used to show his strength by lifting heavy bags of maize just with his teeth. He started carving notches in his machine gun for every person he killed, and sometimes he would even cut the ear off his victims and put them on a string until he got back to the farm where he would keep them in a jar. The hatred drove him forward.

We managed to drive the enemy back towards the Limpopo and as suddenly as the shootings and the intense, ugly noises had started, now we were left with this deathly silence that only exists in the jungle.

After an open-fire battle, you called up the helicopters on the radio, the chopper came, you put the dead bodies in the net, and the chopper took them away before you carried on following the rest. But you had to get the bodies out first. That was the Rhodesian Army's war rule. You didn't leave a body behind – not your own, not the enemy. The freedom fighters would, on the other hand, leave your body if they killed you.

If one of you got injured, they brought another man to your stick of four and took the injured one away, and you carried on following the enemy. Once you'd followed them for more than 30 kilometres, headquarters relieved you and they got the other soldiers in to scout.

I was not proud of killing my first man, and then there were more. I never got used to killing, even though I killed men who wanted to harm me as much as possible. But I was in a war situation. A war, full of brutality and destruction, that never should have been a war.

ALTHOUGH ITS ROOTS LAY IN THE COUNTRY'S COLONIAL PAST, THE Bush War was, in essence, an uprising against the big farmers in Rhodesia, although it was also complicated by Cold War and post-colonial politics. In the military we were sent to watch and protect the farms out in the bush, to police the Mozambique borders, maintain order, and stop the regular incursion of freedom fighters attacking the white farms and spreading anti-government propaganda among the blacks in the Tribal Trust Lands (land reserved for farming by the black population). We were also encouraged to contact the local FRELIMO (Mozambique Liberation Front) army across the border, to exchange cigarettes, chocolate and, most importantly, information.

As early as 1964 a white factory worker named Petrus Oberholzer had been murdered by political agitators from the Zimbabwe African National Union (ZANU). Following this, ZANU, along with a rival faction, the Zimbabwe African People's Union (ZAPU), were banned, its leaders imprisoned and other members either forced underground or into exile in neighbouring countries. Here they received training, weapons and financing from their host countries as well as China and the USSR. Guerrilla raids were periodically launched across the borders with Mozambique and Zambia, often against isolated white farms. When I was a teenager in the early 1970s these started to escalate.

In the early days of the uprising, single farmers got attacked when they were out driving. Often the rebels – or freedom fighters as they are now known – would chop down a tree to block the road, and when the farmer stopped they jumped out of the bush and hacked him. There were basically no guns at that time, but it mushroomed from that. They were always looking for soft targets – farmers' families and children. The army were trying to stop the terrorism; that was until the wars came and other countries started infiltrating, teaching the black revolutionaries to fight, with camps being put on the other side of the border.

As time went on, isolated attacks on farmers with *pangas* and machetes became increasingly daredevil operations. Land mines were put down. Foreign forces taught new and inventive ways for our opponents to terrorise people. By the middle of the 1970s it had become a civil war in parts of the country.

The one thing I am very grateful for was that we never had the war and terrorising in Rhodesia's cities; this would have caused even more victims. It was always in the rural areas. I think there was only one attack right near a city, in Bulawayo. So while the ideologically motivated conflicts today in Europe and in Asia are concentrated mainly in the big cities, because they want to take the destruction to the people, this was a rural war where the Africans wanted their land back. But they ultimately went about terrorising their own people. Who did they think worked on these farms? Serving the military, we were fighting people that were terrorising not just farmers, but their own kind.

A lot of our duties were trying to keep control of our borders. We carried out patrols to stop people trying to get in because we knew what they were going to do. Rhodesia bordered six countries, stretching for over 3,000km, many in remote and inhospitable areas. It was quite a challenge.

I WAS STILL JUST SEVENTEEN YEARS OLD WHEN I JOINED THE ARMY. The day before I signed up, my brother-in-law, Joe Roy, was just coming out from his conscription. He was lucky getting out before it got really ugly. He was at my home and offered me some good advice. He gave me an extra set of eating utensils, which would always be spotlessly clean for inspections – because they were never used. He sent me to a reputable barber to get a short haircut so the army's barbershop wouldn't butcher me on arrival.

Finally, he told me about the boots. 'Tomorrow when you get in, they'll give you a spoon, a candle and a tin of polish, and your boots. You will to have to get your boots like my boots are now,' he said, showing me a pair of gleaming boots. The idea was that you'd heat the spoon and use it to stretch any creases out of the leather. Normally you could see dimples on the leather; on his, though, the dimples had all been ironed out. You had to get them flat, and then polished until you could see your face in the toes and the heels. It was a very time-consuming business.

He said, 'Take my boots and just swap them and those are your presentation boots. And take this little mini-iron, it will help you sort your shoes faster and better.' It was advice that served me well. I went into the army the next day in Bulawayo, and we got our backpack and all our kit. And sure enough, they gave us a brand-new pair of boots and told us, 'Tomorrow morning we want them to shine.'

As we marched to the barracks there were some black Africans walking by, and one of them lit up and shouted, 'Ah, Jungleman!' He started running alongside us. 'You coming in?' This was Thomas, who recognised me as he used to go to the stadium during the weekends to watch Matabeleland Highlanders. He would end up as my batman, and we would do great business together.

We got into the barracks and were shown our dorm. I made sure I was second-last to the door. Why? Because at the door you can't see the door being opened, but as second, you can see if someone comes; you can open and close it. The sergeant was in the room screaming and bawling at us: 'Tomorrow morning you've got to have your beds square, have your shirts inch-thick; get it squared on the corners and everything in line. And your shoes are going to be like this, shiny like mirrors!' With that he went out, with the parting words: 'Remember, tonight you might get a surprise.'

I went to see Thomas, who said, 'I can burn your boots.' So I took out my brother-in-law's shoes, and said, 'Like this?' He said, 'No problem, I can do it.' So I suggested, 'Do you want to make some money?' I showed him my brother-in-law's little iron, as small as an iPhone with a pointed end. And that was used to burn and flatten all our dorm's boots for $2 a pair. Thomas took 30 per cent and I was making money too. I would also be paid in beers and cigarettes, and eventually some of the guys owed me so much they would carry my kit for me when we went out on ten-mile hikes in the bush.

That first day, Thomas and two of his other batmen started polishing the boots, and they sat all night ironing and polishing, until they heard our superiors coming and they gave the boots back. Now we were sitting, pretending we were working on our shoes, when all these instructors came in, then closed the door after a quick look at all these 'hard-working' fresh soldiers. When they had gone, Thomas and his men continued to work on our shoes. In walked the instructors again for a new inspection. They pulled everything we had out, because we had done our shoes so quickly, and flipped the beds over.

'Your boots – how come your boots are so clean so quickly?'

'We must be good, Sergeant.'

'Don't you talk to me like that!'

The first days were rough, even though we found ways to soften them a little. It is quite demotivating when you tidy up everything and the sergeant pulls everything apart. At the same time they motivate you with this behaviour, to make sure that you can pick yourself up, because when you're going into the battlefield, you will be demoralised because of things that you will see. You've got to be able to pick yourself up, and that's why they broke us down when we first entered the army.

Despite being one of the youngest conscripts I'd say I was quite independent and had experienced more of the country than most through football. Only months earlier I had been riding my bike through the black townships, playing for the Matabeleland Highlanders in a place where white people didn't go. I had learned to adapt to different environments.

I only spent one weekend in seven weeks in the first phase in barracks. On the Friday night I was smuggled out by one of the instructors. He was a mate I used to play water polo with, so what did he do? He snuck me out, so I could go home and see my girlfriend, Theresa Wyley. I got in between the back seat and the front seat, in the well, and put a blanket on my head. Because he was an instructor they waved him through and off we went. If I had been caught, I would have been given 28 days' detention.

I went back home and had a nice time, and then he picked me up at 5 a.m. to get back into the barracks underneath a blanket.

I knew many of the guys in the squad from school and which sport they played, and there were some great rugby players among them. It was still the rugby season so I went to the captain and suggested we could organise a game for the weekend to play against one of the local sides. Sure enough, we got to pick a squad, so we picked fifteen that were going to play and another eight that were going to come on as substitutes. Of course, the major and the captain wanted to be involved, and they played too.

Every weekend for a month we played rugby. After those four weeks, the baseball season started, and we played two weeks of baseball too, where the captain was my catcher; I was pitcher. It was great. We picked up all these guys and we went out every weekend, and we built friendships.

Again, sport saved me. Playing sports was highly welcome, as the induction weeks were all about getting us fit for the bush. We went running up the hills, doing 45 kilometres, and you also had to do another 45 at the weekend, but we went out playing rugby or baseball instead.

During the week you got revved by the instructors. Luckily my brother-in-law had warned me, saying I should never get more than two letters from my mum a week. If you did, you would be branded as 'missing Mummy' and suffer accordingly as the letters were handed out in public. I was receiving letters from my girlfriend Theresa, but the letters arriving from my mother confused them.

'Grobbelaar!'

'Yes, Sergeant.'

'Why are you messing about with a married woman?'

'What do you mean, sir?'

'It says, Mrs Davies.'

'That's my mother!'

'But your name's Grobbelaar.'

'Yes, she's remarried.'

'I don't believe you. Get up the pole!' They made me climb up the flagpole.

They tried to humiliate you, but you learned to carry on.

Stooge's girlfriend insisted for quite some time on writing him letters on perfumed, coloured paper, and poor Stooge had to climb the flagpole and shout out, 'I love you, darling!' for every letter handed out from her, in front of everyone. Those letters didn't fit the macho army image.

We could have intense fatigue, having to run around the airfield with the captain, who was a marathon runner. If you beat the captain, he'd make the squad run again, so you made sure you stayed behind him. The captain did three laps every morning with his dog, an Australian shepherd, but the dog only ran once and sat down and watched him do the other two. Even the dog was more intelligent than the captain.

Being able to play sports helped us clear our heads, and would keep us away from lots of pestering. We knew what was happening on the weekends at the barracks, because when we came back the guys that didn't play sport used to tell us how much they were getting revved while we had our games in the afternoon. We, on the other hand, got to stay out and drink with the captain until 11pm and then we'd come in. It was good to play sport.

After six weeks we were getting ready for the bush and they had to cancel the game of baseball, because we had to do a 75km hike, with a full pack. You all had to get back. It took us about ten hours; it was a long way and even the fittest guys couldn't run. You had to do the walk through the bush. But we did it, we got back in time. We passed out the next day, with parents allowed to come and see. We were marching and doing our assault course first, and then we got into our number-ones, our best kit, and went and did the parade. Two days of time off awaited, before we were deployed in the bush with all its brutalities.

5

The Bush War

MY INTAKE, NUMBER 147, WAS A DOUBLE INTAKE, SO THEY SPLIT US UP. Half of the intake went to 3 Independent Company in Inyanga, up in the Eastern Highlands, and we went to 5 Independent Company in Umtali, close to Rhodesia's border with Mozambique.

Adams Barracks were positioned adjacent to a boys' school and a convent school, with the border right in front of us, about a kilometre away. We went into the bush and set up a camp near an abandoned school, just in and around the buildings there. We put up our bivouac, which was just a line and waterproof sheet in case it rained, and slept underneath that.

It was here that I met my next girlfriend. She was a girl called Jean McDougall. She came driving past us in a jeep one day with her sister. Both of them were absolutely stunning and all the boys just dropped their jaws. Jean was tall and slim with blonde hair. Her sister Lorna had darker hair, and Mahiri the smallest sister had blond hair. All three were beautiful.

Jean was the head girl of the convent school. It was my stick that went to the mother superior to make sure that we had people guarding the school at night. A stick comprises four soldiers. There was a leader, a corporal or the sergeant, which was my role in the stick from early on; a machine-gunner; a medic; and a signaller. You might have another person that could track – but I was a tracker as well.

At the convent school I made sure to put myself in to do the guard duties, and that's where I met Jean again. Her father was the managing director of the Katea

Tea Estate in Honde Valley – a big tea area in the Eastern Highlands, which was about an hour-and-a-half drive from Umtali. One day Jean and her sister came with a case full of ice-cold beers and magazines, and I insisted on taking the empty bottles back, whereupon her dad invited us in for scones and tea. Soon we were regularly visiting them on their estate and in their flat.

For the first four-and-a-half months of our service we went down to the borders of Burma Valley, Silverstream, on border patrol. We went up to the Mozambican border and just walked along.

On Christmas Eve 1975 we had done our daily border control and were shaking hands with the FRELIMO, swapping chocolates for cigarettes – we gave them cigarettes, they gave us chocolates, because their chocolate was better, it was from Europe, and ours was only local. They liked the cigarettes so we were both happy swapping. They warned us that they had heard of increased enemy activity in the area.

Around eight o'clock that evening we came back into our bivouac, and suddenly all we heard were missiles exploding, as we came under mortar fire. We ran for cover and first hid anywhere we could, then went to work for our lives changing our whole camp. It was clear that we weren't safe there and that a bomb could just come through the canvas roof at any time. Overnight we had to build bunkers, digging with a shovel, filling up sandbags and building walls with them. We tried to make our place secure, with the sandbags going over us, creating a bunker with viewing holes. This wasn't just a border patrol for us any more. Christmas 1975 was the start of the proper war for us. People were injured, people would die. Fortunately in this first attack, no one died. There was only one soldier who suffered a slight shrapnel wound to his arm.

We felt so sorry for ourselves having to be spending Christmas under fire rather than with our families, but when the local people came with food and drinks for us, we felt so grateful. A local woman dressed as Santa Claus gave us a dozen bottles of beer each, and we were presented with a whole pig. I do not think warm beer has ever tasted better. This wasn't, nevertheless, the time for goodwill. The enemy started mortaring again, a bomb hit our camp, and one of my fellow soldiers dived to cover one of the local women. He saved the girl but got caught in the back with shrapnel. He was evacuated by helicopter and operated on that night. That was when we knew these guys from the other side of the valley weren't playing.

We used to play music to keep our spirits up. We played Jimi Hendrix and shouted obscenities at the FRELIMO and gooks across the valley. Down the road there was a little motel, the Wise Owl, where you could skinny-dip in the pool and rent rooms by the hour rather than the day, and where the local discos were held. This was the sort of place where the McDougall sisters would never stop. Drugs would soon be a big part of our army lives, especially marijuana, known locally as dagga. When we were going into action, we would smoke some to take our minds off what was waiting for us. The marijuana was even grown on the main base camp, despite the threat of penalties for smoking it there. But out in the bush no one would punish you for trying to calm yourself before battle. Drinking alcohol or being hungover could, on the other hand, be lethal in battle.

WHEN YOU WENT INTO THE BUSH YOU DIDN'T WASH YOURSELF WITH water and soap. You'd wash with fine sand. You go to the river and get the fine sand and rub your skin with it. Then you get a leaf, like a herb, and rub on just for a bit of smell. If you used soap or toothpaste you could smell that from a kilometre away.

The freedom fighters used to wait in the bush. They could smell the new boys coming in, because it took time to get the bush smell on them. Freedom fighters were not the only threat in the bush. Elephants, lions and rhinos close-up could give us plenty of challenges, and I conquered many snakes during my time in national service. When you were experienced, you learned the ways of the jungle. Climbing up a tree to get out of the way of a curious elephant wasn't uncommon.

Snakes were a continual problem. Waking up, you'd sometimes find one had crawled into your sleeping bag. You'd call a colleague and he would come with his hessian bag and a hook for the snake, put it around the snake's neck, pop it in the hessian sack and tie it up.

Later we'd eat it. Behind a snake's head is the poison sack, so we would cut the snake about two inches behind that, chop its head off, then slit the body, skin it, slice up the meat and barbecue it. It's protein, after all. Whenever we had a snake in the bag, we used to chop it up and have it for dinner, instead of our ration packs. In the bush we had ration packs, and we had biscuits and a bit of snake; we had powdered soup and used to sprinkle that on the snake and cook it up. It gave it a little bit of flavour. Puff adder were the ones that we normally ate because they're nice and thick. Cobra you could eat, then there's the black and green mambas. Green mamba you can't eat, black mamba you can eat, but you've got to watch out how far back you cut it, because if you cut it too close to the head you could be dead. Boomslang is very thin and one of the most dangerous snakes in Africa. You can definitely not eat those.

Africa is full of snakes, but most of the time they won't attack you. With the puff adder's venom you get paralysed and lockjaw. If you get bitten by the black and green mamba and you don't get the venom out, the poison will close down all your organs and you suffocate. If you get the spit of a cobra in your eyes it will blind you; and if it's big enough it might eat you. The cobra will spit at and blind a rabbit and wrap itself round and squash it and swallow it whole.

Scorpions were not so bad in the Rhodesian bush, but if we found them at the camp we had certain men knowledgeable about insects and arachnids who would extract their poison and make a mix with other chemicals which could be injected into you as an antidote if a scorpion stung you. If you don't get an antidote in a certain time, you'll not be in a happy place.

There were also a couple of dangerous spiders in the bush. There's the baboon spider, which is a sub-family of tarantulas, and others, including one with a red abdomen. You certainly don't want them in your sleeping bag or crawling into your mouth while you're sleeping outdoors.

We ate many flying ants though. When it first rains the termites become flying ants when they come out of the mound you've got to catch them. You put them in a bag and shake them, then you take them out, take the wings off them and throw them in your pan with a bit of hot butter, then cook them over the stove. A little bit of salt and pepper, let them sit, and then you eat them like peanuts. They are full of protein. Once you bite them they are like crunchy peanut butter because you've burnt the skin in the pan and you're frying them in butter, and that's what you taste. I even ate flying ants when I lived in Ottawa in Canada recently and some Zimbabwean friends came to visit.

Anything that moved in the bush you ate. A rabbit, boom, there we go; we're having rabbit tonight. Any birds you'd shoot with a little pellet pistol, make sure it's got no worms, pluck it, debone it, and cook it up. If we went near a village and chickens came out, you'd take a chicken and wring its neck quickly. It flaps around until it calms down and then you'd put it in a bag and cook that up at night.

We would also eat mopane worms, which live on the leaves of the mopane tree; grasshoppers and locusts too. They are still a speciality among Zimbabweans.

In the army we had to cook, otherwise we would not survive. Food is your fuel and it doesn't matter if you don't like meat, or if you're a vegan or vegetarian – you have to find what you like to survive. There's a joke that I like to tell: what's the definition of a vegetarian? A very bad hunter who can't make a fire.

WHEN I WAS FIGHTING IN THE BUSH, THINGS WERE NOT TOO GREAT at home either. I didn't know this, however, until I was given a telegram from my Aunt Pam: 'Sister gone insane. Believes you are dead. Come as soon as possible.'

I was unaware of my sister and her husband Joe's battle in trying to have more kids. Shane had been born when Jacqueline was only sixteen, but their Mormon faith encouraged large families. Although she struggled with miscarriages, finally they had a daughter. However, Natalie was born prematurely and complications made them lose her within a week after she was born.

Jacqueline became really distressed and was put in a psychiatric ward and was close to being put into an asylum. She got so ill, believing that everyone she was close to was dead unless she could prove they were physically there and not ghosts. With me away and not there for her in this condition it made her absolutely sure I was gone too. She was suffering from enormous distress.

I got the telegram five days after it was sent, and I realised the army had held it back from me. I was furious, storming into the major's office asking what was going on. I couldn't believe the heartlessness in his reply: 'We need your tracking ability and knowledge of the area for one more patrol before you go on pass.' I knew a vehicle was leaving, and I threatened to go without leave; eventually I got my pass.

I hadn't had a shower for days when I started my three-day journey to get to my sister in the hospital in Salisbury. I only had two days to convince her I was fine before I had to return as my pass ran out. Even after my arrival, she thought I was a ghost. Eventually I had to take her into the hospital's recreation room and play table tennis with her, where over and over again I let the ball hit my chest for her to realise I was real and well. A few days later she started recovering and in 1982 she gave birth to David. She and Joe also ended up adopting Debbie and Tracy Lee, children from my father's second marriage, which had also ended in a divorce.

I didn't find it too hard to return to the army camp as I only had less than a month left of my one-year service. Or so I thought. However, on my return I learned that because of the intensification of the war compulsory military service was now increased to eighteen months. That put my life in so much more danger, and it would also result in the loss of some of my best friends.

THE VEHICLE IN FRONT OF YOU HITS A LANDMINE AND THREE BODIES blow out of the side of it, right before your eyes. It could have been you. Three metres ahead of you a friend is shot. Not you. A helicopter dives towards the ground, trying to pick you up while others are shooting at you. The guy next to you is shot through the leg by a machine gun. It could have been you. There are so many things that could have happened to me, but didn't.

One of the scariest experiences happened in Mozambique. We were told we would have to make our own way back after an ambush. I heard over the radio that the enemy was on its way, so I was abandoned with just three other men. The border was 25 kilometres away. It was always about getting out of trouble. My four-man unit ran towards the border, but they would never have made it there in time, with one of us injured in the foot. Finally, we managed to contact a helicopter, shouting 'Casevac!' into the radio. It meant somebody was shot and they needed an escape.

The helicopter pilot was my cousin Archie. Thank God for family in the air force, and thank God the helicopter came and picked us up. Our lives were saved, once again.

What haunts me still now all these years later are the images burnt into my memory bank when we went into a raid in Mozambique. There was a camp where they were training people to become freedom fighters.

You got called in to do the morning raid, seeing the lights from the helicopter that would drop you, getting your map. I, as the stick leader, went inside the call centre; four stick leaders gathered and our captain. We got a briefing: 'You're going to Pafuri.' Pafuri is an area where three borders meet; Mozambique, South Africa and Rhodesia, right at the top end of the Kruger National Park. The Pafuri River comes down there, and we were going in on the Mozambique side, about ten kilometres into the neighbouring country.

Helicopters took us up and we landed on the Rhodesian side and waited for the helicopters and the jets to come and drop the first bombs. These bombs burn everything. And then we went in.

We were dropped right into the middle of the battle zone. But in this instance, the rebels had learned from the North Koreans, the Chinese and the Vietnamese how to burrow underground. So when the bombs landed, many didn't get hit, they scurried into their holes. The bombs only killed half of them, and we were dropped in, thinking that most of them were dead, but that wasn't the case. We were suddenly in a real fight.

There were 16 of us against probably 200 of them, and we had to go through and try to wash them out. People got shot and maimed. We found out that they were burrowing, and they had to come out somewhere, and we worked out that was on the Pafuri River.

Sure enough, there were many holes in the side of the bank of the river where they were coming out. The whole of the Pafuri River was full of rebels. We called for air strikes onto the river. They came and dropped the bombs in the river and killed most of them.

This is the image that haunts me the most. With our rule of bringing all the dead bodies back to civilisation, we had to go into the river to get the bodies out, to see how many people had been killed. But their corpses attracted crocodiles, so while we were taking them up from the river, we had to put our guns under the water and shoot at the crocodiles. That was the only way you could get them away.

In the end everything was cleared. My stick was the last of the four there, and as the helicopter took the last bodies away in a net hanging underneath, I called for a helicopter to take me home. My cousin Archie, who was in a helicopter, radioed through: 'Don't worry, in ten k's you'll see the border post, you can walk.' He was joking.

Yet when we heard an engine approaching, we thought they were trucks from the enemy coming, so we began making a run for the border. But it wasn't the enemy. The noise was a helicopter coming in very, very low. It was my cousin. After such a terrible assignment, in which we were so heavily outnumbered, coming out alive welled up mixed emotions.

People go into the army for different reasons, whether it's political, whether it's just the thrill and desire, the adrenalin rush that you get from a war situation, or they simply have to. Like me. I didn't want to be there, but I had no choice. We had been told by a superior to undertake that mission. Again, there was no choice. If you didn't you faced a court martial.

*

WE ARRIVED IN CHIPINGE ON INDEPENDENCE DAY, 11 NOVEMBER 1976, and the four of us stank. We'd been in the bush, hiding. So we smelled like the bush, having spent days washing in cow dung. It's OK; it's grass in the main. We brushed our teeth with fine sand and rinsed it out. And even after a proper shower we still had to put on our dirty clothes again before heading for the bar, where, to our surprise, we were invited by the president of the Independence Ball to join in the festivities.

At the party they put us at a table well away from the other guests, in the corner by the servants, where the waiters were. All the locals at the other tables were coming up and giving us money. 'Buy yourself a drink, buy yourself a drink.' We had all this money and at the end of the night we were completely drunk.

The band stopped; they went to take a break. There were three people dancing with this band. So Stooge said, 'Come on, Bruce, get on the drums; get the microphone, Mark. Full crew. Lieutenant Jackson, can you play the bass? Go with Bruce and he'll give you the eyes, and hit the bass drum, and you pluck that one.' We played a Doobie Brothers song, 'Long Train Running', then 'The Wizard' by Uriah Heep, Mark's favourite. We played three songs and everybody in the audience was dancing. Mark Torrington was a great singer, while I was beating the drums like Animal from *The Muppet Show*.

The band members came out because they heard us playing; and when they saw everybody was dancing they stopped and watched. So they knew what to play now and ended up playing the Beatles.

The relief was brief. The next day we were flying out, going on Fireforce missions. We took over the Fireforce the next day at 0600 hours.

Two weeks later, Mark got shot by a sniper and died in his best mate Stooge's arms. Mark's parents gave his guitar to Stooge. A few years later, I was asked to be the godfather of Stooge's daughter Kelly, an honour which I happily accepted. But I know I was second choice after the war had taken the obvious candidate.

IN JUNE 1976 WE WERE IN THE SMALL KATEA TEA ESTATES OF THE Honde Valley. We were two on either side of the road, eating a little, before going into ambush position.

I told my fellow soldiers, 'Not long now, lads!' I had only signed for a year – this was before I was told I had to serve another six months. And I told them that one day I was going to play for Liverpool FC. They said, 'Yeah, right,' and laughed. 'We're going into ambush tonight – you could get shot!'

At first I had chosen Derby County as my dream club – but then found out they did not play baseball after all. That was just the name of their ground! When I first saw the Liver bird I thought it was a funny-looking bird, so I chose Liverpool as my favourite team in England. All because of that red bird!

WHEN WE ONLY HAD THREE DAYS TO GO FROM OUR EXTENDED service of eighteen months, we came back from Fireforce patrol, finished our stint, got back in the trucks on the Friday afternoon, showered and changed. We were passing out on the Monday. We returned our kit to the quartermaster's stores – our rifle, all our arms, took all our gear off. We were in civvies, jeans, T-shirt, playing darts in the mess, snooker, drinking, having a great time. Saturday night after dinner we were in the mess again playing darts, then sure enough at midnight we're still in the mess when the captain came in. 'Guys, sober up quick, we leave at 2 a.m.; get your stuff out of the quartermaster's stores, we're off. You have to do another six months.'

What?

This was beyond demotivating. Two of our guys took their weapons, went in the toilet, and blew their heads off. Boom, simultaneously. One of them was in my stick. They just couldn't bear to carry on in the war, didn't want to be there any more. We didn't leave at 2 a.m. because we had to clean up their brains from the ceiling. Then I had to get another two guys, and that was my stick for the last six months. We had to regroup and eventually got two chefs that wanted to fight to join our stick. Into the bush for another six months.

Within our stick in these final six months, Stooge and I were trackers. We had a machine-gunner, Sarel Vermaak, the ex-cook, who was sick and tired of cooking, so the last six months I gave him the machine gun. Phil Crewe was the signal and the medic. That was our stick.

Four sticks were sent to Chipinge airstrip. Sixteen of us altogether, meaning two sticks would be on duty at all times, while one was to stand by and one was resting, meaning they would drink beers or smoke some wacky baccy. One day there were fights between the local rebels, the Makendangas, and our two patrols and we were all called out to help in Chimanimani Valley.

We were dropped off in a forest with such high pines that we couldn't get proper cover, as the branches started twelve to thirteen feet off the ground. We were shot at by snipers and we managed to kill three of them, and all sixteen of us managed to get in line to move forward to take out the other snipers. The problem was, we couldn't see them, but we were fired on and it was lethal. A bullet went though Totland's rifle magazine and into his stomach. Another bullet injured Vermaak on the machine gun, Smith-Rainsford got a toe shot off and Phil Crewe got hit between his eyes.

It was raining bullets around us. We had nowhere to hide and could not understand where the bullets were coming from when Doe, in pure fury at losing his close mate, Crewe, turned his gun upwards towards the trees and shot in frustration. Two rebels fell out of the tree: one dead and one still alive. Doe, wanting to avenge his friend, cut off the rebel's genitals before we got to him.

I'VE BROKEN MY NOSE SIX TIMES – FIVE TIMES IN FOOTBALL AND once with a punch from my mother. Christmas 1976, we got a pass to go home to our families for a few days. I got dressed nicely and my brother-in-law arrived with his fatigues and in his army uniform, and we drank some Scotch that wasn't ours. You see, in the house there was this one expensive Scotch we were told not to touch, it was for mothers, fathers and uncles only. It was too tempting not to drink it. My cousin Archie stayed in the house, and he was the culprit, saying we could open it. So we took a tot each, then put the bottle back in the box as if nothing had happened. Unfortunately, my mother found out what we had been doing.

When my sister put my nephew to bed, I went out to the veranda to look for Joe, and my mother said, 'And you, my boy,' – *pow!* She punched me in the middle of my face and broke my nose, and said with a strict voice, 'Get your kit and get out of my house!' So Archie and I went out into the road. My sister came out, asking, 'Where is everybody?' Our mother responded, 'And you, my girl, get your stuff, get out!' My sister got the baby, put it in the pram, and joined us out there in the road.

That night we went to Joe's sister's home in Bulawayo after getting a lift in the back of a pick-up truck. The next day I phoned my mother and apologised for drinking the Scotch, and she said, 'Come back for Christmas lunch. Happy Christmas!'

My mother had had to bring up three children on her own; and it didn't matter who you were, if you disrespected the owners of the home you were in, you were not welcome. So we weren't welcome that night.

IN APRIL 1977, THE RHODESIAN FOOTBALL TEAM WAS GOING TO PLAY against the South African Springboks in a two-game affair. It wasn't a high-profile game, just designed to get some proper exposure to show our talents to teams outside Africa, as both our nations were banned by FIFA because of apartheid and, in Rhodesia's case, the Unilateral Declaration of Independence (UDI). The Rhodesian Football Association picked a side and I was selected. I went to my CO, Major Taylor, and told him.

'Well done, Corporal, very well done. When is the game being played?'

'It's getting played on Sunday in South Africa.'

'Right, you need to get to Salisbury. Let's see if we can get you there by helicopter; you've done well in the bush. OK, here's your pass, make sure you're back on the Monday morning by six o'clock.'

A helicopter took me to Salisbury, and I went and joined the team. Guess who was the manager? Jack Meagher from the Chibuku brewery team who I'd told to stick his football club up his behind. It was he, the guy who'd told me I would never be a goalkeeper as long as I had a hole in my backside, and that I could never play anywhere else in the world because he had my contract with Chibuku. But while I'd been in the army Chibuku had folded, gone out of existence. So my contract became null and void and I could play anywhere.

Meagher looked at me after two training sessions and said, 'You haven't played for eighteen months; I'm not going to be playing you this weekend, so you might as well go back to the army.'

Since I had my pass to come back on the Monday I decided to go to Durban City FC. They had a seminar for goalkeepers and Roy Bailey, the former Ipswich goalie, was hosting it. I participated, but later overheard Bailey telling the owner of Durban City that this Grobbelaar chap would never be a goalkeeper. You could say I had lost a little bit after two years in the army, but this was still deeply disappointing.

I flew up to Johannesburg for the game and I was sitting in the stands. Rhodesia lost 7–0. I went back with the team that night, and then travelled back to the army base. We got back to Salisbury round about 10 p.m., I got on the road, hitchhiked, and was back at the barracks before 6am.

I was there in time for the 6am pass, but awaiting me was a nasty surprise. The sergeant came down and said, 'Let me take your pass.' He said, 'Corporal Grobbelaar? Take the laces out of your shoes; take the belt off; give me the dog tags. You're arrested, you are going to the jail.' I was double-marched by two guards and taken to the jail. I was perplexed. And nobody would tell me what was happening.

At 9 a.m. I was double-marched up the hill into the major's office. He was taking books off his shelf and putting them in a box with his back towards me.

'Corporal Grobbelaar?'

'Yes, Major Taylor.'

'Do you know why you're here?'

'No. I've just come back from pass.'

'Never mind about your pass; you didn't play in the game in South Africa. You should have been back here the next day.'

'Well, I've got this pass signed by you, sir, to come back today. I got back this morning at five o'clock.'

'You're found guilty of being absent without leave.'

'How can it be that I'm found guilty when I've got the signature by you?'

'Yes, but you should have been back when you didn't play the game in South Africa. I'm charging you AWOL.'

All I could think of was going to the detention barracks where they'd shave my hair off so everybody would know I'd been there. There'd be shame, and my mother would be furious.

'May I ask why, sir?'

'Well, you've made it difficult for me, because as you can see I've been promoted and I'm taking my books down. If you were here on time, or should I say, if you had come back, you would have passed out with all your mates.'

I'm thinking, *All my guys have passed out.* I didn't say anything.

'I'm charging you AWOL, and your punishment is to take all your stuff to the quartermaster's stores and get out of here, and go to the mess, as your mates are waiting for you to pass out properly with them. They stayed here since last night waiting for you.'

He laughed. The major had had the last laugh, but my army days were at an end.

I went back to the barracks, got showered, changed into civvies, took my kit down to the quartermaster's and said cheerio. Then I went into the mess and there were my guys. The ones that didn't like me had buggered off, but the majority of them stayed. We had a few drinks and then we jumped on the train and off we went back to relative normality.

First we went to the Wise Owl motel by the edge of town and stayed the night there because we were quite blitzed. Next stop, Salisbury. We all went on the train to Salisbury, got blitzed there. Went to Bulawayo, got blitzed there. Then I was told, 'Next week get to football training back up in Salisbury.'

IT WAS FINALLY OVER. NO MORE GETTING SHOT AT. NO MORE witnessing friends and colleagues dying. No more weeks spent in the bush, caked in animal shit to put off enemy trackers. No more picking up dead bodies that have been shot or burnt by the bombs, and no more piling corpses on a big hill ready for a helicopter to take the bodies away.

If my military service had gone to plan we wouldn't have been in Fireforce, we would just have been a unit that went to guard the border, with a couple of patrols. But we had a very inspired leader in Captain – later Major – Taylor who was very fit, and he wanted to get us out there.

As much as I wish I had done without my army years, and as much as I wish the war had never happened, one good side effect was the discipline it instilled in me. Learning to be on time. It taught me extreme determination, the will to stay alive, and the gift of being alert. You have to be alert at all times, be aware of your colleagues; keep your colleagues safe. Keep your family safe. Be patient. A lot of people, families, couples, aren't patient. It's often an 'I want something now' attitude. That can be a mistake.

In the army they taught me patience. You go to an ambush position; you've been told 150 gooks are coming through; there are only four of you, so be patient. Imagine you have a killing zone probably twenty yards wide. You have all your weapons pointing in those twenty yards. You've been told there are 150 enemies approaching. You don't want any of them to take another route and get in behind you. But if you pull the trigger too early you will only take out those at the front and allow the others to regroup and attack you from all sides. Patience. How many do you let through before you do anything to make the rest of those who are coming through turn around and run away?

The army also taught me to function well under pressure. You go in at seventeen, you come out at nineteen. You ask a youngster today, 'What did you do aged between seventeen and nineteen?' 'Oh, I was in university.' Great. 'And what did you come out with on the other side?' 'Oh, I got a BA in Finance,' or 'I did another couple of years and got a doctorate.' That is good. It's tangible skills, something on paper. I came out the other side of a war, wondering, *What am I? What do I have?* It's hard, but the knowledge of life can help you a lot more than a doctorate. I have been to the university of life and it took me to the very top. I'm fortunate that I've been able to dine with the Queen at Buckingham Palace, dine with many kings (and I'm talking African kings) and just earlier today – ahead of working on this – I dined with King Kenny.

We stand in front of these crossroads every day; decisions we are making in our lives. Some of them we just take on intuition; some of them we don't even think about as crossroads, we just act, and others we make a big deal of choosing. I do believe someone is looking after us, whether it's God or your father, your grandfather or grandmother. I believe that happens. There are too many people in the world that have said that sometimes they've frozen and not taken action on something and it turned out for the better, and had they done that, they would have not been here today. It's remarkable.

In the war days there were so many times where you could have been maimed. You're going through the bush and you've tripped a wire, but you have to stay there, because if you pull out of it, a bomb is going to go off. So you have to get someone to go and disarm it; someone has to get to the bomb and make sure that the pin is replaced.

It happened to me. My mate went in and tripped and he froze and said, 'You guys better get out of here.' Doe, the madman, said, 'I'll do it with you, because you need two pairs of hands.' It was a Claymore mine with a pin by a rock. Everything is blasted away when that detonates. It would have taken all of us. We found the pin, replaced the trip switch and made it safe.

What we called terrorists back then – the freedom fighters – were terrorising everybody with a strategy to get their country back. When it's all said and done, Britain gave them that chance to govern again with Mugabe in the lead. All of that war could have been averted. We should never have been in the middle of the Bush War, because it could have been negotiated, and should have been negotiated. But wars are there to make politicians remain in power and to make a lot of people a lot of money.

It was a war that should have been fought over a long table with all parties around. It was a senseless war. It really was a senseless war.

Surviving a war makes me think I'm lucky, I'm fortunate. A lot of people haven't been. When I came out of the military I thanked God that I came out unscathed. The only thing that wasn't quite sound was my mind.

We saw shocking things, which is normal in war. When you come out, you thank your lucky stars that you're alive. You must love every day like it's your last. That's probably the attitude I had in my early football career.

It has instilled in me to live my life for today; don't worry about tomorrow, because if you live your life well today, tomorrow will take care of itself. If you can do things today that people appreciate, and if you can make some people laugh today, tomorrow will be better.

Of course you're going to have ups and downs on the way. When it happens you have to deal with it, not dwell on things. I believe my sense of humour and general good mood has developed from some of my life experiences. You need a good mood. This world is a messed-up place. But if you can keep sanity in your family, and you can bring joy to them and your friends, that's the best thing you can offer. Yes, you can go through hard times. I've been through a few. It's like my mother said, and I'll always remember this: 'Life is full of disappointments, it's how you get over those disappointments that make you a better person.' Her wisdom is true.

The war definitely helped shape me as a goalkeeper. In goal, I felt I was in a unique position. The area around my goal was all mine, just like I felt about my stick and the areas we protected during the war. As a squad leader I had to look after my team in the same way I felt I was taking care of the defence. If someone did something wrong, you told them, and if they did something right, you encouraged them. It was just like during the war.

I learned a lot about team building during my time in the army, which proved to be very useful on the pitch. I don't think I am unique with this war experience in top-flight football in England; there are players to this day who carry war experience with them, who have been involved in war one way or another. Some went through the Balkan conflict and I'm sure quite a few lived in countries with uprisings and social turmoil in South America and in Africa. There are players who are in danger of being kidnapped when they go back to their home countries because of their high profile and because the rebels might want something from the government. It happens. Like when the Togo national side were shot at in Africa when driving through Angola.

I'm a light sleeper. I've always been a light sleeper, but every now and again bad memories from those days still wake me up.

6

Saved by Football

I CAME OUT OF THE ARMY UNSCATHED. SO MANY WENT INTO THE
Bush War with expectations of finding adventure or excitement and they're
sadly not here with us any more. Between December 1972 and December 1979
around 20,000 people were killed, including more than 8,000 civilians.
After almost two of those years in the armed forces I considered myself lucky
and blessed to be alive.

For me, the army wasn't a way of life I wanted to pursue. Did I want to carry out
the duties expected of me in the army? Jeepers, no. I realised that as soldiers we
were largely powerless to have a lasting impact on the destiny of our country.
It's the power of negotiation that can prevent conflict from escalating. I also saw
that the influences behind war are rarely recognised – those who depend on arms
being sold. Without wars, they are not getting paid. Governments are complicit in
all this because they want to get rich themselves.

The war in Rhodesia was a stupid war and the outcome was even worse.
Of course, the black population wanted their country, but they should have worked
with Ian Smith's government rather than outside forces – whether those of Britain,
China, Zambia, Mozambique or North Korea – who used the conflict to fight their
own proxy wars. That was the big problem. It fed all sorts of false perceptions. In
Rhodesia it was believed the British government was siding with the rebels against
the Rhodesian government, while many in the black population thought that the
Rhodesian government was trying to uphold British colonial rule, which wasn't
true either. The two sides were on different pages. Long before it escalated into
the Bush War they could have sat around a table and formed a consensus that

would have allowed them to work together and maintained Rhodesia's status as one of the most peaceful and prosperous countries in Africa.

In 1979, after a ceasefire had been agreed, the Smith government ended minority rule and held multi-racial elections. The leader of one of the factions, Bishop Abel Muzorewa, won the election and he became the country's first black head of government. As a result of this so-called 'internal settlement', the country briefly became Zimbabwe-Rhodesia. But because Muzorewa wanted to work with Ian Smith, the outside world – Britain in particular – said no, claiming those votes were rigged, and called for another election. Britain retook control for a transitional period, in which the country became Southern Rhodesia and was ruled by Winston Churchill's son-in-law, Lord Soames, ahead of multi-party elections and independence the following year.

Southern Rhodesia lasted for barely six months, and if you want to know about rigged elections, the next elections were 100 per cent corrupt. There was no way Bishop Abel Muzorewa or Ian Smith were going to be allowed to govern our country. Amid voter intimidation, rumours of coups d'état and Lord Soames's colonial administration not doing its job as a neutral arbiter, the UK handed the country on a plate to their designated successor, Robert Mugabe. Mugabe was educated in the UK, and probably the most intelligent African leader in the world. He lent the perception of being a moderate and modern post-colonial leader and joined forces with key figures in the white minority to promise a future for the new country that resulted from the period of conflict – Zimbabwe.

The fallacy of allowing Mugabe to take control would show itself over time. For the first ten years, Mugabe was OK. The Western world liked him and he was popular in Zimbabwe. After that, something changed and he became what is written now. Mugabe showed himself to be the very worst sort of leader and far from a moderniser. He fulfilled every worst European preconception of a tinpot African dictator: corrupt to the marrow and a tyrant. In the medium term the white population played a part in the new country and believed Mugabe's promises about national unity. The farmers remained and Zimbabwe was the breadbasket of Africa at a time when the continent was synonymous with hunger and famine.

Then, in the 1990s something triggered a switch. I couldn't tell you what. Maybe it was simply his desire to hold on to and consolidate power, but Mugabe turned on Zimbabwe's white population. Farms were taken away from white farmers under his so-called land reforms and nominally shared among the black population, although often they were just given to his henchmen. Productive farms that had once made the country prosperous were turned over to subsistence farming. The new black farmers farmed enough to sustain their own families – and sometimes not even that – but much of the land fell fallow. A country that had once seen its food exported all over Africa and beyond became reliant on food aid. The economy collapsed and hyper-inflation became rampant. White farmers lived in terror. Many were forced to flee and some took up the offer of land in Zambia, which has a similar climate and has since – like Rhodesia once was – become Africa's breadbasket. Meanwhile democracy was eroded to the point where Zimbabwe became for so many years no more than a dictatorship, with Mugabe seemingly a president for life. It was an outcome those of us who fought for our country's future in the Bush War considered abhorrent. Not only those fighting on the same side as me but the freedom fighters as well. They were promised things that never happened. It doesn't matter which side you look at it from, the war worked out badly for everyone other than Mugabe.

COMING OUT ALIVE FROM SERVING YOUR TIME IN A WAR MAKES you see life with a new perspective. Of all the everyday luxuries we can easily take for granted, what I appreciated the most was getting on to a football field again and playing. Knowing that I had legs and arms, and eyes and ears to play this great game again was such a relief. I was relieved too that my closest family had seen service and come out the other side unharmed. My brother-in-law and stepfather had served; later, my brother would serve after the Bush War had finished. Any man under the age of sixty could be called up as a reservist. Only the fact that my father had lost a leg prevented his own call-up. Three of us in the close family had to go in and fight. Sometimes I used to contemplate how it might have been if one of us hadn't come back.

I did not know what the future held when I left the army. I was still a boy, with only an elementary education. One option would have been to remain in the army through six-week shifts, alternating the time with another job. But I didn't want to go back. I saw destruction in people, and it could have been me. I think I was saved from the worst war traumas because I got into playing football again straight away. I was picked for the Rhodesia team to play South Africa, who a few months earlier, in April 1977, had hammered our national team 7–0. After that result nobody gave us a hope when South Africa were invited to Salisbury's Rufaro Stadium in July, not least since wholesale changes had followed the previous demolition. A new coach called John Rugg came in and he picked a mixed team, with me – a debutant – in goal. It was a 1–1 draw after Shaw Handrede hit a 35-yard screamer into the top corner to level the South African opener. I'd played well and coming so soon after the catastrophic 7–0 defeat it was considered a remarkable and unexpected score. We were all hailed as heroes, but for me the game was to have life-changing consequences.

Next came an important phone call. Norman Elliott was the chairman of Durban City. 'I believe you played well for your country, and I want you to come down and play for us in South Africa. We saw the Rhodesian game. An independent spy was looking at you play.' That spy – to use his word – was Harry Weir. He came from South Africa and monitored me and then told Elliott that Durban City should sign me.

My prospects in war-ravaged Rhodesia were not great. The war was intensifying and while there were jobs, if you wanted to earn more and live a little Rhodesia wasn't the place to be. I had gone back to play for the Callies on being discharged and our team, ravaged as it was by military call-ups, embarked on a run of ten straight defeats. We were only playing for pleasure, but we were not happy. The side had collapsed, just like the country.

Durban City was my first introduction to professional football after leaving the army. Everything happened so quickly, but looking back I think it saved me from post-traumatic stress disorder. I knew the problems that I would have encountered had I stayed in Rhodesia. In many ways John Rugg, who picked me for the Rhodesia team, saved me. Rugg was a tall Scotsman, who had previously played for Berwick Rangers and Queen of the South before emigrating to South Africa and then Rhodesia in the 1960s. He coached a gold-mining team called Rio Tinto from Kadoma, 100km southeast of Harare, and transformed them into one of the best teams in the country before being invited to coach the national team for the first of two spells in 1973. On being asked to return as national manager in 1977 he was there for years and years, always very well dressed in chinos and a chequered shirt. When he was representing Rhodesia, he wore a suit. He was very respected in football and continued to be involved with the national team until the 1990s. I remain grateful to this day for his intervention.

*

DURBAN IS A GOOD CITY. THE COAST HAS MILES OF WHITE SANDY beaches. Piers go out into the ocean where people fish for shark. The surf is fantastic and the whole city smells of the sea. Everywhere you go, there is a salty whiff of fish. The air is different and has a really sticky feel to it because of the humidity. If you go walking around town in Durban, depending on which area you go to, you can also smell the Indian spices; the Indian curries. Walk another few blocks and you can smell the African food, the real Zulu food.

Durban has had its upheavals. In the 1940s there was a clash between Indians and the Zulus, then there was a clash between the Indians and the whites, then there were clashes between whites and the blacks – and finally whites and the Zulus. Now they say that it's quite harmonious, but nevertheless it is a city which has had its problems and it remains a mixed bag of cultures, mainly Zulu and Indian. I call it the capital of India because it's the largest group of Indians in one city anywhere in the world, outside of India. That's why I say I was born in the capital of India. And they say, 'Oh, Delhi?' 'No, Durban, South Africa.'

In Durban I lived with Harry Weir, the gentleman who had spotted me playing for Rhodesia. They converted the servants' quarters at the back of the house to a self-contained maisonette that I was able to rent from him. I had my own door so I could come and go without disturbing them, and that's where I resided while I was playing football: 335 Cowey Road – a little one-bedroom place. He had a lovely property in a nice area with a swimming pool, overlooking the racecourse and the sea.

Harry had gone from Northern Ireland to Rhodesia to play for Salisbury Callies and then gone on to play for Durban City, and then he became a coach. He was married to a lovely lady in Anita, and they had three children, three girls. Michelle was the eldest, then Joanne, and Adele. Michelle was the prim and proper one. I taught all three of them to swim in the garden pool. Anita was like a second mother to me. 'What did you do last night?' 'Why were you coming home at three o'clock in the morning?' She was very protective of me and didn't want me to screw up.

Harry was coaching AmaZulu, an African side in Durban. He had encouraged the manager of his former club, Durban City's Bill Williams, to sign me. Later, I would guest for Harry at AmaZulu. Harry and his family were really positive influences. I wanted for nothing. We'd eat curries, fish and chips, and roast dinners on Sundays after matches.

Because of the country's apartheid policies, football in South Africa was very different from Rhodesia. In South Africa they had three leagues: one for white players, another for those of Indian and Coloured origin, and the third one was the black league. We played in the white league. The first six months we were an all-white team. The next season we had one African player, named Mophat Zuma. South Africa was still banned by FIFA for its apartheid policies, but at the time there were some attempts to bring racial integration in football and a competition named the Mainstay Cup was introduced, so all those teams from the different leagues based on their skin colours could play against each other.

We used to call our chairman Norman Elliott the 'Silver Fox'. Whenever Norman pointed at you with his crooked forefinger, he used to give it: 'You, young man!' He had an absolutely gorgeous wife, Marilyn. She was tall and elegant, but he, by contrast, was a short, grey-haired, pot-bellied fellow wearing glasses. The Elliots lived in a fantastic place in Umhlanga, an affluent resort town north of Durban City.

Norman was an uncompromising fellow. He was always rowing with Harry Weir over who should pay my rent; in the end I'd pay it and then argue it out with Norman. Other players were always fighting with him over money too. I remember he asked a Scotsman to come and play with us, a striker with a fiery character. He was that tight he gave the Scotsman a Volkswagen Beetle to drive around in, even though we had a deal with Toyota. When he saw that I and my teammates had a club car, a Toyota in my case, the Scotsman wanted one too. Much to his disgust, Norman told him, 'No, you get a Beetle.'

One day the Scotsman wasn't getting paid for some reason so he went to Norman's house. The chairman wasn't there, so he started talking to his wife, and asking: 'Where's the Silver Fox? I know that he's called the Fox because he doesn't want to pay me.' Next minute Norman comes back and the Scotsman tells him, 'Listen, you haven't given me my money; and also another thing – you've just given me this bloody car, and that's not on. I want the same as the others.' Norman Elliott wasn't used to being spoken to like that and told him to jump in the bay. 'OK,' said the player, whereupon he went outside and drove the VW Beetle into the swimming pool. Inevitably, the player was sent back to Scotland.

The Silver Fox used to get players from all over the world – but particularly Scotland and England. We built great friendships in the team and even today I still keep in contact with several of them, like Tony Paris, the bodybuilder who now lives in Florida.

Durban City played in blue and white hoops with red numbers, blue shorts with red stripes, and then blue and white hooped socks with a red trim at the top. As the goalkeeper, I wore red or sometimes green. In those days my boots were Adidas. I didn't have gloves. I used to lick my fingers and catch the ball. Saliva counted; it was sticky. When it was raining I used to wear gloves, but never when it was dry.

It was July 1977; my debut for Durban City was against Maritzburg and I did well enough to be selected for the big game against Wits University in Johannesburg. We played at Kings Park, which is on the same ground as the brand-new stadium in Durban, the Moses Mabhida stadium. In goal for the other team was a South African goalkeeper of great promise, Gary Bailey. Before his arrival in South Africa South Africa, Gary's father, Roy, had been a goalkeeper with Ipswich Town and Crystal Palace in the 1950s and 60s and had become one of the first players to earn championship winners' medals in England's top three divisions. Gary had inherited his old man's talent, and the game was portrayed as the battle of the young stars in goal. Little could either of us have imagined that just a few years later the two of us would be coming face to face in one of English football's biggest rivalries: the Liverpool v Manchester United matches.

It was a typically hot, sticky, sun-shining Durban day. There were 32,000 packed into the stadium. In the main stand were mainly white people; on the right-hand side were Africans, and behind both goals were Indians. The skin colours were all segregated; that was the reality of South Africa.

I had left the army appreciative of what I had. I thought: *This is my opportunity*. Yet it would be a theme of my football career: glory laced with a touch of controversy. I don't think that I played badly; it was just one misplaced kick. I'd collected the ball by the edge of the area; I was on the left-hand side, in the corner of the eighteen-yard box. Someone was standing on my right side so I couldn't kick with my right foot, so I kicked it with my left and the ball squirmed only to the edge of the centre circle. I'm pretty good at kicking with both feet, but it just wavered a bit and it went from the left-hand side of my box to the very spot where the opposition centre-forward was waiting and he just half-volleyed off the bounce and it was perfect strike into the back of the net. Da-ding: 45 yard into the goal.

After that mistake, I played very, very well. I had some good saves. Wits were a very strong team, but we lost 1–0 and I found it all a bit embarrassing. I will always remember the headline in the *Durban Star* after my debut: 'Bruce boobs and Schoeman shoots home the winner.' I recall in the wake of the game one of our Indian fans saying, 'Ay, man, who's dis chap playin' for us? Ay, can't he kick properly an' all?'

*

TO HELP COVER THE COST OF LIVING, I DID OTHER WORK. IN THE first weeks at Durban City, I sold men's clothes at a shop called Markham's. Here, the manager, the former Blackpool player Brian Peterson, taught me all about the art of salesmanship. After that, I went to Toyota, our club sponsor, where I learned how to sell cars.

It was a tricky apprenticeship. Initially, the more experienced staff would walk up and say, 'All right, I'll take over here,' and then go and clear the deal. I didn't get a sale, not a sniff. Since we worked on commission, I came up with a plan. I said to the receptionist, a young Indian girl, 'If people ring up to speak to a salesman, ask them if they play golf, and if they do, put them through to me and not to any of the others.' She looked at me a bit strangely.

The next day I got a call put through on my extension. 'Hello?'

'Yes, I'd like to have a look at some cars.'

'Which cars would you like to look at, sir, and may I ask, do you play golf?'

'Yes, I do.'

'Well, have you got an afternoon free? I'll have the vehicles there at the golf course, you can have a look at your leisure, then we play nine holes and then you can look at the other vehicle and we can play the other nine. Afterwards you can drive one of the vehicles back to the showroom and I'll follow you in the other car and then I'll give you the keys and I'll jump into the car and you can drive back to the golf course to pick up your vehicle. And if you like any of them we'll just come back to the showroom and sign the papers.'

'Oh, that sounds like a good idea.'

I arrived at the golf course and we played while we talked about the cars. That's how I got the sales done, through developing a rapport with the buyer. When we finished, he did the two test drives, and then he got into his car and he followed me back to the showroom. And I said, 'Come into my little cubicle; now, which vehicle did you like?'

'I liked the Camry.' Then the next minute he signed. One sale down and an afternoon of golf included.

Soon, I started getting more commissions than any of the others, and I got a reputation that if you wanted a good deal for a car, go and play golf with this fellow, and it went round town.

It was good as long as it lasted. I worked there for eighteen months while playing football in Durban.

At the time I had an extra incentive to earn money as I was supporting my girlfriend Theresa and – as I then thought – my son, Hayden. I was there to witness his birth at the end of 1977, and he was a blond-haired, blue-eyed bouncing boy, and therein lay the problem. I am swarthy, dark-haired of Afrikaner background, while Theresa was a brown-eyed, raven-haired beauty of Spanish ancestry. I wondered about it at the time but, being naïve, I signed as the boy's father when the birth was registered. It was only later that serious doubts arose, particularly when I bumped into an old friend, a handsome, blond-haired, blue-eyed man who I had asked to watch out for Theresa while I was in the army. Just quite how attentive he was I'll never know; Theresa would never say. We split, inevitably, but I continued providing for the boy.

My time in Durban was also drawing to its conclusion. One day I got a government letter in the mail saying:

> *Dear Corporal Grobbelaar, you're hereby notified; in six months' time you will be coming into the South African army, and you'll be sent to 32 Squadron in Angola.*

I panicked. I wanted to be a footballer. I didn't want to go into the army again. In South Africa they were fighting the Cold War. South African soldiers went up to Mozambique, Angola, Namibia and other African countries to stop communism, because the Cubans and Russians were there helping them. The old regime in South Africa did a lot of bad things, and this so-called war was just one of them. It wasn't a war in South Africa – the war was fought on the borders. That's why they called it the Border Wars. The South African army wasn't fighting the ANC on the borders, they were fighting the armies of other countries.

South Africa had an influx of white Rhodesians who had left the country either after they had served their time in the army or later to escape the army when Mugabe took over in 1980. But because of their military experiences, the South African army took in a lot of ex-Rhodesian soldiers. They had the right to call you up into the army if you had lived in the country for two years in total and were over the age of eighteen. And because I'd done my military service they wanted me to go into the army.

The 32 Squadron that I was called to join was where all the nutcases that had fought in the Rhodesian War ended up. They went to South Africa because they were spoiling for a fight. It wasn't a good place for a sane man to be. They were truculent and desperate for a fight with the Cuban-backed forces because they hated communists and saw it as part of the Cold War. I had no interest in this at all, but the South African army wanted me in that squadron because I had been a tracker; I could follow people in the bush and they were skills they needed.

That was not for me; I had done my stint in one stupid war and this one was even worse. I decided there and then: That's it, I'm leaving.

I told Harry Weir, 'I don't want another war; I've had it up to here.' He was sympathetic to my plight and started helping me look for ways to escape the South African army and started looking for an overseas club for me. He utilised his big network in the game and came back to me six weeks later saying, 'We've got you a plane ticket to get you out of here; you're going to West Bromwich Albion on a trial.' The manager, Ron Atkinson, wasn't a name familiar to me, but his assistant, Colin Addison, had once been the manager of Durban City and was well known in South Africa. On April Fool's Day 1978 I left for Britain ahead of a trial that was to commence that July with West Brom.

7

The Green Mamba

IT WAS HARD LEAVING AFRICA BUT I WANTED TO KNOW IF I COULD
actually play this game at a higher level, and I certainly didn't want to be
conscripted again. I'd also had enough of Norman Elliott. I knew he wouldn't have
allowed me to travel to England without some form of payment so I told him I was
going to the US with a view to starting a baseball scholarship. Yet there were
other barriers up against me from the outset. I travelled to England on my South
African passport because it was easier to travel with that than with a Rhodesian
one. That passport wouldn't have got me anywhere, because ever since Rhodesia
had made a Unilateral Declaration of Independence against Britain in 1965 it had
been faced with sanctions.

Yet little did I know that it was like a green mamba travelling on a South African
passport. Like a snake it came and bit you on the behind, because every country
you went to, you had to have a visa and a work permit. As a South African footballer
that was impossible, because the country wasn't recognised by FIFA. I was sent to
the Home Office in Croydon and faced a Kafkaesque questioning but it got me
nowhere. It was so frustrating, but at least I was allowed to train and play some
friendly matches as an unpaid triallist.

I stayed in the Norfolk Hotel in Edgbaston and went to training to show what
I could do. Ron Atkinson was great. I went pre-season training with him and his
team in Oxfordshire, an area he knew well from his many years spent as Oxford
United's captain. We ran all over the Cotswolds. I trained with Cyrille Regis,
Laurie Cunningham, Brendon Batson, midfielder Len Cantello and the left winger
Willie Johnston. We did these two-mile runs through the hills and I used to lap

the others. By the time they got to the finish line on their first lap I was finished with my second; that's how fit I was in those days. The other players said, 'Hey, you, Grobbelaar, you stay behind us; you're not going in front of us!' So I made sure I was behind them in the second round.

I played the second half after we'd gone in 3–1 up at half-time, but sadly this was my only first-team experience in a West Brom shirt. The other goalkeeper was Tony Godden, and we had a great time together. I was at West Brom for five months and I did OK both in that pre-season outing and the reserve games I played in. The work permit, however, was a seemingly insurmountable problem. I was running out of savings and had to book a flight back to Africa. I remember ringing my mother and saying, 'I might be coming back to Rhodesia.'

'Oh, you need to get a proper job then.' Every time I returned to my mother, she said the same: 'This playing football, what kind of job is this? You've failed there, so you come back to get a proper job.' So I said, 'OK, yes, Ma.'

Ron Atkinson suggested I spent some time on the south coast at Bournemouth, in the hope that the greater promise of first-team opportunities might bring that elusive paperwork, but I came up against the same barriers. They had a goalkeeper called Kenny Allen, a big, tall guy – ugly as sin – unlike his wife, a South African lady. I spent my 21st birthday on the beach in Bournemouth alone with a bottle of rosé wine, ticked off with the world because I couldn't get a work permit with Bournemouth either. On the Monday I went back to West Brom, shook their hands and said, 'I'm going to go back to Africa.' I was gutted.

Colin Addison said, 'Listen, don't go yet. Go down to Derby County; Tony Waiters from Vancouver Whitecaps wants to see goalkeepers, and he's holding trials down there. Beg, borrow, or steal a car!'

I did the latter. By then, I had very little money left. I asked the girl behind the desk at the hotel if I could borrow her car. She said no. When she went in the office, I found her keys in the reception. I took them and drove her car to Derby, did a two-hour training session. I was having a shower when Tony Waiters appeared and said, 'I want to sign you. What are your movements?' I told him that I was planning to go back to Africa. 'OK, Thursday I'll give you a call and your tickets will be sorted out. I'll find out if there's a travel agent in Bulawayo that I can work with.'

I gave him my mother's phone number and the name of a travel agent in Bulawayo. I drove back to Birmingham, and as I got to the hotel there was a police car parked in the front, and the receptionist was speaking to a policeman. Quickly I went around the back of the hotel, parked the car, hid the keys, went from the side to the front of the hotel and walked in.

'Someone's pinched my car!' the receptionist exclaimed.

I said, 'Just hold on, I'll put my things down.' So I went in and there was no one at the front desk; I put the keys there and some papers on top and came outside. 'Where was the car parked? I'm sure you parked it at the back, because I just walked round there.' The receptionist, the policeman and I walked around the back and there – miraculously! – was the missing car.

That night I went to the airport, got on the plane and flew to Bulawayo via Johannesburg.

I arrived in Bulawayo on the Tuesday. My mother and my stepfather came and picked me up, then we went into my mother's shop and sat down in the office. She said, 'So you failed in Britain, you failed in South Africa, now you need a real job.'

'No, no! On Thursday night I will get a phone call. Vancouver Whitecaps in Canada want me; I'm going to play professional football for them.'

'Thursday?'

Thursday night came, but there was no phone call.

At five o'clock the following morning my stepfather woke me up. 'Get yourself a shower, shave, and put some clothes on.'

He took me to the railway yard, where they had invented a job for me – a refrigerator mechanic inspector. With my assistant Phineas, we had to check all of the refrigerated wagons in the yard. I was following in both my father and stepfather's footsteps in the railways now.

IN RHODESIA YOU GO TO BED EARLY, ESPECIALLY IF YOU WORKED ON the railways like I did. Yet my experience in the army had conditioned me to need five hours' sleep or less. The phone was in my mother's bedroom when it rang late one night, waking her up. I could hear one end of the conversation. 'Hello, who is this? From where? Just hold on.' Next thing she called my name.

Tony Waiters was on the line. 'Bruce, I'm going to give you some instructions for tomorrow. Listen carefully and take them down. There's a travel agency in Bulawayo. Go to that travel agent, she's got your ticket to fly via Johannesburg, via Heathrow, via Toronto to Vancouver. Those are your stops. The first stop tomorrow morning you have to get to Pretoria with your passport to go to the Canadian Embassy to get them to give you a work-permit stamp. They know about it. Get back to the airport early in the evening to catch the flight. If you don't get here by Saturday morning the contract might not come.'

'OK, thank you very much…'

My mother was still rubbing her eyes with tiredness: 'Who's that?'

'Vancouver! I'm going to Vancouver!'

'What time is your flight?

'I don't know until I get to the travel agent tomorrow.'

'Right; make sure you go to the railways with your stepfather before you go to get the ticket.'

'What for?'

'Just to apologise that you are leaving and disappointing them.'

I packed my boots and everything else I needed. The next morning I was up anyway because I couldn't sleep. I said goodbye to my sister and my brother and went off with my stepfather to the railways, into the foreman's office, announcing that I was leaving.

'Where are you going?'

'I'm going to a place called Vancouver in Canada.' All the Africans within earshot of this news responded, 'Ha – hey, Jungleman going to Canada!'

We used to get a little brown envelope with our money and the weekly slip. The foreman came and gave me the money – though not for the Friday. And I gave it to my mate and said, 'All you guys, go for a nice drink in the bar. Cheerio!' Then I turned towards the foreman: 'Mr Foreman, I'm going to Vancouver now. Cheers; make sure you stick this job right up somewhere I don't like. I'm off!'

And with that I walked out the door and back towards football.

8

A Football Gypsy

A FOOTBALLER'S GYPSY LIFE BEGAN.

There was a ticket waiting for me at the Atlas Travel Agency in Bulawayo from Vancouver Whitecaps, and my intercontinental football commuting started that day.

I went to the airport, said cheerio to my mum and stepfather, and jumped on the aircraft to Johannesburg. Then it was a one-hour drive to Pretoria, where I reached the Canadian High Commission at three-thirty, knowing the embassy closed at four.

At four o'clock I was still waiting to get my stamp while the clock was ticking fast towards my flight to Canada. At four-thirty I got the stamp and it was now a 90-minute journey back to the airport in Johannesburg because of heavy traffic.

I got there in an hour, went through security and I could finally relax when I reached the departure lounge.

I flew to the UK, landing at Heathrow at about 7 a.m. My flight from there was in the evening, flying then from Toronto on the Friday afternoon and finally arriving in Vancouver on the Saturday morning.

It was winter and minus-20 degrees Celsius in Toronto. I had gone from a southern African summer and was in shorts and a T-shirt, and there was no gangplank – you had to come out of the aircraft, go down the stairs into the bus. I went into the building, got warm again and panic-bought a thick jacket.

In Vancouver, Les Wilson, the reserve coach, picked me up at the airport and drove me to the hotel. I checked in and thanked him for taking me there. He said,

'What do you mean, thanks? Put your stuff in, get your kit, your boots and gloves, we've got a game tonight!'

I had flown across the world from Africa, through two nights and a day, and now I've got to go and play a game…

We played a reserve game against Seattle Sounders at Swangard Stadium and drew 1–1. I was pretty tired before the game but now I was knackered. I came back to the hotel sleepy.

'Get some sleep, because tomorrow afternoon you're playing the same team again,' was the message as I got dropped off.

The next day we beat them 1–0. I had a pretty good game and at the end of it was presented with a one-year contract, which I signed, too tired even to check the small print. It was such a relief. For me, the start of my journey to become a top-class professional footballer had come in such a roundabout way. Dreaming of making the big time in Africa, I had always thought I could go straight to the UK to pursue my career. Scarcely could I have imagined that the journey would take me to Canada. But in essence playing in Vancouver was like playing with professional footballers from the UK because half the team were from England.

In my trial with West Bromwich Albion, Willie Johnston was at the club. When I got to Vancouver he was playing with me there as well; so there was a familiarity. I really haven't thought about it before now, because as much as I'd been hoping and dreaming of playing in England, my career could have turned out very differently had I been able to get a work permit and signed for West Brom at that time. Instead I had to take the journey towards English top-flight football through Canada, and training and playing for Vancouver gave me my first real test of games that involved high-profile players. I played against Franz Beckenbauer, Pelé, Johan Cruyff, Giorgio Chinaglia, Teófilo Cubillas, George Best, Rodney Marsh. Alongside me at Vancouver was Alan Ball, England's World Cup-winning midfielder, and Ruud Krol, who had been part of the Netherlands team that had reached two consecutive World Cup finals. Although I was second choice to the former Wolves goalkeeper Phil Parkes I was made to feel very much part of the set-up. Before every game every player would be introduced to the crowd, whereupon I would return to the substitutes' bench and playing for the reserves, waiting for my chance to come. When Phil went out with his wife, I'd babysit his kids. Because of what had happened to me in the army, I adapted quickly to my new surroundings. Going to Vancouver and becoming familiar with some great players was no big deal in the grand scheme of things.

The North American Soccer League (NASL) was doing very well at this time and so was our team. We played against some big teams. As the champions of the National Conference, we played the American Conference title-holders, Tampa Bay Rowdies, on 8 September 1979 in the final of the Soccer Bowl in front of 50,700 at the Giants Stadium in New Jersey. Phil Parkes was in goal while I sat on the bench watching my team win their first North American championship. Alan Ball was man of the match.

Vancouver were in so many respects like an English club stuck on North America's Pacific seaboard. Our manager Tony Waiters had played for England, Blackpool and Burnley. He was a good goalkeeper and a good coach. At the back we had Roger Kenyon, who had captained Everton, and John Craven had played for Coventry City; in the midfield were Jon Sammels, who had played for Leicester City, Derek Possee (Leyton Orient) and Willie Johnston. Up front we had Kevin Hector, the former Derby County player, Trevor Whymark (Ipswich), Carl Valentine (Oldham Athletic) and Ruud Krol (Ajax).

Playing alongside such figures and seeing how they approached the game improved my professionalism. Above all else I learned how to prepare properly for games, to take my time on a match day so I was never rushed. Like in the UK, we had a steak before the game: a minute steak, a thin one with an egg and some chips. Nowadays it's frowned upon because science has told us that it's not good for your body. But in the 1970s and 80s, you ate what your body felt was comfortable.

In North America there is always a demand for entertainment that goes beyond sport. It was here that I developed my repertoire of pre- and in-game gymnastics and clowning: climbing on goalposts, handstands, spinning the ball on the tips of my fingers. I understood my duty to entertain as well as keep goal. It was ingrained in the American sporting culture.

Tampa Bay had a mascot, the Rowdy, while a chicken represented the team from San Diego, and then there was Buffalo Bill. If the game was boring in San Diego, for example, the chicken mascot would jump into the crowd and be passed above the heads of the supporters like he was surfing. It ensured that everyone always had something to watch.

I can remember playing one game in San Diego where the chicken mascot really infuriated me. When a shot flew past my post and went wide, the chicken caught it and didn't want to give me the ball back. We were losing 1–0 and pressing for an equaliser. I said, 'Give me the ball!'

'No, no, no!' the chicken shouted back at me. In the end, the referee gave the chicken a yellow card. The chicken then fell down crying in front of the fans. For them, this was entertainment.

AT VANCOUVER THERE WAS A FELLOW RHODESIAN NAMED GRAHAM Boyle, a right-back who had played for Arcadia and Rio Tinto in Rhodesia but came across to play in Canada because his parents lived in Calgary. His nickname was Iron Man, because he was hard as rock. By 1980, Mugabe had taken over and our country was renamed Zimbabwe and Graham told me that our renamed country was going to play against Cameroon to compete for a place in the 1982 World Cup. It was the first time our country had entered the tournament since 1970. The manager John Rugg wanted me to come and represent Zimbabwe in goal.

I wanted to, but thought that my South African passport would now be a problem. He told me not to worry, that they would swap it over for me and provide me with a Zimbabwean one. It was through football, therefore, that I got my first Zimbabwean passport. I took the long journey to Harare – as Salisbury was now known – and collected my passport, and then travelled with the team to Douala where we played against Cameroon at the Stade de la Réunification in a two-legged qualifying tie. It was six days after my 23rd birthday.

Douala was the old capital of Cameroon and a seaside port. Once you leave the city and go inland a few miles, it becomes a tropical jungle. The stadium dated back to Cameroon's colonial past and was a multi-sport arena. There was a football pitch surrounded by an athletics track, circled by a concrete cycle track. You could only see around ten rows of seats from ground level, because the stadium was dug into the ground. It officially holds 40,000, but they had another 20,000 sitting on the concrete velodrome and they had a makeshift fence around the middle of the running track. No breeze would help us in the heat as the spectators blocked any air reaching the pitch. The heat was intense. So was the noise around us.

We kept them at bay for eighty minutes and then their striker scored, the reigning African Footballer of the Year, Jean Manga Onguéné. From the eightieth minute until the final whistle there were 60,000 people whistling until we got this ringing in our ears like bees. It was a nightmare. Then they scored again in the

85th minute through their midfielder Grégoire M'Bida.

The return game in Zimbabwe was at Rufaro Stadium on 16 November 1980. The game was played in a thunderstorm, and as much as the official number says we played in front of 20,000 people, I think there must have been about 40,000 in attendance. People had even climbed up on the floodlight poles to watch the game, and lightning struck a pole just outside the stadium. The referee, a Sudanese chap, thought the weather was quite nice because he came from an arid country and they hadn't had any rain for a long time. So he made us carry on in this weather, while any other referee might have called the game off. Cameroon's goalkeeper, Joseph-Antoine Bell, had a magnificent match and pulled out some fantastic saves. David Muchineripi scored the only goal to win us the game 1–0 but Cameroon went through to the next round of qualifying with their 2–1 aggregate win. The following year they would become only the second sub-Saharan World Cup qualifiers after beating Zaire and Morocco on the way to Spain. For me – at a time when only two African nations qualified for the finals – it would be the closest I ever got to a World Cup tournament.

Nevertheless I was very proud to represent my country and thereafter I flew back to Africa as much as I could for games.

BACK IN CANADA I KEPT IMPROVING AS A GOALKEEPER. EVEN though I only got to play three games for Vancouver in my first season, I learned so much. I owe a great deal to Tony Waiters, who lent his experience as a goalkeeper to me. He passed on advice and was able to tell me when I was making errors. Although I was only Phil Parkes's understudy he always found time for me. He was an excellent manager, a taskmaster who demanded excellence from all of his players. I thought I was fit until I played under him, but I soon found I was quite wrong. He was nevertheless aware of the shortcomings of reserve football in North America and saw that an ambitious young player needed a higher standard to improve. He talked of a loan spell to England, but I was disenchanted after my previous ordeals over a work permit. Only if Liverpool, Arsenal or my boyhood favourites Derby County had made a move would I have considered it. Tony assured me that it was vital for my development as a player that I went to play in England. When I expressed my reservations, he told me not to worry. He'd been talking to 'the strongest team in England' and there was clear interest.

When he revealed who that was after a loan had been agreed a few days later, I couldn't hide my disappointment.

'Crewe Alexandra? I thought you said I was going to the strongest club in England?'

'You are,' said Tony. 'They are ninety-second in the league, bottom of the Fourth Division and holding everyone else up. They've got to be the strongest club to do that!'

Whitecaps' joker had fallen for the oldest joke in English football. But when I got to Crewe in October 1979, I faced a familiar problem: I still didn't have a work permit to play in the UK. In desperation I called my mother in December asking her to turn over every rock to see if I had any blood links to Britain; I would get an ancestral visa thanks to the knowledge my mother gave me.

She told me how my great-grandfather was in the Welsh Fusiliers. His name was Charles Ernest Banning. They were stationed in Cape Town Fort, the castle, in South Africa during the Boer War. This was a British stronghold and as such designated British soil. So by virtue of my great-grandfather being a commissioned officer and him being able to stay in that area within the walls of the castle, my grandfather was born in that castle – officially British soil – in 1903.

When I went once again to Croydon to try to get my work permit, the same people behind the desk said wearily: 'Oh, it's you again.'

'Yes, but I've got some more information for you.' Then I told them about my grandfather. Remarkably, that was enough to convince them and they stamped my passport with an ancestral visa which enabled me to start playing. If I'd known that a year earlier, I would have been playing for West Bromwich Albion.

Crewe is a railway town halfway between Birmingham and Liverpool. It was a real awakening going to the town's football club, Crewe Alexandra. The style of football was so different from what I knew in Canada. It was hard and fast, with hefty aerial battles. The club itself seemed a long way from Vancouver with its heavy resources and smattering of world-class stars. Crewe were indeed used to the strongman act, holding everybody on their shoulders – the bottom of the Fourth Division was a home from home for them. In a time before automatic relegation to the Football Conference, applying for re-election to the Football League had become a regular occurrence for the club.

At Crewe I played under Tony Waddington, the legendary former Stoke City manager, who was nearing the end of his coaching career. Tony knew a thing or two about good goalkeepers. Twice he had shocked English football by signing the current England goalkeeper for Stoke: in 1967 he'd bought the World Cup winner Gordon Banks, and seven years later Peter Shilton, both from Leicester City. I think some of his experiences with those two rubbed off on me.

The English Fourth Division wasn't without its colour and occasional glamour, however. Playing for Crewe, I played against Ian Botham, 'Beefy', the famous English cricketer, a very strong, powerful guy who was later knighted and regarded as one of the best all-rounders in cricket history. He came on as a substitute when Crewe played Scunthorpe United. On a corner I went up for the ball and he banged me from the back and it hurt. So at the next corner I said, 'Hey, listen, blockhead, I'm going to come through and when I shout "keeper", get out of the way.' I came out, hit him on my way for the ball and got him back. I looked at Beefy and reminded him, 'That's 1-1!' Since that day, Ian Botham and myself have been firm friends.

Now it is a big industry bringing African players into the English leagues, but back in the early 1980s it was a completely different story. The English game was very insular, and there were very few foreigners at all. Manchester City's South African-born midfielder Colin Viljoen was one rare example coming from Africa. In the 1980s the Stein brothers – Mark, Brian and Eddie – would make names for themselves in the English game; they had all been born in South Africa but were forced into exile as children due to the political activism of their father. There had been other South African footballers in the past, such as the Leeds United winger Albert Johanneson, but in the 1970s and 80s we were trailblazers for our continent.

While at Crewe, Tony Waddington sent me to Nottingham Forest to train with Peter Shilton and gain some experience. Forest were European champions and on their way to retaining that trophy. They were, of course, managed by the temperamental genius Brian Clough. After the training session Clough called me over into his office. 'I think I remember you, you were supposed to come to me a decade ago. People talked to me about you in Rhodesia. Now you're on loan at Crewe and training with the greatest goalkeeper England has ever had. Whom are you signed by at the moment?'

'I'm playing in Vancouver in the North American Soccer League.'

'Oh, that Mickey Mouse league across the pond! If you want any advice son, forget the Mickey Mouse Yankee Doodle Dandies league and get your arse back here. It is not bad over here, son!'

By their standards Crewe had a reasonably good season. From being seven points adrift at the bottom when I joined, we were eight points clear of the bottom spot at the end, though 23rd in a 24-team division. They had to apply for re-election and, like the rest of the bottom four, were successful.

For me it had been a tough but steep learning curve, yet I always had fun, and my stock was rising. Waddington would tell me about all the teams that would come to watch me play. Twenty times out of 24 games I played for Crewe, Man City were there watching. Tony Book from City's coaching staff seemed to have his doubts about me, though, and was forever coming back for a 'second look'.

In April 1980 we played away against Portsmouth and Tony Waddington said, 'There's a scout here today, he'll be watching one of our midfielders, and he's from Liverpool.' His name, Tom Saunders, meant nothing to me at the time, but I was to soon learn that he was one of the most influential people at Anfield in the Shankly and Paisley eras.

Our opponents that day needed two points to remain with a chance of promotion. They thought it was going to be an easy victory because we had nothing to play for but we fought hard and they had to come back from behind to draw 1–1.

During the warm-up Tom Saunders was standing with some local guys behind the goal, and he overheard a conversation between two of them. One guy said, 'I don't think we're going to get the two points today.' The other one said, 'Of course we are,' smoking a rolled-up Woodbine cigarette. 'What are you talking about, of course we are, mate.'

'Now, have you seen the goalkeeper? Have a look at his warm-up.'

In those days I still used to do crazy warm-ups, the habit that I'd picked up and developed in Canada, sitting on the crossbar being one of them. Tom Saunders took a note, *goalkeeper*; even though he was there for a midfielder.

I played the game well and in his notes to Bob Paisley it read, 'Forget the midfielder, have a look at the goalkeeper.'

The next weekend we played Stockport County at Gresty Road. Tony Waddington said to me, 'Come here; two very important people are coming to see you play today.'

'Oh, let me guess: Manchester City?'

'They'll be here as well, but these two are from Liverpool. Try not to do anything silly.'

I went out and did my warm-up, a crazy one again. It started raining when we went out for the warm-up so I took an umbrella to keep dry walking out on the pitch, shook it out and did my normal thing – throw the ball at the crossbar from the penalty spot, and when I hit it three times I started my warm-up. I was always superstitious like that. Years later at Liverpool, I would have to hit the light switch in the dressing room with the ball three times before entering the pitch. It would drive some of my teammates nuts having to wait for me. It tested everyone's patience, particularly Ronnie Moran, who would tell me week after week: 'Get the eff out of here and play.' I think superstition is a trait I've carried from Africa. To this day I always put my left shoe on before the right one. I don't know if it makes any difference, but I don't want to risk it by putting the right shoe on first.

At Crewe my pre-match superstition and warm-up involved swinging on the crossbar to stretch my back. I'd pull my legs up and then drop down; roll, do a few flicks, walk on my hands, jump back on top of the crossbar with the ball, throw it at the person on the eighteen-yard line, and as soon as he touched it I'd come back down off the crossbar, land and then make a save before the ball went in. Messing about like that in the warm-up could take about 20 minutes. When I was done I ran in with the umbrella – it had stopped raining by then – and the manager Tony Waddington was standing there looking at me, shaking his head from side to side.

'What's the matter, boss?' I asked.

'You know those two people that came to watch you play?'

'What do you mean *came*?'

'Yes, they've already gone to watch another game.' Apparently Bob Paisley had told Tom Saunders, 'I've seen enough, let's go,' and made Saunders drive him down the road to go and see Port Vale play.

The last game of the season and my last game for Crewe we played York City at home. I was captain for the day and it was a May bank holiday weekend. I have always loved taking penalties and I wanted to leave a mark by taking one for Crewe. Tony Waddington told me I could take one if we were at least 2–0 up, but that day, when we were awarded a spot-kick in the 58th minute, we were only 1–0 up. Nevertheless, I was undeterred by this. I ran the length of the pitch and told Bobby Scott, our regular taker, 'Oi, Scotty, hold my cap, I'm taking this penalty, get out of here, I'm the captain.'

I put the ball down on the spot and the York goalkeeper, Richard Taylor, came up to me and said, 'Listen, Bruce, don't take the mickey out of me, I don't want to look like an idiot with a penalty being taken by a goalkeeper sending me the wrong way. Which side are you putting it?'

'You just dive to the right.' He did as I told him, the ball went to the right, but it flew so close to the goal frame you could almost hear the contact as it whooshed past it into the net. We won 2–0 and the next day I flew back to Vancouver.

9

To Liverpool on a £1 Bet

I DIDN'T HEAR ANYTHING FROM LIVERPOOL, AT LEAST not immediately.

The English season might have been over, but the American one was not long under way. Phil Parkes had departed Vancouver for Chicago Sting. I had fully hoped to succeed him as the Whitecaps' number one, but in my absence Tony Waiters had signed the Scotland international David Harvey. That move was ill-fated and after an indifferent start I replaced him as first-choice goalkeeper for the rest of the 1980 season. As my reputation grew in the NASL so too did speculation about a return to England. Tony Waiters told reporters: 'My phone has been red-hot recently with English clubs chasing Grobbelaar and if I were to make him available, a deal would be on immediately.'

Liverpool as it turned out were just one of those clubs. In the midst of this speculation I was told to travel to England to meet Bob Paisley.

I was excited but apprehensive as well because I'd learned quickly how fragile the world of football is. It had seemed that I had a chance of signing for West Bromwich Albion but I didn't. It had seemed that Bob Paisley was interested in me for Liverpool but then the line went dead for a while. Would it happen again?

I flew direct to London Heathrow and caught the train to Birmingham, as Liverpool were playing Birmingham City that day. I was asked to meet Bob Paisley and Peter Robinson, the club's secretary, in a quiet room but the meeting would raise more questions than answers.

Paisley eventually shuffled in and mumbled: 'You've played in the UK at Crewe, well, this is not Crewe, this is Liverpool Football Club. This is Peter Robinson who does all the admin. I see that you've got an ancestral visa. Good, you'll hear from us.'

Then he walked out the door. I was confused and looked at Peter Robinson, who just said, 'Well, you've heard the man, you can go back now.'

It didn't make me any wiser. So I returned to the airport and took the long journey back to Vancouver. I didn't even get a ticket to see the game.

Months passed and nothing came from Liverpool. The NASL season was coming to an end at Vancouver. After losing 1–0 to San Diego at home, Tony Waiters came to me and said, 'Listen, two very important people have come to see you. Bob Paisley and Tom Saunders from Liverpool want to ask you a few questions.'

As I walked into the room, Paisley says, 'Grobble-de-jack, would you like to play for Liverpool?'

'Yes, Mr Paisley, I'd love to play for Liverpool.'

'That will do for me.' And with that they turned round and walked out the door. I didn't see them again for another six weeks.

What I wasn't aware of then was that there was a reason for these long silences. A months-long battle between Liverpool and the Home Office had ensued for them to get me a work permit in England. Without one there was no way they could complete a transfer. The conditions then were much more onerous then than they are now: Liverpool had to convince them there was no one in the UK who could do the job I'd be able to do as understudy to Ray Clemence – who was 32 years old at the time.

It was only when working on this book that I was shown the letters of correspondence going back and forth between Liverpool Football Club, the Department of Employment's Overseas Labour Section, the Football Association and the secretary of the Professional Footballers' Association. And it was quite moving reading Bob Paisley's arguments in a letter of 3 December 1980:

> We wish to make application for a work permit for Bruce Grobbelaar a professional goalkeeper of outstanding potential who at present plays for Vancouver Whitecaps in the North American Soccer League.
>
> He is a Zimbabwi [sic] National and also the holder of a South African Passport.
>
> You will appreciate that in an effort to maintain our position as one of the most successful clubs in Europe it is necessary to extend our scouting activities far and wide to find an understudy for Ray Clemence, who is now thirty two years of

age and we are convinced that Bruce Grobbelaar is the player we require. He is a current International player having represented Zimbabwi [sic] since that country became independent.

Mr. Tony Waiters a former English International Goalkeeper and one time employee of this club, is of the opinion that Bruce Grobbelaar is the best goalkeeping prospect he has ever seen and we are sure that we cannot possibly get a player of equal status in this country.

To be able to employ someone from abroad, the club also had to 'guarantee that no person who is ordinary resident in the United Kingdom will be displaced or excluded in the consequence of the engagement of the overseas worker in question'.

In the application it also said the club had 30 contract players at the time and seven apprentice professional players. It said I would be getting £450 per week plus the same bonuses as the other players. The bonuses were '£10,000/20,000 per annum, depending on success'.

It also said that at the end of 1980 the highest rate of pay was £952 per week.

I know that Tony Waiters thought highly of me, but it is still touching to find his words about me in an official document all these years later. I feel proud and very honoured to be thought of this way – that Bob Paisley would make the effort to try to convince the authorities that I was the only man for the job as Clemence's understudy, instead of not having to go through the extra trouble by signing someone from Great Britain.

But the Department of Employment – Overseas Labour Section – was not convinced; I had only played two games for the Rhodesia national team and two for Zimbabwe, so they did not see why I would be this extraordinary international reinforcement that couldn't be found in the UK. So they asked for advice from the PFA and the FA in a letter of 14 December 1980:

On the evidence available we have some doubts as to weather [sic] Mr Grobbelaar can be regarded as satisfying the 'Internationally established' rule. Moreover, there is no indication of any search for a suitable resident or EEC footballer.

We would welcome your comments on these aspects of the application and on any other relevant matter, including the question of understudying for Clemence.

Luckily the Professional Football Negotiating Committee backed Liverpool's application, answering the very next day:

> *...in [the] opinion of the Professional Football Negotiating Committee the application from Liverpool meets the requirements of the work permit scheme.*

That wasn't enough for the Department of Employment, who in a letter of 13 February 1981 wrote to the Football League:

> *As I mentioned to you over the telephone yesterday, we are not satisfied that the application made by Liverpool F.C. in respect of Bruce D. Grobbelaar meets the rules of the Work Permit Scheme.*
>
> *Grobbelaar does not seem to meet our skills criteria; he has played only two international games for Zimbabwe – not a major football nation. Therefore, he can hardly be said to be an 'established international player with significant contribution to make to the game'. Moreover he is required only as an understudy goalkeeper.*
>
> *In addition, the club has not provided us with evidence of having made a search for suitable resident players.*

Luckily Bob Paisley got his way. The Department of Employment finally granted me a work permit in the UK, and I would start an unforgettable thirteen-year journey with a club and a city that hasn't left my heart since.

On 15 March 1981, I came to Liverpool on a bet. Tom Saunders and Bob Paisley staked money against each other that I wouldn't find my way to Anfield, or figure out what to do next. I didn't know where I was going. I was a big signing of £250,000. That was quite a lot of money for a goalkeeper after only seeing a 20-minute warm-up, and one game that we lost in Vancouver against San Diego. So signing me was a big gamble.

I landed at Heathrow. They hadn't given me a ticket to Liverpool; I had to find my own way from Heathrow to Anfield. I went via Manchester Airport by plane, hired a car, got into Liverpool city centre and did not have a clue where I was going.

I asked a black cab where Anfield was; he laughed ironically and replied, 'Do I know where fucking Anfield is?!' You don't ask a cab driver that question in Liverpool without them laughing at you.

On arrival at Anfield. I realised the gates to the stadium were shut. It was 5:15pm, the working day was over, so I had to go and find a hotel. What did any person do when visiting Liverpool in the 1980s if they needed a room? They checked the Adelphi first. As I walked through the door towards the reception, I passed the lobby area, not taking any notice of the people sitting there. I asked the girl if they had any rooms and she apologised: fully booked.

As I turned around I saw Tom Saunders give Bob Paisley a £1 note, saying, 'I never thought he would get here.' One pound poorer, he gave me the keys and said, 'Here's your room for tonight, see you tomorrow at training.'

10

In at the Deep End

BOB PAISLEY WAS A MAN OF FEW WORDS, BUT HE WAS ALWAYS FIRM in his instructions. That evening in the Adelphi Hotel in March 1981 he imparted the final directions for my journey to become a Liverpool player. I was to take a taxi for the short journey from Liverpool city centre to Anfield at eleven o'clock the next morning. If I encountered a pack of photographers and journalists upon arrival – as I may well do – I had to stay inside and tell my driver to take me back to where we'd come from. There I'd get a phone call with new instructions.

The next day at 11 a.m., I arrived at Anfield in a taxi to sign for Liverpool but I could see straight away that my signing would be delayed. Stood in front of the main gates when we arrived were a herd of photographers, so I did as I had been told and asked the puzzled driver to take me right back to town where I came from. At 2:30 p.m., once the press had left, Paisley called the hotel and said I could come back up to the ground, so I went back to Anfield and signed the contract.

This wasn't actually the final journey to being a Liverpool player. As I was to learn, there was to be a final detour to France. My contract was actually dated for the following day – 17 March – because, officially, I needed to enter the country with my work permit. To get around this Peter Robinson arranged for me to fly to Paris for the day so that I could re-enter the country with all of my documents properly stamped.

Liverpool booked me a plane ticket to Charles de Gaulle Airport in Paris, but upon arrival I couldn't get through the airport with my South African passport – I needed a visa to enter the country. At the same time, I couldn't fly back to England after only staying in transit in Paris. I was stranded and desperate. I was so close to realising my dream of becoming a professional footballer for Liverpool Football Club, but here I was stuck in an airport far from anywhere.

As I pondered my next move, I saw a little lady with a South African passport in her hand. I asked her how she had gotten through and she told me she had obtained a 24-hour shopping visa, and pointed me to a counter, where I was able to purchase one. Finally I had a way out. Slap-bang, the stamp was in my passport, providing me an entrance into Paris, where I stayed the night at the home of the city's most eminent dentist, an eccentric called Dr Peter Heuith, who Peter Robinson had put me in contact with. We spent the night at the famous Crazy Horse Cabaret, just off the Champs-Élysées, and enjoyed a memorable night.

The next day, 17 March, I returned to Liverpool and completed my move. I signed for £250,000, with a weekly salary of £250 – less than Liverpool had claimed in their original application to the Department of Employment. Finally I was a Liverpool player.

FOR THE REMAINDER OF THE 1980/81 SEASON I WAS TOLD I WAS going to be playing in the reserves, alternating with the club's other young goalkeeper, Steve Ogrizovic. Steve was a former police officer who had signed for Liverpool from Chesterfield four years earlier, but had spent all his time in Liverpool's reserve team. There was no disgrace in that. Many considered Liverpool's reserves one of the best teams in the country, not just at reserve level – the team had dominated the Central League for a decade – but in all of England. With players like Steve, Ian Rush, Ronnie Whelan, Kevin Sheedy, Craig Johnston and Howard Gayle, it was an understandable contention.

Steve was to play the remaining home games, while I played the three away games. My first game was against Everton, which we won 1–0; in the second game we beat Bolton Wanderers by the same scoreline and in the third game we drew 1–1 at Leeds United. One goal against me in 270 minutes of football wasn't a bad start to my Liverpool career, but it was the fixture against Bolton that got me noticed. In that game I was up against the former Manchester United and England forward Brian Kidd. He was in his early thirties and I let him know about it, telling him he was too old and should swap his boots for a pension book. I could tell I was getting under his skin and he responded as any good footballer should do by trying to make me eat my own words. He fired a piledriver at the top corner, but not only did I save it but I held on to it as well. As I picked myself up I told him he needed to do better if he was going to score past a young star like me. He responded soon after with another fierce drive and I saved again. I knew I had won the battle when he began to rant and rave, shouting, 'Get that gorilla out of goal!' I know that Roy Evans, our reserve manager, was impressed by my performance and went back to the Boot Room saying so. The performance put me on a real high.

At the same time as playing for the reserves I was training with the first team, and I worked as hard as I could to show them that they were soon going to have to make a decision, not on their number two, but on who their first-choice goalkeeper was to be. Steve still thought he was second in line behind Ray Clemence, since he had played the home games for the reserves. I had other ideas in mind.

Ray had been at the club since joining from Scunthorpe United in 1967, and had been first-choice goalkeeper for more than a decade. He was a truly great player and at the time the most decorated individual to ever play for Liverpool. Only the excellence of Peter Shilton, whom he alternated with in the England goal for many years, limited him to 61 caps. In any other era that would have been 161 international appearances. Ray was 32 at the time of my arrival, and while relatively young in goalkeeping terms, it was clear that I was considered a long-term replacement for him. Ray was aware of this too, but I don't think he fully appreciated how I had more immediate designs on the number-one jersey.

Soon after my arrival Ray and I were interviewed jointly by a journalist named Matt D'Arcy of the *Daily Star*, who started by asking the club's number one how much longer he envisaged himself being at Anfield.

'I'd like to be here another two years and teach Bruce how to come through the ranks,' was his answer.

When D'Arcy probed further, asking if he had any intentions of moving on, Ray reiterated that it'd be another two years before he left the club.

The journalist then focused his attention on me, asking for my thoughts on Ray's words. I turned to my teammate and said, 'That's what he says, but if he's here for another two years I'm going to take his place anyway.'

'What do you think to that, Ray?' D'Arcy continued.

'Well, he's a very confident young man.'

'When will you take his place?' I was asked.

'I'll probably take his place next season,' was my instant response.

Without another word, Ray got up and walked away.

AT THE END OF MY FIRST SEASON LIVERPOOL MADE IT TO THE 1981 European Cup final in Paris against Real Madrid. In the first round of the competition they demolished the Finnish side Oulun Palloseura 10–1 at Anfield, with Graeme Souness and Terry McDermott both scoring hat-tricks. The team then comfortably defeated Aberdeen and CSKA Sofia in the next two rounds by a margin of five goals on each occasion, before a tight affair against Bayern Munich in the semi-final. We eventually progressed via the away-goals rule after two even legs.

Paisley soon told us the team for Paris and named me on the substitutes' bench, but I went to him and told him he should select Steve Ogrizovic instead, someone who had been at the club far longer than I had and had actually played for the first team before.

'Don't you want to play?' Paisley asked.

'I won't be playing anyway – I'll be sitting on the bench.'

'Well then, you go and tell him.'

It was therefore left up to me to tell Steve that he was going to be sitting on the bench, and would potentially be winning a medal if the team was victorious. Meanwhile I was in the stands with Craig Johnston watching what was the first European final we were involved in. I could have got a medal had I sat on the bench, but you give the person who has been there the longest the opportunity. I didn't think I deserved it at the time.

I was sitting there with all the wives of the players as the Reds took on the famous all-whites. They were so quiet, so Craig and myself got them some scarves and told them to start shouting. You can't go to the football, sit down and just say, 'Oh, good shot.' We gave them a little supporter crash course. 'Come on! Shout! Jump up and down! Jeepers! When your husband kicks the ball, shout louder.' We warmed them all up for when Alan Kennedy scored the winner towards the end of the game.

Afterwards I went away to Hawaii for my holiday. My lawyer Ron Perrick and his wife were also there with their kids. Ron and I were playing golf at one hole near the condominiums by the sea when his kids, Kit and Otis, came running over.

'Hey, Dad, there's a phone call for you.' He went on the buggy back to the flat, returned and said, 'Bruce, you must tee up. You are first because you won the last hole.' As I put the ball down and pulled the club back, twisting my body and lifting the club, he said, 'Ray Clemence has gone to Tottenham.' I couldn't stop mid-swing, so instead I just slashed the ball out of bounds. I think I broke a window. 'What do you mean, gone to Tottenham?'

'Signed for Tottenham, you idiot,' he said. 'Now you've got a chance, it's you or the big guy, Oggie.' Thousands of thoughts were flying though my head. Clemence leaving came completely out of the blue. Just weeks earlier he'd said himself on the record that he expected to be at Liverpool for another two years.

I hit the next ball, finished the round – which I won – and as victor let Ron pay for dinner that evening. It was a good night all round.

WHEN WE RETURNED TO PRE-SEASON TRAINING AHEAD OF THE 1981/82 season, it was the first time in fourteen years that there was no Ray Clemence at Melwood. Against all expectations, Bob Paisley had sold him for £300,000. Steve and I were now battling it out for the number-one jersey.

In the brief period I had spent with Ray, I had managed to spend a little time studying him. In particular he taught me how to sweep behind the back four. Although I was doing it in North America, he taught me more subtlety as to where you need to position yourself. He was a very good sweeper-keeper, though later on I think I took it to the next level and would go a little bit further up the pitch.

That summer we went on pre-season tour to Switzerland. I played every single game against Neuchâtel Xamax, FC Zurich and Servette. The setting of the stadium in Neuchâtel was breathtaking, right on the edge of a lake.

Paisley paired us youngsters up with one of the more experienced players who could look after us. He had his own way of addressing you and he was always getting names wrong. 'You, Grobble-de-jack, you're going with David Johnson.' David taught me very well. On the night before games we had a curfew, but nevertheless he'd say, 'Don't you want to come out for a drink?' so out we went. We sneaked out to town and went to a couple of bars before ending up in a nightclub with Ronnie Whelan and Ian Rush.

David and the other senior pros taught me how to be a Liverpool player. It was one thing performing on the pitch, but so much of Liverpool's success was attributable to the team spirit and bonds built off it. You needed to fit in, because if you didn't it could be a ruthless place. As a newcomer in the team, I didn't have any problems asking David if I needed something. So, if David was going to do something, I did it too, even though it wasn't always the smartest idea. He was fantastic; he was one of the old boys. He'd been there, done it, and was an important member of the group. I'm very proud to say I'm still a good friend of his and I often see him when I go back to Liverpool.

David also had a great sense of humour and, my goodness, he used to take the mickey out of some of the youngsters. There was a time when young Ronnie Whelan wanted extra tickets for the Manchester United game, because his family were all United fans. Knowing full well what his response would be, David suggested he went and asked Bob Paisley for the tickets.

Ronnie went up to Bob's office and knocked on the boss's door, went in, and with that sixteen pairs of feet went down the corridor to listen in.

'Yeah, sit down, what do you want?' we heard Paisley say.

'Well, boss, growing up as a youngster in Dublin, I was a Manchester United fan. I had a great game last week and scored, so this week I was hoping to bring my brother and sister over for the match as well as my parents, and we've only got two tickets, so I'd like two extra.' There was a silence and then Bob Paisley said, 'Yeah, that's OK; you can have five, because you're not playing!' We were running down the corridor in fits of laughter.

If you played badly you'd get the mickey taken out of you in front of all the players. Alan Hansen would make up things like, 'The coaches want to see you, so go to the Boot Room,' or 'Gaffer wants to see you.'

Of course, you went to knock on the door. 'You wanted to see me, boss?'

'No I didn't. Stop disturbing me, go away,' would be the inevitable reply.

The Scottish mafia – Graeme Souness, Kenny Dalglish and Hansen – were always together, and they were the most active in taking the mickey out of us foreigners, not just me and Craig Johnston and our Israeli teammate Avi Cohen, but Ian Rush too, who, of course, was Welsh. Avi didn't take too kindly to the Scots and when I asked him on my arrival at Anfield what advice he could take from his experiences he warned me darkly, 'Don't trust those Jocks, they are all cheats!' This was a reference as much as anything to the five-a-side games we had in training, in which they'd all team up together and be unrelentingly competitive, claiming any dubious decisions as their own. Fortunately, I had experienced the

Scottish humour in my days at Salisbury Callies – a club with long connections to Scotland. I had also been with a Scottish girl, Jean McDougall. What did they bring? A dry wit, stability and a great professionalism. In Souness, Dalglish and Hansen you were looking at the three best players in the team and the spine. If you played with them and made a mistake, Hansen would not speak to you for a week. He wouldn't even pass you the ball in training. In the same situation, Souness would be on to you all of the time – trying to improve your standards and remind you of what his were. Kenny, meanwhile, would make some sort of subtle remark to the other Scots about you that, if you didn't know him, would make you think he was being sly. The three of them were impregnable. You couldn't take them on. When Stevie Nicol came – another Scot – he was the brunt of all their jokes until he eventually joined forces with them and became another leader.

I soon got the hang of it. Once we flew to Sudan and everybody had too many drinks on the way there. Many of the players fell asleep on the aircraft. We lifted Sammy Lee into the overhead locker, put a pillow on the side and closed it. When we came down to land the door popped open and out dropped Sammy Lee. He must have thought, 'What the bloody hell am I doing up here?' The pilot warned us that he could actually get us arrested – what we had done was dangerous. Later he drank with us in the British Embassy in Khartoum.

I don't think any other team had the laughs we had. I was on the receiving end of plenty, especially in the beginning, but given I had seen so much at a young age in the war – more than most others in the team will have seen in their lifetime – I was pretty well equipped to take everything that was thrown at me.

Not everyone warmed to the style of banter. Some of the other players would wind Howard Gayle up about my record with the Rhodesian army, which, as the club's only black player, he didn't take kindly to. Ian Rush also found it hard to deal with in the beginning. It made him insecure, especially in the first year. Rushy took the brunt of a lot of it, because he was quite shy. Eventually he wanted to leave because it was so harsh. He even asked Bob Paisley to put him on the transfer list. The way Rushy eventually stopped people taking the mickey out of him was by sticking the ball in the back of the net all the time. Eventually he did leave for Italy, but returned after supposedly complaining it was too much like living in a foreign country. Maybe he missed our banter too.

11

The Clown Prince

RAY CLEMENCE WASN'T THE ONLY BIG NAME TO DEPART DURING this period. Despite winning the European Cup for the third time in May 1981, Bob considered it the moment to bring some fresh blood into the main squad and let some of the older, more experienced players go. As well as Ray, Jimmy Case would leave, while Terry McDermott, Ray Kennedy, David Johnson and David Fairclough would be edged out over the following year. Much was expected from Ronnie Whelan and Ian Rush, who had made their first-team debuts the previous season. Mark Lawrenson was signed from Brighton & Hove Albion over the summer of 1981 and Craig Johnston was still to make his debut having signed from Middlesbrough for £650,000 shortly after my own transfer.

After playing only three reserve games and the pre-season matches as preparation, my first-team career with Liverpool commenced on 29 August 1981, the opening day of the new campaign, against Wolves at Molineux. Mark Lawrenson also started his first game for Liverpool and Craig Johnston made his debut as a 72nd-minute substitute for Ray Kennedy. It was an inauspicious start for all of us: we lost 1–0.

Naturally, Steve Ogrizovic was unhappy. He would eventually go to Bob Paisley and said, 'Boss, I think I should be playing week in, week out.'

Paisley responded, 'You will be playing week in, week out; I've just sold you to Shrewsbury Town.' Bang, Oggy's Liverpool career was over. We had got on great. We had a mutual interest in cricket.

I was a very confident young man taking over from Ray Clemence, but to be honest, the first six months playing for Liverpool's first team was a real struggle.

The near invincibility the club had shown over the previous decade was dented in the first half of the 1981/82 season. In this day and age, I don't think a manager would show the same faith in a struggling player like Bob Paisley did in me. It helped him that, in the bigger picture, Liverpool were still getting results and still winning trophies but criticism was flying around and he could have signed any goalkeeper in the country if he'd really wanted to. Bob never said anything positive about anyone but I felt like he trusted me when many others did not.

Initially I had some misty-eyed ideas of Liverpool supporters getting behind you, because they were known as the best supporters in the world. But they had no patience, at least with me, and the clowning and showing off didn't go down well with them. They were fed, to an extent, by the local media. I felt the local papers in particular didn't like me.

Things weren't helped by the fact that we initially hovered around mid-table until after Christmas, losing games Liverpool would never have usually expected to lose. There were rumours about Bob's long-term future and talk of his impending retirement, with the Swansea City manager, John Toshack, tipped to take over. In the dressing room there were tensions when Bob replaced Phil Thompson as captain with Graeme Souness at Christmas. Phil felt Graeme had stolen the captaincy from him and was especially hurt because some players on the team had known about the change before him. The two didn't speak for months. Though they reconciled to some degree for the benefit of the team, a feud has existed for decades since, ramping up again a decade later when Graeme became Liverpool manager and sacked Phil as reserve-team coach.

At this stage in my Liverpool career I made many errors and hadn't figured out how to communicate efficiently with my new defenders. The first months were far from promising from my perspective. My style was very aggressive. I would rather go and meet the problem – the problem being the ball – than wait until it came to me. But in goalkeeping there are only certain times you can go and do this; either when there is a through ball or the play is in your area. In your area you can use your hands, and you are therefore at an advantage as long as you can judge the flight of it, which I often did. However, sometimes I was prone to error – that was just the way I played. I enjoyed enough of a rapport with the centre-halves that if I shouted, they'd know to drop behind me onto the line so they would be there to sweep up if I missed it. It was exactly the same procedure when coming out for a through ball. An important principle to remember, and it seems like many goalkeepers don't know this, is that when a through ball is coming towards you and you're moving towards it, you're moving towards the ball at twice the speed as the opposition player trying to score, because he's chasing the ball. The fact that it is coming towards you means it's going away from the striker, so you should be able to get to the ball before they have the chance to shoot, provided you judge it properly. It's all about timing. The speed of your feet is also important as a goalkeeper. You do not need to be a good sprinter; you just need quick feet to get into position. You have to be a good dancer, light-footed and able to move around. I love to dance, of course. A goalkeeper should never stand on his heels, but be ready to move on his toes, and then it's easy to shift position.

But I wasn't dancing too well in goal for the first half of my debut season. We were reigning European champions, but in the following two campaigns my mistakes sent us packing in the same competition. I had never played in Europe before, where they'd punish you if you were not up to it. You're playing against the best, only the league winners from each country.

In those days there was a lot more pressure in the European Cup as it was a knockout competition straight from the beginning. There were no group stages where the top two progressed. It was all or nothing. In the quarter-final of the 1981/82 edition we played the Bulgarian champions, CSKA Sofia. We were the dominant side, but they defended well. At one point I went up to claim a ball, and one of their players bumped into me as I jumped. The ball dropped to the ground and a forward stabbed it in. For their second I just completely misjudged it. The ball went over my head and straight to their striker: 2–0. If the ground could swallow you that would be the moment you wish it would eat you up. We had won the home leg 1–0, but my two mistakes in Sofia had cost us. I was solely to blame.

Do you think the players spoke to me until the next time we played? Not a chance – not even on the plane. There was nowhere to hide. You learned to cope with it that way. There were other players that didn't play particularly well, and they were able to get over it. But as a goalkeeper, I had cost my team and my club progress in Europe. The punishment of silence would end by the time the next game came around, but during training in the first couple of days after the event they wouldn't even pass you the ball – certainly not Hansen.

For the first six months I tried to do things that were not to Liverpool's liking. I came from playing in North America, where it was all about entertaining people. They don't want a second without something happening. I used to walk on my hands around the pitch while the game was going on. Coming to England, I was trying to entertain the crowd like I did over there. In truth, I was trying to relieve the pressure of playing in front of thousands upon thousands of passionate Liverpool supporters through entertainment. I had never seen passion like that before. I had played in front of 35,000 at Barbourfields in Bulawayo, Zimbabwe, when I was a teenager, and Matabeleland Highlanders had a big stadium, but the passion there is a little different. At least I had the experience of playing in front of big crowds, so those who thought I didn't do well because of the size of the crowd were wrong.

What made me fail was probably the fact that I felt the need to put on a good performance, and the way I could do so was to entertain. However, entertainment off the ball was not what the Liverpool fans wanted to see. They weren't bothered about the handstands and the gymnastics off the posts, they just wanted you to do your job and then you'd be OK.

Some thought I lacked confidence, seeing as I was making so many mistakes. That wasn't true. It was actually the opposite: I was ultra-confident then. I'd come out of a bush war after nearly two years fighting for my life, got to Vancouver and lived on my own for eighteen months before Liverpool happened. I was probably too confident. That is why things transpired the way they did in the first six months.

My teammates had not told Ray Clemence what to do in his area, and therefore I felt that they shouldn't tell me what I should do in my area. But for the first six months, that's exactly what they did. Eventually I learned to be humble and take heed, realising I had to listen to what other senior players said. It was the Liverpool way. They had been around a lot longer than me. With this hierarchy, the oldest and most experienced in the team were the leaders and therefore told the youngsters what to do and what not to do. It made it extra challenging being new to the team. As a keeper you need to take a leadership role in your box and over your defence, and at the same time you're new and trying to find your place in the side, and therefore you need to be humble. It is a conflict of interests.

Maybe clowning around, walking on my hands and sitting on the crossbar was me subconsciously trying to take some of the pressure off, so I could blame 'the clown' if I didn't play well.

The Everton fans gave me the nickname. The Blues started the clown thing in my very first derby game at Goodison. The press loved the metaphor, and would call me a Clown Prince as often as they had the chance for the rest of my playing days. Three fans dressed as clowns came over at 1–1 and gave me this big picture of me saying, 'Bruce is the Clown'.

I put the clown's face facing the Gwladys Street end, and I had a brilliant game in the second half. When we won 3–1, I picked up the clown face, walked up to the fans and said, 'Who's the clown now? You or me? Me? No. You? Yes.' And I walked off. I looked back over my shoulder, and the three jesters were getting beaten up by their own. Karma.

WHEN I STARTED PLAYING FOR LIVERPOOL'S FIRST TEAM, MY WAGES doubled. I bought a a three-bedroom cottage in the Welsh village of Gwynfryn. The third bedroom was very small so I knocked it through from the bathroom and put a Jacuzzi in. Bob Scott, who was our captain at Crewe, helped me – he was from Liverpool but now lived in Coedpoeth, just outside Wrexham. When I first signed for Liverpool he advised me not to buy a house there, but out in Wales instead. 'After a game if you go into town and you drink, you'll be like George Best in a few years – a pisshead,' he said. 'Buy yourself a house in Wales so you can drive back. It will give you some leeway to get out of town.' It actually helped for a while. I drove a Jeep to and from my house in Wales to Anfield. Buying the cottage was the best thing I did in my early years.

Nevertheless, I ended up partying in that area as well, and still ended up getting myself into some trouble during that first year for different reasons.

In December 1981 we were flying to Japan to play the Brazilian team and winners of the Copa Libertadores, Flamengo, in the Intercontinental Cup. I woke up in my Welsh cottage a little too late and saw snow covering the ground. '*Oh shit*,' I thought. My Zimbabwean mate Graham Boyle was visiting, so I asked him to take me to Speke Airport. The roads were terrible; covered in snow and very slippery. Finally I got a police car to escort us along the chaos on the motorway. When we finally made it to Speke everybody was waiting on a bus because they couldn't fly out due to the snowfall, so we were going to Manchester. As I stepped foot on the bus Bob Paisley said, 'We've been waiting for you. Where have you driven from?'

'Wales.'

'Buy yourself a house in Liverpool!'

It wasn't a suggestion. It was an order.

We flew via Anchorage on the first leg of our epic journey to Japan, where we would play the final. When we got off the plane Craig Johnston spotted a well-known face: 'I know that fellow; I'm going to see if he wants to play football.' So in the departure lounge all of us were playing five-a-side with Rod Stewart, using plant pots as goals.

On 13 December we played Flamengo at the National Stadium in Tokyo. They had Zico – nicknamed 'the white Pelé' – as their captain and attacking midfielder, a very creative and technical footballer who was one of the world's best players. He and his teammates hammered us. We lost 3–0.

Straight after the game I was given a shocking message. Bob Paisley came to find me and said, 'Do you want to sit down? Sorry to give you this news, but your dad died on Friday.'

I looked at him. 'It's Sunday.'

'Yeah, we didn't think you could handle the news on Friday and then play the game. So speak to the secretary. You've got a funeral to go to.'

Then he walked out the door. No hug or pat on the shoulder from Bob. Bob didn't know that I wasn't particularly close to my father but I don't think he knew how to deal with the issue of mortality sensitively. When I look back, though, at the time it didn't occur to me that he could have done anything differently to make me feel any better about it because my emotions towards my father were conflicted. On the other hand, if it had been my mother I would have been devastated.

PETER ROBINSON ARRANGED FOR ME TO TRAVEL BACK TO Johannesburg business class. I left that night straight after the game, first to Paris, then from France down to South Africa. Maybe this would have annoyed other players but not me.

His death came as a shock to us all, despite the poor health he had suffered from. He was only 51. Buerger's disease ultimately took his life. The arteries in his legs weren't getting blood to his feet. It's similar to Raynaud's disease, where it's very difficult to get blood to the extremities. They had his artery and his vein reversed so it pumped the other way, and that saved his left leg. Then they tried the same procedure on the right leg, but he got a verruca at the bottom of his foot and when they cut it out the sore went septic and gangrenous. They then told him they had to cut another part of that leg off too, but during the procedure they did not operate high enough, missing the gangrene they were hoping to eradicate. He carried on living with this gangrene and it eventually went to his stomach, and that's what killed him. When I had a burst duodenal ulcer later in life, I thought it might be the same disease that my dad had suffered from, but luckily it wasn't.

Looking back now I suspect he must have known the end was coming. A couple of months earlier he asked to borrow some money from me, £3,000, and I thought nothing of it because I had access to it – I'd signed for a lot more than that. I asked my mother if I should give it to him, but she advised me not to. I thought about it for a while and then concluded, 'Ah, you know what, he's my father; I'm going to give him the money.' I asked him what he wanted it for, and he told me it was to pay all the debts that he owed to various people in South Africa. Neither my mum nor I knew of these debts and I realise now that he did it so that it wouldn't leave a trail to me, my sister or any of his family. I sent it out to him in November, and made sure my cousin Archie gave it to him. Dad died just a few weeks later.

The funeral was a strange occasion. As well as my sister and brother-in-law, his second and third wives were there, along with his latest girlfriend. My mother didn't attend. Not everybody got along, so you can imagine what the atmosphere was like in the chapel. As well as his collection of wives, there were priests from three different churches – the Dutch Reform Church, the Anglican Church and the Presbyterian Church – sharing the altar, as he had visited all three at different stages in his life. There was also a Mormon priest present, as my brother-in-law was a preacher by then. In total he had four eulogies done by four priests. I am not sure what faith he belonged to at the end, but everybody was looking after him.

The funeral was on a Thursday and I was in a hurry to fly back to England as we had a game in London against Tottenham that weekend. When I got there, I found the game was called off because it was snowing.

My dad really hurt us when he left my mum and us children while we were small. The scars lived with us for a long time. Have I forgiven him? Yes. I gave him his dignity back before he died, which gave me my dignity too, because had I not given him that money then the debtors would have been on to me. He could leave the world with a clean conscience. He was complicated – a drinker, a smoker and a womaniser – but for all his faults he was an honest man too.

It's ironic because before my mother died some years later she told me, 'Bruce, I know you're going to South Africa. I want you to go to your father's grave and tell him that I've always loved him, and that he is forgiven. I will see him in heaven.'

I went to the Boksburg cemetery between Benoni and Brakpan and lit a cigarette by the gravestone – because he used to smoke – and I told him what my mother had said. When I finished, three Africans that looked after the graveyard came to me as I was walking back to the car, and one of them said, 'Why did you, as a white man, kneel and pray to the headstone?'

'Because that's my father, and I had a message from my mother who just died.'

'You've done it like a true black man. We've never seen a white man do that. And do you know what happens after that? You have to have a drink.'

'I'm sorry, my father smoked, I had a cigarette with him,' I replied, and they said, 'Yes, we saw that; but now you're going to have a drink,' and they took me to the office and they gave me some beer. One was a Zulu, one a Xhosa and one a Pedi. They had been working at the graveyard for many years but they had never before in their lives seen a white man kneeling to the same height as the gravestone, looking down, talking to their ancestors. They asked me how I knew what to do in African style, being a white man. I said, 'No, I'm African; it's just the colour of my skin that is different.'

Every year when I go back to South Africa, I kneel at my father's grave and talk to him in the same way.

WALKING ON MY HANDS AND SWINGING ON THE CROSSBAR DIDN'T go down well with the football purists who came to watch Liverpool on a weekly basis. They would all say the same thing: 'Who is this guy and what is he doing?'

I was showing off my fun side, but the truth is a lot of people saw that as disrespecting the club. They thought that by messing about I was not focusing on the game, and consequently other people's livelihood.

The first six months was a disaster. We were knocked out of the FA Cup and the European Cup, while the Brazilians had humiliated us in the Intercontinental Cup. We had been sinking like a heavy rock in the league, hitting a low on Boxing Day, losing 3–1 to Manchester City at home, sending us down to twelfth, with a nine-point gap between us and Swansea City at the top. This was the first season where three points were awarded for a win instead of two. I had played seventeen league games for the club so far, and I had conceded nineteen goals. Against City I had a bad day. Three goals went in and I was at fault for at least one, maybe two. I blamed our captain Phil Thompson for the second one, and he blamed me. We were fighting a lot in those first months. Our communication was poor.

After the City game, Joe Fagan was given the green light from the boss to tell us off. He was screaming furiously in the dressing room, picking every single one of us apart, except the youngsters Rush and Whelan. He told Kenny he should have scored twice as many goals as he had this season. To me he shouted: 'Grobbelaar, you look more like a ballerina in goal. Why don't you catch the round thing like you are supposed to do?' You could hear a pin drop – the place was deadly silent.

Bob Paisley came in and gave me a hooked finger, meaning 'come to my office', and that was what you dreaded the most after a loss. For you to get the crooked finger meant one of two things. You were either going to get dropped, or you were going to have to work hard to convince him from here that you were worth perservering with.

He said, 'There's going to be some changes.' Then in front of everyone he turned to me: 'You, Grobble-de-jack, come here.' Everybody thought I was going to be dropped. Finished.

When I went to his office, I knew once I walked in that door there would be sixteen sets of feet coming down the same corridor, because the whole team was going to come and listen to what he was going to say.

He told me to sit down. 'How do you think that you have played so far?'

'Well, boss, I think I've had a reasonable first few months. I have tried hard to adjust from North America to here. I suppose I could have played better.'

'In North America they entertain. Here, we win. If you don't play better you'll find yourself back in Crewe. Now eff off and think about it.'

I was about to walk out of the boss's office when I heard everybody outside the door running away from it.

As soon as Bob Paisley swore at you, you had to react. I asked Ronnie Moran, Joe Fagan and Roy Evans for advice. They repeated the mantra: it's about winning. I had to forget all about walking on my hands and swinging off the crossbars.

The next weekend, we played Swansea in the FA Cup. There was a lot resting on the game. Not only was it the FA Cup and a game we were coming into on the back of a poor result, but Swansea were riding high in the league and there were rumours about their manager John Toshack replacing Paisley as Liverpool manager. I was convinced I was going to be dropped. The day before, Paisley reminded us, 'Yes, there's going to be some changes.' And I thought, 'Oh, here we go, another goalkeeper's going to get it.'

Instead of me, he dropped Sammy Lee and Craig Johnston, but the big change was Graeme Souness replacing Phil Thompson as captain.

Bob was matter-of-fact about it all – 'Right, let's go and play' – but Thommo was furious at losing the captaincy. Thommo had always dreamed about being the captain for his favourite team, and assuming the role was one of his life's proudest moments. In fact, he is probably one of the proudest captains in the club's history. Losing the honour was deeply hurtful. Yet while Thommo and Souey developed an ice-cold front between themselves off the pitch, on it they would help each other like before.

The truth was Thommo's performances had gradually declined during his tenure as captain because he carried too much responsibility. He was like a union leader to us all. Whenever anything went wrong with the players, Phil Thompson was the one to go to. If he got a sponsorship deal, he would negotiate the same deal for everybody. It was Thompson as captain who carried the burden when Paisley introduced a host of fresh faces into the first team. Not only did he have to get used to playing in front of me and alongside Mark Lawrenson, there were also two new midfielders in Craig Johnston and Ronnie Whelan, and a new striker in Ian Rush. We all came in at more or less the same time. That was a lot for him to carry, as he would take the blame if we messed up.

After the captaincy was taken off him, we argued a lot less, and I probably gained some confidence. Phil used to be really hard on me. He and Alan Hansen could be brutal. They knew how to really put you down.

The change of captaincy worked straight away. It took the pressure off Phil, who rediscovered his form, and that rubbed off on us all. Graeme Souness was a strong enough character to take the captaincy off Thompson. It was another stroke of genius by Paisley.

AFTER THE TONGUE-LASHING BOB PAISLEY GAVE ME, I STARTED finding my feet. My confidence grew and I started fully justifying my place in the starting eleven. From December 1981 onwards it was business as usual for Liverpool, and if we got comfortably enough ahead in a game I would mess about. Paisley didn't have anything to say about that.

Ray Clemence had left us to win trophies and seek new challenges at Tottenham

Hotspur. I had been struggling to fill his gloves as the new goalkeeper without his tutelage – which I had expected to last for two years. How would I fare against my old teacher when we did battle with each other on the field?

Liverpool were League Cup holders, and on 13 March 1982 we were once again in the final defending our title, and that so happened to be against Ray Clemence and Tottenham. The master meeting his understudy. At the old Wembley Stadium we came out behind the goal. Clemence and I met in the tunnel, shook hands and walked out together, wishing each other luck and then we played the game in front of 100,000.

After eleven minutes Steve Archibald went through on goal. I came out to try and close him down, but he slid it under me and made it 1–0. I did make a few decent saves during the match. I made a good stop from Glenn Hoddle, and then another one from Archibald in the first half, and I denied Hoddle in the second period as well.

This was going to be a game Ronnie Whelan would be remembered for, as he curled one in past Clem only minutes before full time, sending the game to extra time. In the 111th minute Whelan scored a second to make it 2–1, and Rushy added our third just before the end of the game.

Ray came straight up to me at the final whistle and shook my hand, while I offered my commiserations.

Maybe I didn't need a teacher after all. Believe me, though, I would have rather stayed behind Ray Clemence for a couple of years to learn and develop, even if I had told the press early into my Liverpool career that I would take his place by the end of the season.

Onstage at a charity event in Liverpool a couple of years ago, Clemence was summing up his time as a player and said he was very grateful for how Tommy Lawrence taught him how to play for two years before he became Liverpool's first choice. I didn't get that with Ray. When the time came to speak about me, he said, 'I knew from the moment I met Bruce that he had a strong enough character to go on without me.' That is very big praise from such an incredible keeper and I was overwhelmed and very thankful to hear it.

AS MUCH AS THE FIRST HALF OF THE SEASON HAD BEEN A BIT OF a disaster, the following four months were very good. In the second half of

1981/82, we won 20, drew three and lost just two of our remaining 25 league games. I only let in thirteen goals in those matches, my best record for Liverpool. We went on a spectacular climb up the league table.

The League Championship was secured with a 3–1 victory over Tottenham with a game to spare. That result lifted us up to 86 points – an insurmountable tally after second-placed Ipswich lost their penultimate game to Nottingham Forest. Ian Rush would take over the throne as our top scorer, netting 30 that season, 17 of which were league goals. If we had been more successful in the cups, he would have scored many more.

We faced Middlesbrough away in the last game of the campaign. There was nothing for either side to play for: we had finished top and they were already relegated. Craig Johnston and Graeme Souness had both previously played for Middlesbrough and had got to know the singer Chris Rea while living in the northeast. At the time, Chris was involved with a new wine bar and he invited us there the evening before the game. It was with the approval of Bob Paisley, who was realistic about keeping us in check ahead of a game with nothing at stake. 'We think you're going to go out for a drink – just make sure it's only two,' was his warning.

It was a fine place to go out and invariably we had more than two drinks. We were drinking and dancing until a glass mezzanine floor collapsed when Terry McDermott's foot went through it and he got injured. While all this was happening the owner of the bar rang a Middlesbrough player and said, 'Put some money on yourselves to win this game, because these guys are getting drunk in the bar.'

We got back to the hotel at 4 a.m., sneaking into our bedrooms. A few hours later we had to get up to prepare for the game.

Terry McDermott was sitting on the bench and every time we got a corner, they poured a little nip of Scotch for the coaches. 'Oh, we've got a corner; that's a tot. Cheers.' Soon it was, 'We've got a throw-in on the far side; I think that's another tot.' We got a throw-in close to our bench and Sammy Lee came into the dugout and asked for a drink, so Joe Fagan gave him a cup. Lee took a big, thirsty sip and his eyes soon widened when he realised it was Scotch burning down his throat and not water. The game ended in a 0–0 draw and I don't think there was a sober man on the bench. Fortunately for Terry, his services weren't called upon.

Although it seems inconceivable now, in an era of sports science and nutritional plans, whisky was part of the Boot Room regime. When it was cold, we used to call the Scotch – invariably a Johnny Walker Red Label – our 'medicine'. Phil Neal would say, 'Where's the medicine?' He used to have a little tot and then pass me one. The first time I went, 'Jeez, what's that for?' 'To keep warm outside,' he said. We all had a little mouthful and out we went. It was our winter games ritual, and became one we'd happily repeat in May, when the trophies had been brought home.

They say that the first medal is the best. I'd won my first one two months earlier in the League Cup, but winning a league title is more of an accomplishment and that first championship was especially momentous. I had played my own part in that victorious campaign, and I kept nine clean sheets in the final fifteen games. Only one other goalkeeper – my old rival Gary Bailey, who was now at Manchester United – had conceded fewer than my 32 goals. It was special not just because it was my first title, but because it had been such a turnaround, especially with so many youngsters in the team. Looking back, it is only the European Cup triumph in Rome two years later that beats the feeling of this first league medal.

Once the title had been secured I was desperate to have that league medal in my hands, but we had to wait. You got your cup-final medals on the day if you went to Wembley, but they didn't give us our league medals until July. Ronnie Moran would bring them in during pre-season in a cardboard box. Unceremoniously he would put them on the massage table and say, 'Right, if you think you deserved it, come and get a medal.' And then he'd walk out. We'd won, but we were brought down to earth straight away. I don't know if the players today would put up with that approach.

That first time I sat and waited and saw the old boys go and get theirs, and then I went to get mine. There was no ceremony, no big speeches and pats on our backs by the Boot Room staff. That first year we just had a few beers on the bus coming back from Middlesbrough. I'm sure by that stage the thoughts of Bob Paisley and his Boot Room were simply focused on getting ready for the new season and winning the next trophy.

12

Match Days

ON BOB PAISLEY'S INSISTENCE I HAD TO MOVE AWAY FROM WALES and buy a place in Liverpool. I bought a show house in West Derby, but the move was ill-fated.

To keep me company I had bought two cockatoos from the local pet shop; one white and one grey. One day, soon after buying these birds, I came home to a smashed kitchen window. Someone had broken in, looking for things of value to steal. I got the window fixed, but the burglars soon returned and this time they ventured upstairs to look for valuables. When I came back on this occasion both the birds were missing – the burglars had let them out of their cage in the kitchen. You could see where they had initially hit the windowpane, but the window was open so they had hopped out and flew away. The grey one returned, but the white one never came back.

From there, the problems continued. I liked to dress well, and I had spent a bit of money on clothes, as turning out smartly was part of my upbringing. I had purchased some Lacoste T-shirts when I was in the south of France, and one day while I went to the local pub I left them hanging on the washing line in the garden. When I returned, they had disappeared. Later on I had more shirts go missing.

I decided to investigate and found out that the boys at the local borstal were jumping over my fence and had easy access to my garden from their yard. I took myself into the wooded area of this yard, and soon found a plastic bag underneath a bush. I opened it and, sure enough, there were my missing T-shirts. In order to prove that it was the kids stealing my clothing, I decided to set a trap. One morning I hung a fresh batch on the washing line, put a camouflage jacket on, and went and hid in the woods. It didn't take me long to catch the culprit, and when I did I took him to the headmaster of the institution. He was aged around fifteen. The borstal's aim was to help him and other troubled young kids before reintegrating them into society. But this boy had stolen from me, and in front of his headmaster I asked him to open this bag full of my shirts. After a period of questioning it soon became clear that he intended to sell my items, and that he had already found a buyer. That was the final straw for me. I decided to move. If you can't protect your home, you have to relocate somewhere else. Kenny Dalglish suggested I buy a house in Southport, but I ended up choosing the Wirral, the area on the opposite side of the River Mersey to Liverpool.

On the field things were happier. My second full season as a Liverpool player, the 1982/83 campaign, was another huge success. We started off by winning the Charity Shield 1–0 against Tottenham at Wembley, meaning that after the League Cup final earlier that year I had gotten the better of Ray Clemence for a second time in a row at Wembley.

During a normal week, approaching match days, we were meant to get as much sleep as possible, but sleep is something I always struggled with. When you're in the army you sleep for three hours and you have to open your eyes again. You've got four people in your stick, so you sleep three hours before doing an hour on guard. Three hours' sleep became the norm, and it has stuck with me since. Added to that, my experiences both in the war and later at Hillsborough regularly come back to haunt me to this day. Nowadays, five hours asleep is unusually long, and my body has subsequently adapted. My mother used to say, 'You can sleep when you die.' However, your body does need a little bit of downtime and if you can take a nap of 20 minutes, it rejuvenates you. That's what I had to do back then. If you're in the army you take all the opportunities you can get. If we were in a position ready to ambush those we were fighting, we would sometimes have to climb up a tree and nap there.

On match days I would have my breakfast at home and do my usual routines, before driving to Anfield about two hours before kick-off. Later, when I was married and had children, my family would make the journey with me, and on other occasions they travelled later with others. We would always make the journey back home together. At Anfield we would sort the tickets for our visitors later that day, before heading to the dressing room for our pre-match rituals.

Later in my career we'd have to go to a hotel the night before home and away games. That way no Evertonians could keep us awake at night on purpose by constantly knocking on our door or windows. This practice started when Kenny Dalglish became manager, and continued under Graeme Souness. We got to the hotel, had dinner, and then slept. Those of us with small babies would perhaps pick up more sleep than we would at home. My first born had colic, so my need for little sleep came in handy, but it was good to get a proper rest before the games in silence.

My roommate in the earliest days was David Johnson, and when David left the club I got put with Craig Johnston. I shared with Craig for around five years until I had a fight with Steve McMahon and smashed his nose after a heated argument, the sort that happens inside football clubs all of the time. Craig was scared that McMahon would come to our room seeking revenge. Craig turned out to be right, and on that very same evening he did come back to our room in the middle of the night to get me back, but I was ready and smashed his nose a second time. He never troubled me again, but I lost a good roommate in Craig because he thought McMahon would come back again and he didn't want to miss out on any of his beauty sleep. For the rest of the time at Liverpool I roomed with Stevie Nicol, and that could be pretty wild. After dinner with the team I'd leave Nicol in the room on his own for a couple of hours, because all he did was eat and drink. He would have his meal, followed by three bowls of crisps and a couple of pints of lager tucked up in bed. He'd talk constantly. At night when he rolled over you would hear a crunching sound.

THE BOOT ROOM STAFF HELPED ME PREPARE FOR THE GAMES AS a goalkeeper by studying the teams we were facing. It seemed like the staff knew everything about everybody. When facing penalties, I was well briefed about opponents. They would say to me, 'Don't worry about penalties. If they get one, look over to the bench and we'll tell you which side to go.' They would issue subtle signs. Often, they had seen the player in question take a spot-kick before.

My first game against Manchester United was a very close-run thing. In my first year we went to Old Trafford, and they had Frank Stapleton playing for them and he was their penalty taker. Before the game I went through my usual ritual in the changing room. I was sat on the toilet reading the programme, just to get the nerves out of my stomach, when I stumbled upon United's and therefore Stapleton's recent sequence of penalties. I stored that information, and sure enough they were awarded a spot-kick. Who steps up? Frank Stapleton. I remembered the sequence in the match programme, which told me which side he normally put the ball. I threw myself to that side and saved the ball, and we went on to win the game 1–0, Craig Johnston getting the goal.

A reporter asked me afterwards, 'How did you know he was going to put it there?'

'Well, when Manchester United are stupid enough to put it in the programme, it is easy.' They probably never did that again.

There were some penalty takers I feared more than others, like Alan Shearer, who scored 45 of his 50 penalties during his career. He was one of the best in the history of English football, and his shots would almost rip the net with sheer force. Still, I managed to save a penalty of his while he was at Southampton, and then I later saved one off him in an Old Boys' charity game up in Newcastle. Matt Le Tissier was another one. He later became my teammate at Southampton. In training he'd tell me which side he was going to put it in and I wouldn't be able to save it most of the time. He only missed one penalty in his Southampton career, scoring 47.

IN MARCH 1983 WE WERE BACK AT WEMBLEY CONTINUING OUR good run in the League Cup, beating Manchester United 2–1 in the final, our third triumph in a row.

We had our share of luck on that afternoon though – I should have seen red. In the final minute of normal time an injured Gordon McQueen somehow raced through our offside trap and headed towards goal. I came flying out, but he reached the ball before me and knocked it to my left. Instead of catching the ball cleanly my leg connected with him and took him out completely. I turned around and ran back to the goal, hoping the referee wasn't going to do anything, and thankfully he only booked me. In truth, I was very lucky not to get a red card. Today I'd be off straight away.

We then won the league again, my second in two years. That meant another box of medals was placed on the bench in the dressing room at the start of the following season, carrying the same implicit message: don't get complacent. Meanwhile my trophy cabinet at home was starting to fill up. Liverpool had done it again.

In the beginning I thought it was great to put the medals and trophies on display in the cabinet at home, before someone warned me that I should not have my most valuable possessions on show. From then on, I kept my medals in a sock in the sock drawer. If you didn't trust the bank, you kept money at home as well, and in the 1980s the world of finance was a bit shaky. I would stash my money in the bottom of the same drawer, bundles worth £1,000 each, then I'd put the socks on top. Everything was hidden there. We still had money in the bank, but there was always cash in the house, especially from when I got married.

When we won the league in 1982/83, it was Bob Paisley's sixth league title as Liverpool's manager and my second league championship in as many years. It proved to be the last with Bob in charge. He had taught us over the years to forget our triumphs straight away, and he had plenty of practice in preaching his own mantra. In total he won the European Cup three times, the Charity Shield six times, the League Cup three times and the UEFA Cup and the Super Cup once each. On top of that he had also six runners-up medals, but coming as he did from Shankly's school of management, first was first and second was nothing to Bob.

Paisley was funny and cutting. If he called you to his office it was serious. I wasn't scared of him, but he would cut you off at the knees. 'Jimmy Case, you're gone.' Off they'd go, their reputations and history at Liverpool counting for nothing. Paisley was ruthless when he got rid of players who had brought him lots of success, and he knew when he needed to refresh things in a certain position. 'Yep, time for you to go; piss off.' He was blunt. Some of the players didn't appreciate it and thought he was an absolute arse, but he wasn't. He could tell if a player was injured by watching him run or walk. 'Neal, their left-back, he's got a sore left leg, cut in, then cut outside, cross the ball and we'll score.' So Phil Neal cut in, cut outside, crossed, and we scored. 'I told you,' he'd say.

Bob also had the best backroom staff a manager could wish for, with Ronnie Moran and Roy Evans acting as the good-cop/bad-cop combination. They were fantastic together, absolutely brilliant. And then there was Joe Fagan, who was one of the best. For a man to win five trophies in two years, as he did when he succeeded Paisley in 1983, he has got to be very good. He was gone too soon as a manager. I would have loved to have played under Fagan for longer. He was a man who put his arm around you and said, 'Come on, lad, you're better than that.' He knew how to speak to players. He had this way about him that everybody trusted.

While Paisley was completely ruthless – toughened up by his own war days –

Fagan was Mr Calm. They complemented each other so well. Fagan told us everything. He also acted as Paisley's interpreter, because you couldn't understand anything that Bob was saying. He'd come out with expressions like 'He fling the far-flung one.' Naturally, we had no idea what he was talking about.

If players asked for extra input, like Souness, who once said, 'Excuse me, there's no instruction of how I should play,' Paisley would answer, 'Yes, we bought you for a shitload of money; you can figure it out. Why ask me?'

Shortly after signing, Jan Molby asked Joe Fagan a similar question, bemused that the team had been offered no guidance.

'We've paid a lot of money for you. You're playing in the middle; just play in your area and you'll be OK,' was the response on that occasion. Young Molby soon picked the ball up, dribbled it all the way through and scored. When he returned to the bench to get some feedback from the coaching staff, Ronnie Moran turned to him with a stern look on his face and said, 'I thought we told you to stay in your own area?'

13

Falling in Love

I MET MY FIRST WIFE IN HONG KONG. WE FELL IN LOVE AND I MADE a trip to the South of France to surprise her not long after we first met. It was a trip that ended up giving me an even bigger surprise, one that could have even sent me to jail.

We had been in the Far East at the end of the 1982/83 season for a friendly match to mark the opening of the new Hong Kong Stadium.

We played Arsenal and beat them, and afterwards Graeme Souness asked me to go and find a place where we could party. I went and asked the concierge where people go drinking in Hong Kong and found out that the Dickens Bar in the basement of the Excelsior Hotel was the place to be.

This was where I first saw her. She was standing together with a few ladies and a couple of men, all from British Airways, wearing a pair of jeans and a white blouse: Debbie Sweetland.

Debbie was very beautiful with striking features. She was petite, with short, brown hair, and had lovely blue eyes. She held herself well and spoke well too. When I told her I was African she said she'd never been there, despite working for an airline.

She then introduced me to the pilot, Captain Van der Merwe, who was a South African. We were chatting in a group, having a nice time, messing round, dancing a little bit. Then all of a sudden she disappeared into the night. I decided I had to find her.

I went to the phone, rang the hotel reception and said, 'Hello, this is Captain Van der Merwe from British Airways. We came in this morning and I would like to know the names and rooms of some of my crew, because I'm going to have a room party in the suite and I'd like to invite them.' The switchboard operator said they could invite them for me. I politely turned the offer down, explaining that I wanted to pick and choose, so I just needed their room numbers. The receptionist went down the list and as soon as he got to Debbie Sweetland I said, 'Thank you very much, that's enough for now.' It hadn't taken me long to obtain the information I needed.

I went and purchased a Portuguese bottle of rosé wine – a Mateus – and headed up to her room with two glasses. I knocked on the door, knocked again and then for a third time. It was actually the door of the room down the corridor that opened first, and out came another British Airways hostess with a towel around her, and one of our players behind.

'Do you want to join in, and is that bottle open?' she kindly asked. I shook my head and told her I was on my way into the room next door. The door in question then swung open, and there was Debbie, whispering to me that she was on the phone. She signalled I needed to be quiet with a finger over her mouth – she was on the phone to her boyfriend, telling him their relationship was over. With hand signals I asked if she wanted a glass of wine, and she shook her head, so I drank a glass anyway as she continued to speak on the phone. The time soon came for me to have a second glass, and again I asked in silence whether she wanted one. No.

I ended up drinking the whole bottle myself. When I finished it, I stood up and walked straight out through the door. She put the phone down and a pillow over it, followed me and said, 'Sorry, come here tomorrow and I'll take you around and show you Hong Kong.'

The following day she showed me around the Asian metropolis together with one of her friends and Craig Johnston. We went to the beach and had a fantastic day. I thought Debbie was very nice and after we returned to England, I couldn't stop thinking about her. I wanted to see where she was from, so I went to visit her in her flat in Sunbury-on-Thames and we went out for a date at an Indian restaurant. Again she was in a pair of jeans and this time a pink blouse.

She then went on a holiday to Juan-les-Pins, which is in the South of France. I was in love, and I needed to do something. I was playing tennis on a Thursday afternoon at the West Derby Tennis Club with some friends. 'What are you doing this weekend?' I asked them. They looked at each other before saying, 'Nothing.'

'Fancy going to France?'

I had a Ford Capri as my sponsored car, so I rang up the sponsors and asked if it was OK to take the car down to the South of France, but got a swift no. I had also bought a metallic-pink Ford Cortina convertible. It was absolutely beautiful, a red onion colour – I have never been afraid of standing out. However, I had given this to a mate of mine who was an insurance broker in Bolton. I rang him up and we agreed to meet on the M6 motorway at Knutsford services, where we would swap cars. He took my Capri so I could drive my Cortina convertible to the South of France. Problem solved.

Nineteen-and-a-half hours later I was in Juan-les-Pins. We got down there on the Saturday and surprised Debbie on holiday with her mates.

That night when I took her back to the hotel, I was told by reception my broker wanted to speak with me. I thought I would just leave it – I was not interested in talking business this weekend. We went down to the beach the next day, and finally I rang him back. 'Bruce,' he said. 'How's the car? Have you got the top up?'

'It's the South of France; I took the top down when I went past Paris.'

'Where is the car now?'

'Parked on the beach.'

'Go and check it; look under the passenger seat under the carpet. Come back and tell me if you find anything,' he said, so off I went, and find something I did: two gold bars – one white gold and one golden gold – plus a bag of stones. Diamonds, to be precise.

I had driven from Liverpool, got on the ferry, crossed borders and driven through France with two gold bars and a bag of diamonds. I rang him up that night: 'What the hell are you talking about?'

'Did you find anything?' he asked.

'Don't pull my leg; there's nothing there.' Silence. 'There's nothing under both seats,' I repeated. 'I've checked thoroughly. What are you on about?'

He broke down crying. 'I'm going to get my legs shot, I'm going to be done in.'

'Why?'

'Because I've been dealing a little bit on the side with some fellows, and they asked me to deliver this, but you came and took the vehicle off me so quickly, and I totally forgot about it. I had to deliver the goods by Monday.'

'Well, you'd better stall them until I get back, because they're still in the vehicle and they're still under the bloody carpet.'

'Well, you'd better take them out. '

'I'm not going to touch them; it's all staying where it is. It's come this far, and it's coming back with me.' I didn't touch anything. I still had to get back over the border with the goods in my car, so you can imagine what it was like getting the ferry back.

'Anything to declare?' asked the customs man.

'No, just these two idiots in the back.'

'Where are your passports? You're taking the mickey.'

'Yes, I am.'

I had gotten away with it.

I was totally innocent, but I had risked getting into serious trouble by smuggling my broker's valuables across the border. When we swapped cars I thanked him for nearly getting me arrested. Who knows what fate might have awaited me?

THREE MONTHS AFTER I FIRST MET DEBBIE, I WAS GOING TO Zimbabwe with a mate of mine called Martin Prothero, so I invited her along. She was 30 and I was nearly 26. We were at the casino in the Troutbeck Resort celebrating a friend of mine's marriage, and when we returned to our cottage Debbie turned and said, 'You wouldn't marry me, would you?'

'I would tomorrow,' was my reply.

So the following day we went to the District Assistant's office in Mutare, formerly known as Umtali, and did just that. No engagement, we just got married in tracksuits there and then. The tracksuits were Umbro, Liverpool's kit manufacturers at the time. Mine was a maroon top and grey pants; she had grey pants with a light-blue and white top.

We walked straight into the DA's office and told him we'd like to get married. 'Have you got your passports?' was his response. He took both, then asked how long we had been in the country.

'We've only been here a week.'

'Ah, then there's a problem. You have to be here for three weeks before you can get married.' He took a look at Debbie's passport, then picked mine up. It did not take long for him to understand. 'Ah, Jungleman! Maybe we can break some rules here. When do you want to get married?'

'Now.'

'OK, you need a witness.' I had mine – one of my mates was there – but Debbie still needed one, so I asked Mrs Chidehru, who happened to be sweeping the floors at the time. 'Excuse me, would you like to be a witness?'

'A witness for what?' she asked, stopping in her tracks.

'Don't worry – for marriage.'

'Oh, give me five minutes!' She went and dolled herself up with lipstick and everything, just to sign the marriage certificate.

We celebrated with a bottle of champagne, a jug of orange and two beers at eleven o'clock in the morning. Debbie phoned her parents after the ceremony and told them the news: she had just married a Zimbabwean who played football in the UK. Their first reaction was to ask if I was black. They had never met me. I don't think it was the sort of white wedding they had planned for their only daughter and in September 1983 they had the church wedding they had hoped for, when our marriage was blessed in a lovely church in Ubley, near Bristol. The previous day I had kept goal in a 2–1 victory over Aston Villa and afterwards my teammates chartered a bus down to Ubley for the big occasion.

After our Zimbabwe wedding we headed to Harare to tell my mate Graham 'Boysie' Boyle the news and we had another celebratory drink. Afterwards I took my new wife to the airport. She had to fly back because she was working – that was the downside of getting married unexpectedly. Boysie and I headed on to the honeymoon at Lake Kariba, the beautiful, big lake that feeds the Victoria Falls. My favourite place in the world.

I SOLD MY WEST DERBY HOME AND WE BOUGHT A BEAUTIFUL NEW house, Novar, in Heswall on the Wirral. Novar was going to become the family house for the next ten years and hosted some of my happiest years in my life.

Novar, which apparently means first house, was right next to the tennis club on top of the hill. After the gates a circular driveway took you up to the front door of our white house, and then there was a small gate, a wall, and then flowers. The semicircle had a rose garden in the middle and a few flowerbeds around the side.

The house had big double doors, arched like a nook, and the nook was where you took your shoes off. You had windows at the side at a 45-degree angle, so you could see out there before you opened the door. Past the big double doors was a hallway with high ceilings, with my study on the right, and the first lounge – the good lounge – on the left. Beyond that, on the right, was the television lounge with

French doors opening to the garden, and then you walked through to a wine cellar, followed by a toilet and a kitchen. Novar had five bedrooms and three bathrooms.

We renovated the house to make the toilet and bathroom a little bigger. We moved everything over so the builders could make another wall on that side, but as they were drilling the wall on the outside to make an extension, they stumbled across a well. The drill went straight through the wall and dropped into the water, but luckily the worker drilling fell on to a pipe instead, ultimately saving him. If he had fallen into the water he would have electrocuted himself, but the pipe caught him. We hauled out the drill, but we had a problem. We scooped up the water and it was spring water. To combat this we put a feature in where we built up one half of the well to the house and put a grate over it so kids couldn't fall through. We covered it with a glass top so you could see down into it.

We had a long back garden. From the drive was a short walkway down to a little garden, and behind the wall at the end of it was a vegetable patch and a greenhouse. We put a nice little Wendy house there. This was our family home, a fantastic house full of happy memories, by far my favourite home during my playing career in England.

I REMEMBER WHERE I WAS WHEN I GOT THE NEWS. I WAS DRINKING Guinness and watching the Olympic 800m final on the TV while my first daughter was being born. My first daughter, named Tahli, was born a couple of months after the European Cup final in Rome in 1984.

We had a great gynaecologist in Winifred Francis. Mrs Francis was an IVF pioneer and a great Liverpool fan and served as the gynaecologist for the families at the club. We were quite privileged to have her there to look after the wives.

Debbie was induced on 6 August.

Tahli came out, and she was a big, healthy baby. We named her Tahli Mellisa, after Umtali, the place in Zimbabwe where we got married.

My second daughter, Olivia, was born on 17 March 1988. She was slightly premature. Both Olivia and Tahli were delivered via caesarean section at Oxford Street Women's Hospital, making them Scousers.

We named her Olivia because we loved the name, but I also wanted to honour my dad by having a little bit of his name in hers. His second name was Gabriel, so we named her Olivia Gabriella.

My first born Tahli had colic for a while, so you had to rock her all the time. Before games I used to sit in the rocking chair rocking her to sleep. I did the same thing with Olivia, even though she didn't have colic. She just wouldn't settle, so it seemed the simple, efficient thing to do.

The two girls are amazing. They are very different from each other and both have a beautiful nature about them.

The four of us were a good little team. I knew that Debbie would never have another child, so it was quite nice that we kept it that way.

We bought a place out in Portugal, where we went on holidays quite often. We would spend a lot of time with my teammates and their families, as many had kids the same ages as Tahli and Olivia. Quite a few times we went to Disneyland with Ronnie Whelan's and Stevie Nicol's families. Life was good.

14

European Ride

AFTER NINE YEARS, DURING WHICH HE BECAME THE MOST
successful manager in English football history, Bob Paisley retired in July 1983.
Liverpool followed the precedent they had set with Bob's own appointment by
recruiting a new manager from within the Boot Room walls.

Joe Fagan had had a distinguished but war-interrupted playing career with
Manchester City in the 1940s, before turning to coaching with Nelson in the
Lancashire Combination League and Rochdale, where he worked under future
Everton manager Harry Catterick. It was on Catterick's recommendation that he
joined the Liverpool backroom staff, a move that would take him – via the positions
of reserve-team coach, first-team coach and assistant manager – to the Liverpool
manager's job. 'Smoking Joe', as he was known, was practically part of the furniture
in the Boot Room and knew Liverpool like virtually no one else.

His inheritance from Paisley was an excellent one. The team knew each other
inside out, and the next generation of serial Liverpool winners were now
embedded into the team. We could almost read one another's minds from
spending so much time together. The policy to rotate as little as possible, with
virtually the same eleven playing every game, meant we gelled incredibly quickly.
During this season Joe used seventeen players in total, and only fifteen in the
league campaign. The season before, 1982/83, Bob Paisley only used sixteen
players across all competitions.

Ian Rush and Kenny Dalglish had developed a near-telepathic relationship.
Rush would start his runs long before the opposition defenders would react, as he

knew in advance which open spaces Kenny would drop the ball into. At the end of October, Rush had stiff boots before a game against Luton Town and decided to soak them in water beforehand. Playing in these dripping wet boots he scored five, and so he ended up continuing this ritual for the rest of his career – even on the coldest winter days. He managed to score 47 goals in this incredible season.

It seemed like we had a team that could go on and on. Fagan just carried on from where Paisley had left. We were like a train on the tracks, and the train just kept on moving. At the start of the season we had a hiccup here and there, but then we always seemed to start slowly. We were beaten 2–0 by Manchester United in the Charity Shield and lost two league games in a row at the end of September and the beginning of October, but in total we'd only lose six league games all season, two of them at Anfield.

The loss I remember most vividly is the surprising 4–0 hammering away to Coventry in December, with Terry Gibson helping himself to a hat-trick against me. It was simply a bad day at the office where everything went wrong. Sometimes, you can analyse things too deeply. All you can do after a bad result like that is make sure it doesn't happen again. At least we got them back towards the end of the season by beating them 5–0 at Anfield, with Rush getting four. We were properly warmed up by then.

I played in a fantastic side, an unbelievable team. That season was a blur. We played so many games but it seemed to go by so quickly. I had my lapses – as I always did – but taken as a whole I had a pretty good season, keeping 20 clean sheets out of 42 and for the second year running conceding fewer goals than any other goalkeeper in the First Division.

A crowd of 100,000 was at Wembley to see us take on our city rivals Everton in the League Cup final. This was an historic occasion, the first time in ninety years of intense rivalry that the two clubs had met in a major final. The atmosphere was incredible: in a time of hooliganism and crowd violence, the kinship and friendly rivalry between the two sets of fans was an example to everyone who watched. The game was played in a friendly spirit, but with Alan Hansen apparently handballing a goalbound Everton shot off the line and Alan Kennedy having what seemed like a good goal disallowed, neither team could score after extra time, so the game went to a replay three days later. This time we met Howard Kendall's men at Maine Road, where Souness, in his last season for us, scored the winner in the 21st minute. Everton were really shaping up, however, and it was clear that they were going to be one of our hardest opponents in the years to come.

Souness captained us to a third consecutive league championship, as we finished three points ahead of Southampton. It represented a historic achievement for the club, as never before had Liverpool managed to win the league three years in a row, despite the dominance at the end of the 1970s. Only Arsenal in the 1930s and Huddersfield Town in the 1920s had matched such a feat. Coming after the League Cup win, it was a staggering feat, but one which was almost immediately topped.

JOE FAGAN SEEMED TO BE SMOKING WITH BOTH HANDS, LIGHTING up another cigarette before the previous one was finished. He picked Kenny Dalglish as one of the penalty takers, forgetting he had been substituted. And so he had to choose his penalty takers again. Phil Neal was going to take the first; meanwhile I was put down to do the last one, after Steve Nicol, Graeme Souness and Ian Rush. But things didn't go according to plan.

It was 30 May 1984, in Rome's Stadio Olimpico. Liverpool were playing in their fourth European Cup final in eight seasons and the game, against the stadium's usual tenants, AS Roma, had ended in a 1–1 stalemate. Extra time brought no further goals, and so the match had progressed to a penalty shootout.

Our penalty maestro, Phil Neal, was tying his bootlaces when Stevie Nicol thought, *I'm going to get this over and done with now*, and so before Neal had finished with his boots, Nicol had put the ball down on the mark, ready for the first penalty.

'Boss, it's supposed to be me,' Phil appealed. Joe Fagan took a huge drag of his cigarette and said, 'Let's run with it. Leave it, let's go with it.'

Stevie missed, and stood there, rubbing his chin.

As I got ready to walk into the goal, an arm was wrapped around me. There was the acrid smell of cigarette smoke in the air. I could tell by it that it was Joe Fagan.

'Listen,' he said, 'myself and the coaches, the chairman and the directors, the captain and team…' I thought, *Where's he going with this?* '… and the wives and the girlfriends and families, and the ten thousand travelling fans. We are not going to blame you…' My heart sank, and then he continued, 'If you can't stop a ball from twelve yards.'

NOT going to blame me? Oh, that was OK then. I was quite full of myself again, walking out there with a bold chest, and I was about two yards away when he added, 'But try and put them off.'

As I went past Stevie Nicol, I said, 'Thanks for that, Stevie.'

'Piss off and go and do your own job.'

We were never ones to mince our words.

OUR JOURNEY TO ROME HAD BEGUN THE PREVIOUS AUTUMN IN Denmark, where we came up against the country's champions Odense BK. There's nothing like the Danes. Danish people are very lovely, but they are crazy about football and they were especially crazy in those days. We stayed near the Tivoli Gardens in Copenhagen, only travelling to Hans Christian Andersen's home city of Odense for the game.

In a city of about only 150,000 people, almost 30,000 turned up for the match, which is a fair few more than the stadium normally would hold in those days. To give you an idea, Odense's stadium now has a maximum capacity of 15,790 with the new seating regulations. It is an understatement to say it was packed when we walked out there on 14 September 1983. Dalglish scored the only goal to give us a 1–0 win before we later beat them 5–0 at Anfield.

The next hurdle was Athletic Bilbao in October, where Graeme Souness and the 'Butcher of Bilbao', Andoni Goikoetxea, ended up in a proper fight. Souness got taken out by Goikoetxea, who stamped on him. The Butcher had the nickname for a reason – he was a very aggressive player. Only weeks earlier he almost finished Diego Maradona's playing days, breaking his ankle. His tackle on Souness was a bad one too, so everybody rushed over, and things soon turned sour between the two teams. Even Fagan came on, demanding us to clear it up. The game ended 0–0 at home and we knew going to Bilbao the trouble would erupt again.

Before the return game, their goalkeeper Andoni Zubizarreta said something about us having no chance playing them at the San Mamés, which was famed for its intense atmosphere. But we avoided trouble, thanks to our captain. Their fans whistled and booed every time Souness had the ball, but he met the Butcher head-on in his home stadium, and Goikoetxea appeared unusually subdued after Souness made a fair but forceful challenge on him. I think it shook him. We still had to silence their crazy fans though. Sammy Lee had warned us that in this part of Spain, the Basque Country, the supporters were fierce; temperamental like bullfighters. They didn't mind coming out running with the bulls.

Midway through the second half, Alan Kennedy went down the line and crossed for Rushy to head the ball into the back of the net. It was a rare headed goal for him, and I think it actually hit him on the nose. Still, it sealed the win in front of 40,000 mad fans in Bilbao, and up next, the following March, were Benfica.

Benfica were on a fine domestic run, having picked up 40 from a previous possible 42 points in the Portuguese league, and came into the first leg off the back of a 7–0 win over Braga. Our own run-up to the game was marked by the only big fight I've seen internally in our team, between Graeme Souness and Alan Kennedy. It was in a training session before the tie and was over nothing: Souness asked Alan to pass him the ball but his reply was 'No, I'll pass over that side.' They got into fisticuffs on the pitch and Alan had to play the tie with a black eye, punched because he hadn't passed the ball to Souness in training.

That was what Souness the player could be like: he was extremely competitive but that made him the best Liverpool player I've played with. He had everything. Our attacks used to get into first gear in the defence, and then when you wanted to get into a higher gear you just gave the ball to Graeme, and he'd make it change. He could slow it down as well, if that's what the game situation required. He was the cog that made the team tick.

He could play in any position on the field just as well as anyone who already played there, because he had two great feet and great awareness. He could sneak into a position and play that role for ten minutes. He would take over Rushy's role for ten minutes and do it better than him, because he'd move around more. Then he'd return to his midfield role.

The fracas between Souness and Kennedy didn't undermine our efforts against Benfica. We played them at home first, winning 1–0, then beat them 4–1 in Lisbon, with Whelan scoring two for us and my roommate Craig Johnston scoring another. Rushy, who simply couldn't stop scoring, got the other.

After the game in Portugal we decided to have some fun with Joe Fagan and Ronnie Moran. We were staying in the beach resort of Estoril, west of Lisbon, in an old Portuguese hotel with big double-windows. You could push the windows all the way open, and there was a ledge about two feet outside.

Craig and I were on the third floor and I decided to climb out of our window and crawl onto the ledge to the next bedroom and have a look in there. I knocked on the window of this room, which was on the corner of the building. Jim Beglin got up off the bed and went to the door to have a look: how stupid, I thought. I then went around the corner of the hotel to the front side of his room, and when he was back on the bed I knocked on the window closest to him, but this time he saw me and came rushing. He was going to push the windows open, risking knocking me off the ledge. I was going 'Whoa, careful' when he opened it, saying, 'Get off the ledge – are you crazy?' I said, 'Listen, I just wanted to get a newspaper, Craig wants a newspaper.'

'Well, why didn't you just come and ask me at the bloody door? Get off the ledge.' It was a fair response.

'Just give me the newspaper – I can see the newspaper is there, can I have it?' So I took the newspaper and crawled around the corner, passing the other window of his room. He was looking at me, shaking his head. He opened his window, and I knew where he was going. He looked out towards me again, but in the meantime I had got Craig to come and sit on the ledge with me – there were two of us sitting on this small ledge. Beglin was just shaking his head, shouting, 'No, no, no!'

We knew what was going to happen next – he was going to tell the boss. I looked and said to Craig, 'We're going to have some fun.' I heard this knock on our door, and we kept quiet. They had to go down to the reception to get a key to our room, so we crept off the ledge and into the neighbouring room. We escaped quickly out of that door, into the service lift and all the way down and through the kitchen. I took some tomato sauce and we went outside, precisely under our room, and laid down completely still, with blobs of ketchup strategically placed next to our heads. Eventually I look up and I see all the players coming, and then the coaching staff too. I whispered, 'OK, are you ready, Craig?' 'Yes.' We jumped up and started dancing.

Joe Fagan wasn't happy. He didn't see the funny side at all. Craig and I got fined a week's wages for messing about, and we had to give it to charity.

Our final hurdle towards the biggest game in Europe was the semi-final against Dinamo Bucharest, and we were lucky to play at home first. We had struggled against teams from behind the Iron Curtain in each of the previous two years and this fact wasn't lost on anybody; me in particular.

They were a horrible team, and not to be underestimated. They body-checked, spat, kicked and punched. I needed treatment after being stamped on by their captain Lică Movilă. But what I remember best was how Movilă really went over the top on Souness. We thought he'd been so badly injured that he wouldn't be able to play the next week. But Souness got up and he turned to the fellow and said in a manner that made him understand he meant business, 'Don't worry; there's another half and another game still to go.' You could see the fright in his eyes; I think he realised there and then that he'd picked on the wrong man.

It was inevitable that Souness and Movilă would lock horns again at some stage, and that moment soon came. Both looked to win the ball for their team in a duel I believe slightly favoured Souness: 55–45. Souness got to it first and got his pass away, but Movilă was running straight for him. The ball had gone and the camera was following the action. Graeme being Graeme will have appreciated the referee's attention was on the ball and so, he used this moment to catch their captain in the jaw with an elbow. I was standing at the other end of the pitch watching the scene unfold. *Oh shit* I thought. It nearly decapitated him. And yet, the referee had no idea what had happened. He was looking round; nobody was around this player because Graeme was smart enough to get away from the scene. I think Mark Lawrenson got there first and the referee thought it was him, but he was told otherwise.

Movilă walked off, his jaw broken in two places – he would play no further part in the tie. Sammy Lee scored the only goal of the match, and our captain made a point of shaking everyone's hand. The message was nevertheless clear from our opponents. They muttered darkly about what we could expect in Bucharest.

We had a tight playing schedule. We used to play three games a week, and it was beautiful – boom, boom, just rotate from one game to the next between the various competitions.

Behind the Iron Curtain we knew we weren't in for an easy ride. The atmosphere from the moment of our arrival was hostile, first from customs officials, then the Securitate – the country's secret police force – who checked our coach and made threatening gestures towards Souness. This wasn't something I was going to accept passively and I started making gestures of my own until one of the other lads asked me how I fancied spending the next few days in a prison cell.

I might as well have been, as we spent the next few days confined to our hotel instead, the rain lashing down from the moment of our arrival to the minute we left. What little we saw of the streets of the Romanian capital wasn't replicated inside the stadium; where there were food shortages and queues outside shops in the city, there was an abundance of fruit and vegetables inside the stadium – mostly directed from the fans towards us players. I think there were only two cameras – one behind one goal and one on the side – filming the game and if you look back at footage you can hear big, unhappy roars from the crowd every time Souness touches the ball. That seemed to encourage him to play even better and his attitude lifted us all. Rush scored both our goals in Bucharest, sending us to my first European Cup final.

In my second year competing in Europe, I'd made more mistakes against Widzew Łódź, contributing towards Liverpool's exit. Third time lucky. We were now ready for the biggest game of them all.

THEY SAY ALL ROADS LEAD TO ROME, BUT WE WERE TO HAVE A double helping in the final. Not only was the final to be staged in the Eternal City, but our opponents were AS Roma.

Roma had never won a European trophy before but, at a time when Serie A was considered the best league in the world and Italy were World Cup holders, they rightly held a reputation as one of the best teams in Europe. With players like the Brazilian midfielder Falcão, the prolific and very physical centre-forward Francesco Graziani and the lightning-quick winger Bruno Conti they combined all the best aspects of great Italian teams – hardness, defensive resolution and a smattering of Latin flair. They were unable to retain their 1983 Serie A title, but had only finished the 1983/84 season second to Juventus by two points a few weeks earlier. In addition to this the final was to be staged at their own stadium, the Stadio Olimpico. Not that we ever paid much attention to such matters, but the bookmakers made them 13–8 favourites.

The stadium had been chosen as the venue for the final long before it became clear that Roma might end up playing there themselves. The Stadio Olimpico was a stadium that Liverpool had historical connections with. I was living in South Africa, dreaming of becoming a top goalkeeper, when, in 1977, when Liverpool won their first European Cup in Rome, beating Borussia Mönchengladbach 3–1. This gave Liverpool supporters a lot of confidence. It also reassured and excited the players – the chance of emulating what had gone before. It felt like our away form had been better than our home form that year anyway.

At the same time we were aware from the moment that we touched down in Rome of the challenges we faced in taking on final opponents on their home turf. We were kept waiting on the airport tarmac for what seemed like an age and finally disembarked onto army buses hot and bothered. However, no chances had been taken by the club with our accommodation. A Holiday Inn manager from Liverpool had been brought over to run the players' floor at the Rome Holiday Inn and the club had brought their own private security detail. No one, but no one, gained admittance to our floor.

Before the game, Joe Fagan had taken us for a few days to Tel Aviv in Israel. It was ostensibly a training camp and the chance to play an exhibition match against the Israel national team, but also the chance to celebrate our third league victory in a row. It was Fagan's first league title in his first year as a manager, the club's fifteenth in total. Smoking Joe had also made sure we won a double, beating Everton 1–0 in the League Cup. It can't have been without pressure, taking over from Paisley who had won three European Cups in only seven years.

We'd been to Tel Aviv a couple of times. The agent Pini Zahavi had struck up a good relationship with Liverpool, having negotiated the transfer of Avi Cohen to the club from Maccabi Tel Aviv in 1979. Going away, Fagan let us have a few beers to take our minds off the upcoming final. While their players went to a strict training camp in the Roman hills, the Italian reporters dispatched to follow us everywhere looked on in amazement as we relaxed with beers by the Sheraton Hotel pool and lolled around the beach. They filled their newspapers with stories that we would be easy meat as we were simply drunken tourists in Israel.

Roma's confidence might have grown as a result of this, but relatively speaking this was a tame trip. Our previous visit to the Israeli capital had descended into a mass drunken brawl involving every player on the trip after a drinking game called 'Buzz' had gotten out of hand. I'd looked on in bewilderment as my teammates launched themselves at each other in a Tel Aviv square – which we dubbed Madison Square Garden after the fight – and had been an innocent bystander until David Hodgson had jumped on my back. Suddenly I was back in the jungle, and Hodgy went flying over my shoulder and ended with a knee to his chest. Then, just as suddenly as the fight had erupted, so it had ended, and by the time the walking wounded had limped back to the hotel the near riot was almost forgotten about. That's just the way Liverpool were.

There was none of that sort of excess ahead of the trip to Rome, even if our relaxing did surprise our Italian observers. Once there, we were less bothered about the hostile atmosphere. We felt prepared for what was promised. We had already been to Athletic Bilbao, Benfica and Dinamo Bucharest on the run to the final and none of the ties had been easy. We expected it would be a hostile game, and it was.

On the way to the stadium, Roma fans stoned our bus and broke the windows. We were wrapped in aggressiveness, but relatively speaking got away lightly. Our supporters were attacked and ambushed all over the Italian capital and had to run a gauntlet of hatred both before and after the final. The Roma Ultras' habit of *puncicate* – stabbing a rival in the buttocks – was just one of the more unsavoury elements they had to contend with. We weren't aware of the full extent of the horror and intimidation some of them had faced until much later, but it was surely a factor in what was to unfold a year later in Brussels.

There are lots of versions of what Joe Fagan said in the dressing room. Everyone focuses differently in these moments because ultimately as players it's down to us from that point. We have to do what we have to do to be in the zone. If listening to the manager makes you feel more comfortable, then that's what you do. I remember Joe saying, 'We've done our job, we've got here by merit. We're now in the lions' den – go out and show who you are and what character you have. Enjoy it.' Joe was calm in his words when it mattered but you could see he was stressed because he was smoking so many cigarettes.

In the tunnel we waited for Roma to come out for about three minutes. Three minutes just before a cup final is a very long time. *Where is this team?*

Our captain, Graeme Souness, who was soon to play one of his best games ever, said to Sammy Lee, Craig Johnston and David Hodgson, 'Come on, guys, we need something to warm up with. Give us a song.'

David started singing the Chris Rea song 'I don't know what it is, but I love it' and the song spread down our line-up. Adrenaline pumping through our bodies as we joined in singing this song in the tunnel, accompanied by air guitars: 'I don't know what it is but I love it, I don't know what it is but I want it to stay, and I love it, love it!' We were dancing and playing our air guitars and we smacked Roma's dressing room door while we sang as loud as we could. Next thing their captain, Agostino Di Bartolomei, looked outside, and he must have thought, *What is this? English bastardi.*

Souness said, 'Carry on singing. Look them in the eye and walk down towards the pitch and sing.' Imagine looking the Roma guys in the eyes singing 'I don't know what it is but I love it, I don't know what it is but I want it to stay, and I love it, love it!' And when we sang 'love it' we opened our eyes and sang louder in their faces. Our whole team was doing this and the Italians didn't know what was hitting them.

An aggressive and loud wall of nearly 70,000 packed into the stands. The sky was red with fireworks and flares being set off. There was thick smoke and noise. It was electric. There is a photograph of me behind Graeme Souness and his focus now is absolute. He's looking directly ahead. Me? I'm laughing my head off. Why? I have no idea. That's just my way.

After fourteen minutes, Craig Johnston played a high cross from the right side and when Franco Tancredi fumbled the ball under pressure, Dario Bonetti's attempted clearance struck the grounded goalkeeper and the ball deflected to Phil Neal, who didn't waste his chance and scored to give us a 1-0 lead. Only two minutes later Souness netted a volley, but the Swedish referee Erik Fredriksson disallowed it for offside.

Getting close to thirty minutes into the game, I saved a shot from Conti, and only a few minutes later, Neal earned himself a yellow card for taking Conti down. The game waved back and forth, until, with two minutes of the first half remaining, Conti went down the line. After seeing his initial cross from the byline blocked by Mark Lawrenson, he lofted an angled ball into the box and Roberto Pruzzo, getting there ahead of Alan Hansen, flicked it over into the far corner of the net: 1-1.

The loss of a goal was an obvious setback but, on such a big stage, and in the face of such a crazy atmosphere, we soon picked ourselves up. In the second half, Roma went determinedly in search of another goal but our defence worked terrifically well. Lawrenson, in particular, fought like a lion. I managed to save their best chance of that second period, a long shot by Falcão. At the other end, we had our own moments but it just didn't happen. Extra time followed, and when that didn't yield another goal the game went to a penalty shootout.

AS I WENT TOWARDS THE GOAL, JOE FAGAN'S WORDS SWIRLED around in my mind. *What does Joe mean by putting them off?* Subsequently, as a goalkeeping coach I have always said to my goalkeepers, 'In any penalty shootout – for your first penalty, just stand up straight because the ball is going to be coming near you and you probably will have a chance to save it, as they're just as nervous as you. So just stay standing up.'

But silly me wasn't imbued with such wisdom back then. Instead I went one way, put my arm out towards the centre of the goal and the ball clipped my hand. It came right down the middle; if I'd stood up I wouldn't have let it in. I disappointed myself. Roma were 1–0 up.

Phil Neal had finished tying his bootlaces. He came over, put the ball down, and scored.

Bruno Conti, the World Cup-winning midfielder, was up next. I had my hands on my knees, and he was shaking his shoulders as if he was dancing and I looked at him and said to myself, 'You want to dance?' His cockiness set me off. You could almost hear him singing to himself, 'I'm Bruno Conti, I crossed the ball for Pruzzo to score!' All the while I had Fagan's words in the back of my mind: 'Try to put them off.' It is not in the footage, but as he put the ball down and walked backwards, he looked at me, and I put my hands on my knees and I crossed them over quickly. All I hear in the footage is 'Grobbelaar's ready'. Conti's shot came flying towards me. Boom! A brief moment of silence. No explosion of noise from the Roma fans, no sound of the ball rippling the net. It went over the bar.

I was ecstatic. I thought to myself, *This putting-off business might work.*

Souness then came up and put the ball in the top corner; no goalkeeper could ever have saved it: 2–1.

I couldn't get in the goal quickly enough, because next up was a young chap, Ubaldo Righetti, who had been practising his penalties in the stadium after we trained a day earlier. I had hid in the stadium to have a look at him. Every single penalty he took was going in the same corner. I thought, *Hey, I've got you; top right, come on.* I remember taking off to top right, the ball went top left – then I realised I had been watching the penalties from the other side of the stadium. So all my homework went out the window: 2–2.

Rushy, who was at the end of his most successful ever season with 47 goals, came and bobbled one in: 3–2.

Then Francesco Graziani made himself ready by putting his arm around the referee. I didn't like that. I went and bit the net. He carried on walking, sauntering. I thought, *No*, and I bit the net again, like the net was spaghetti. While he was crossing himself I was thinking, *I've got to do something with my legs to put him off*, so I made my knees wobble like pasta softening in the boiling water. When I did the old spaghetti legs, Graziani looked at me and crossed himself again while I made the most of the time, and served him some more spaghetti legs.

Graziani had been the other penalty taker I'd spied on during spot-kick practice the previous day. He had also repeatedly put the ball in the same bottom corner. This time I calculated better and went down towards bottom right. You could actually see him trying to change his position as I've gone down, so he chipped the ball to the far side, but he chipped it too high. It hit the bar and it went over. I felt ecstatic, running around the field celebrating, forgetting I was supposed to take the next penalty.

In my place Alan Kennedy came in, picked up the ball and went to the penalty spot. I said, 'Boss, it's supposed to be me.'

'If it takes you that long to get back here, you can suffer like the rest of us and watch him take the penalty,' was Fagan's reply. I looked over at Dalglish, Souness and everybody else. They all hid their heads in their hands, not even watching. When I looked over to our fans, many of them were not looking either. Then I glanced over at Joe Fagan, who was smoking, asking Roy Evans to tell him how it went, too nervous to watch. We knew where he was going to try to put the ball. He had said, 'I'm always going to put it down bottom right,' but then he hit it top left and he won us the game.

Thank goodness he scored. In Paris he did the same when he scored us the winner after storming forward in the 81st minute against Real Madrid. He was going to shoot bottom right then too – and ended up missing the angle and scored top left instead. Alan is the only one that can boast that he's had two kicks where the intention was something else and won two European Cups from them. Not only that, he is also the only player from a British team who has scored the winner in two European Cup Finals. He's got a record that will stay with him forever. It'll take a long, long time for any English club to do exactly the same.

I'm quite happy that he ended up taking the penalty in Rome, because I might have messed it up and fluffed it. But the massive pressure made us do brave things that night. It reminded me a little of being in the army where the pressure made you do some stupid things, but also brave things. In extreme situations it helps to think outside of the box.

We were so ecstatic going into the dressing room, where beers and champagne waited for us. All of a sudden the officials came in and called for two players to go for drug tests. Of course, yours truly was picked out with Sammy Lee. They gave us two cups we had to pee into, sample A and sample B, signed them off and said we had all the time we needed to take on some liquid.

We sat down, and I said to the officials, 'Do we have to drink this water?

Can I have a lager?'

'Yeah, you can have a lager.' So I went out, followed by one of these officials, and I just whistled outside the dressing room, 'Zico! Stevie! A six-pack.' And a six-pack was slid to me. I picked up the six cans, went into the drug-testing room, and started drinking. I had one full can of lager and I took the two cups and I filled both of them.

I waited there for another hour and a half while the rest of the team was celebrating, because Sammy Lee couldn't produce enough urine – and he didn't want to touch any alcohol. I said, 'Sammy, come on; you've been drinking water, tea and coffee. Just have a lager! I'm telling you, you've had all that water, it's gone down, now if you have a beer, the beer will push everything down, don't worry about it.'

It was getting to about two hours of waiting for him and everybody was shouting in the corridor: 'Come on!' The two Roma players picked for the test had come and gone, but they wouldn't let me go until Sammy was finished. In the end he went, 'Oh, come on, give me the beer.' He had two sips, boom, went in there, filled the cups and signed off the tests and we finally got changed and showered and on our way to party.

We were taken by bus into the hills above Rome to a magnificent villa at the end of a long driveway, named Villa Miani. Guards were on the gate. I don't know who owned the villa, maybe it was something to do with the Vatican, but our sponsors, Crown Paints, had generously footed the bill.

We were dropped off by the bottom of some gorgeous stairs. As we walked up, we were told we could use the left-hand side of the villa; the right-hand side was out of bounds. The first floor had the bar serving us drinks before a meal, and downstairs on the left was a disco – where we went for drinks and canapés first. My wife was coming close to seven months pregnant with my eldest daughter, and Craig Johnston's wife, Jenny, was also pregnant, so they sat upstairs.

We had our meal and came downstairs to have a beer, when Craig and I leaned on this curtain covering a big, wide window. We pulled the curtain to the side and there was a beautiful swimming pool out there. There was nobody around. I said, 'Craigy, fancy a skinny-dip?' We opened the windows, took all our gear off and dived in. We were having races up and down the pool when I saw some army boots on the pool's edge as I came up for air. Then there was a gun. 'No signor, out. Not allowed – out!'

We had to get out quickly, but had no towels to dry ourselves as the plan had been to run around to dry. So we went in and used the heavy curtains as towels and put our gear on. As I came down the stairs, I met my wife who asked, 'Bruce, why is your hair wet?'

There has never been a party like the one we had that night. We went crazy. For me, after three years in the spotlight and with particular attention focused on my foibles, eccentricities and unorthodox approach – even when Liverpool were sweeping aside all comers – it was a particularly sweet moment to emerge as a hero of the night. Night became dawn, and our party carried on until long after the sun had reappeared.

15

Everton

ELEVEN DAYS BEFORE OUR EUROPEAN CUP WIN OVER AS ROMA, our Merseyside rivals, Everton, lifted the FA Cup following a 2–0 win over Graham Taylor's Watford. It was their first major trophy in fourteen years and truly marked the arrival of Howard Kendall's outstanding young team. For the following five seasons Merseyside would rule English football: the League Championship would reside there continuously, as would the FA Cup for three of those years. Everton would also be the last English team to lift a European trophy following our win in Rome until the early 1990s.

It was a great rivalry we had with Everton during the mid-1980s. The rest of the clubs simply couldn't keep up with us. Whatever you say about what happened during the time of the subsequent European ban and the animosity we had with the government and Margaret Thatcher, there is no doubt that we rallied as footballers and supporters. The message was simple: 'You're not going to put us down.' Everton and Liverpool just carried on playing great football. It doesn't matter where you go in the world, football will bring joy to people that are really down.

Leading up to the Merseyside derbies there was always going to be tension. Once one derby match with Everton had finished you started thinking about the next straight away. You prepared properly, which meant that in the period leading up to the game you didn't walk up and down your street quite so much. When we arrived home the day before a derby we'd make sure to get out of our cars and into the house as quickly as possible, because if any Evertonian became aware of where you were living they would come and knock on your door late at night, just so they could disrupt your sleep before the game.

Thankfully my first home was in North Wales, so I could get away to the cottage without being disrupted. However, when I moved to West Derby, near Everton's Bellefield training ground, I was not guaranteed a peaceful sleep, because there were far more Evertonians in the area. Naturally, they'd become especially disruptive in the lead-up to a derby. You could tell them to go away, but that would only encourage them to carry on – bang, bang, bang. Instead you'd try to keep out of eyeshot, and whoever answered the door, usually my wife, would plead with them and say, 'Please could you go away, he's at the hotel.' They would ask her which hotel, so she would just mention a random one and off they went. This was how every night before a Mersey derby would pan out when I lived in West Derby.

After being burgled three times in eighteen months at that home, I chose to move to Heswall over on the Wirral, which is quieter with a lot fewer Evertonians. Because of the rivalry you picked carefully where to live. You also thought through where you ate, what pubs you drank at and what hotels you stayed in by finding out which establishments Evertonians and Liverpudlians frequented.

I could never go shopping before a Merseyside derby. Shopping in town would lead to abuse, and if they were proper crazy Blues they'd start stalking you. I soon accepted this for what it was, and you could go to town afterwards if you'd won anyway. You would still get abused by the Evertonians, but it was bearable if you'd won. If you lost you couldn't go anywhere, because then both sets of fans were having a go at you. The wise thing in such circumstances was to stay away for the week either side of the game; once the week had passed, they had largely forgotten about it. Only then would they leave you alone.

Evertonians gave me my nickname 'The Clown' and it wasn't long before both the press and the Manchester United fans jumped onto this as well, using the moniker as often as they could. They meant clown as a derogatory term, of course. 'Look at that clown goalkeeper, he can't catch anything.'

My style was a bit different from what they were used to in English goalkeepers. It also didn't help that I struggled in the first six months to adapt to the English game and struggled to communicate properly with my defenders. Saying that, my style was also the product of how I was told to play – to be the third centre-half. That was the reason I came out for most crosses.

After my royal telling-off by Bob Paisley in December 1981 I stopped trying to provide the fans with some extra entertainment during the game, though when we scored I still sometimes did a handstand.

Yet despite my performances picking up I was still called the clown in public my whole career. I don't even like clowns – they scare kids. If you have a look at a small kid when they see a clown they are terrified. The way they paint their face scares everybody. It's not very good and it's not particularly endearing. It's not funny. It's a mask; they're hiding behind something. And I don't hide from anything. People can take me or leave me, I don't mind. I'm a clown that won nineteen trophies in thirteen years.

THROUGHOUT THE 1980S EVERTON AND LIVERPOOL WERE THE TWO strongest teams in the league, especially in the middle of the decade.

Perhaps there were signs soon after their FA Cup win that Everton were developing the upper hand. When we faced them at Wembley in August for the Charity Shield they beat us 1–0. Unfortunately I scored the only goal of the game: Graeme Sharp broke through the defence and went to take the ball around me. I got a hand to it, but the ball merely flicked back up to Sharp who drove it goalwards again. Although Alan Hansen blocked it near our goalline, the ball flew straight at me and deflected off my shins and into the net.

Even by our standards, our start to that season was uncharacteristically slow. Everton visited us in mid-October and a Sharp wonder goal settled the game, leaving us down in seventeenth place. Things picked up in the league, as they always did, and by the last Saturday of the season we'd secured the runners-up spot – our highest position all season, but thirteen points behind the champions.

Everton took our title off us in 1985, the only year out of my first five at the club where we didn't win the league. We just lent the title to our city rivals, coming second ourselves. At this point both sides were certainly among the best in Europe. Everton were on their way to winning the European Cup Winners' Cup and we had our own European final coming up against Juventus. This city was a true footballing powerhouse.

We had a rivalry and, looking back, we both had managers who allowed the team to express themselves – on and off the pitch. They allowed the team a bit of freedom. They made sure that when we were off the field we did the right things, but they allowed the players their own judgement, and didn't imprison us with rules and regulations. They gave us guidelines, and you could either adhere to those guidelines or break them. But when you got on the football pitch, you made sure to produce a performance that showed that you were doing the right thing.

Like Liverpool's managers during the 1980s, the late Howard Kendall also allowed his team freedom on their days off. They treated us like adults, not like school kids. It was only later when Liverpool managers started to try and rule with an iron fist that the team failed to produce the goods, and the same happened to Everton as well.

I'VE BEEN AROUND THE WORLD, BUT COMING BACK TO LIVERPOOL now is like coming home, because I always feel so welcome. Liverpool as a city today has everything you want. I regularly visit Ireland too, and I always receive a similarly warm welcome there. The Irish are very similar to the Scousers; very hospitable people. In Liverpool there are two sides, Liverpool and Everton, and in general they're all great people. They are generous, they have time for people, they are self-deprecating and do not take themselves too seriously. Most importantly, they are a great laugh.

Liverpool in the 1980s was quite rough. Along Scotland Road you had a pub on every corner. It used to be said that if you walked up one side of Scottie Road and down the other end you could never manage a beer in each pub, even if you only had half a pint in each.

Some of the pubs were bad. In those days you'd have a smoking room and a separate lounge. If you didn't want your clothes laden with smoke you'd sit in the latter room for a quiet drink. But if people knew who you were, they'd come and banter with you. 'All right there, Bruce? Give us a fiver,' and all that. You'd therefore sit by the door in whatever pub you visited in order to make a quick getaway.

The city centre of Liverpool looked completely different thirty years ago. You'd walk past where John Lewis is now and up the hill, but half of the shops would be boarded up due to the financial crisis that beset the city through the 1980s and early 1990s. The centre was run-down and almost half of the shops had gone out of business.

I continued the tradition implemented by my parents to always make sure I dressed well, and later my care for the way I presented myself would earn me the title of 'best-dressed athlete' in Britain. I used to buy leather jackets and colourful suits, which I considered cool back then. It turns out that not everybody shared my fashion sense: the leather shop I used to frequent closed down because they didn't have the demand and my tailor, Phil Black, relocated to Manchester.

When I got to Liverpool at the beginning of the 1980s the unemployment rate was massive, and it kept rising through the decade. The frustration was huge. It is an understatement to say that Margaret Thatcher wasn't the most popular figure in town.

The whole city was in meltdown when the money moved from Liverpool to Manchester. The docks were the bread and butter for thousands in this city, and Thatcher's decision to move resources to Manchester had ramifications. Liverpool was a city with a strong affiliation to the Labour Party and trade unions, something the Thatcher government didn't like, which set them even further against the city of Liverpool. One government minister spoke openly at cabinet about putting the city into a period of 'managed decline'. Tensions rose because of the sheer frustration of being out of work. There was no hope for a lot of people.

It was a really bad time, full of frustration and vented anger because of what the government was doing. It's not hard to imagine that the animosity that previously existed between Liverpool and Manchester was exacerbated by Manchester receiving all sorts of government assistance to develop its docklands at Salford and fund bids for the Olympic and Commonwealth Games at a time when Liverpool was being squeezed for everything. This subsequently hardened the relationship between our football teams too. It was really, really harsh. During this period, the worst, most dangerous things were thrown at me while on the field of play. It was in this 1980s era that the hatred that came between Liverpool and Manchester really developed and became bitter.

Liverpool wasn't the only place to suffer under the government's economic policies. At the same time in the mid-80s there were miners striking across the country as the Thatcher government tried to force the closure of nearly a hundred coalmines, turning many in the North even further against the government. There were big strikes across the area as well as in Wales and Yorkshire. Later in the decade there would be mass protests against the poll tax.

Later, in the mid-1990s when dockers were striking in Liverpool, Robbie Fowler showed his support by raising up his jersey during a goal celebration to reveal a vest referencing the dispute. Robbie was showing solidarity to his family, who used to work on the docks, and to the city he was raised in. His anger at the injustice the dockworkers faced was also a reflection of the environment in which he'd been brought up during the 1980s.

I think football gave the people that were so angry with the government a sense of relief when there was a game on. They could go and have a singsong with their friends, and if their team won they'd be happy for the weekend at least. It provided a release from going on strike and the disappointment of not having a job. It was an irony that while the city of Liverpool was economically at its absolute nadir in the mid-1980s, it ruled football during the same period.

Football is a tonic for people in bad times. Many in Zimbabwe don't have any jobs, but yet when their team go and play at the national stadium it'll be full. They'll make sure that they've got something to hang on to because it gives them a release – it's a relief to see their team win. If they've won they're happy and they go home happy. Poor, but happy. It makes it even more heartbreaking when you lose, because they are going home sad and they are still poor.

I had grown up seeing some of the same things in Africa that I experienced in Liverpool in the 1980s. The people – whichever team it was, Liverpool or Everton – would go to see their team and hopefully they'd get a little bit of joy from those ninety minutes of sanctity before they went back to their daily toil. Football has done that over the years; given people who are unemployed a place to go, somewhere to belong. A place where you still feel needed. They've got a club they support and they show their loyalty by supporting that club, no matter what.

16

Heysel

WHILE THE 1980S WAS, IN SO MANY WAYS, THE BEST OF TIMES for Liverpool FC, football in general during the decade had become synonymous with hooliganism. Barely a week would pass without some tawdry outbreak of violence making the news. Terraces echoed with the sounds of racist taunts and by the middle of the decade had started to empty of the fans who had simply tired of the violence, unpleasantness and hassle of attending a football match.

As players we were all too aware of the atmosphere in which football was played.

To reach Millwall's ground, The Den, the buses of visiting teams would have to pass a scrap-metal yard. You would know you were close to the ground before seeing it because suddenly objects would start hitting the bus. The projectiles had been taken from the scrapyard and used as missiles.

Chelsea was bad too. At Stamford Bridge, they'd use bricks. Swansea City's old Vetch Field ground was near a prison and an intimidating place to go as well. There, they'd use stones.

I remember playing Manchester United away. We were winning 1–0 and coins came from the terraces, hitting the ball boys behind me. I picked two of those coins up and placed them in my eye sockets. It probably wasn't the most sensible thing to do but I had my own way of dealing with things.

The same happened at Southampton in Phil Neal's testimonial year. I picked the coins up and gave them to Phil. I think he put the money in his testimonial fund.

Burnley's Turf Moor was an intimidating place to go. I got hit by a dart there. It lodged in my back and I placed it by the goalpost. The person that threw it got caught and thrown out of the ground. When the police asked me whether I wanted the culprit charged and I told them that I did, they were horrified. They probably knew the case would involve lots of paperwork and time. I asked, 'What happens if that dart had actually hit me in the eye? My eyes are what I need for football. So yes, I want to charge him.' And he was charged. His punishment was derisory: a ban from football for a year.

The dart, as it turned out, wasn't even the worst thing thrown at me. As a goalkeeper, I was the closest opposition player to the terraces and the obvious target. At Old Trafford, someone used a billiard ball but missed. They used batteries as well and later a potato with razor blades embedded in it. This came from the Stretford End.

From everything I've read and heard about English football, it seems relationships between supporters at rival football clubs began to change in the 1960s. There were many reasons for this, not least the social issues that many working-class supporters faced. It also became easier for fans to travel to away games *en masse*. You must also understand that football then was still a working-class sport. After a hard week at work, football and a fight was a way for some people of releasing frustrations and unwinding. That's not a justification, but for some people this was part of their weekly rituals. Others started to use football to vent their wider social and political frustrations. As social and economic problems increased through the 1970s and early 1980s, hooliganism approached its apex and the game's reputation plunged towards the depths. Ours, as one newspaper reflected, 'was a slum sport watched by slum people.'

Football became an arena for violence. We were the excuse for violence. If we won, the other side would riot and fight against our fans. If we lost, those factions would go and fight because they'd lost. It was in that era where football lost its true support. The true supporters weren't the ones that were going to fight. These were people who wanted to go out to show how tough they were. Football was an excuse to go out and release your anger onto the world. For some hooligan groups that professed a political veneer, like the National Front or Combat 18, violence was almost a military operation.

How did it feel to be in the centre of such violence and such anger? And how did we stay focused on the pitch? Our main priority was playing football; you did the best you could. To stay motivated we went in there, did our job and came out. Bob Paisley and Joe Fagan made us do that. 'Go, do your job, get out, get on the train, off we go back to Liverpool.' It was bad at the time, but we were disciplined. If there was no trouble off the pitch, then it was a bonus. But I think all players knew of someone who was a fan who also went to fight now and then.

WEDNESDAY, 29 MAY 1985, IS A DAY THAT HAS GONE DOWN IN football notoriety. It was English football's nadir. A day that started with the European Cup final between Liverpool and Juventus in Brussels, ended with the deaths of 39 supporters and Juventus winning a match that should never ever have been played. Unfortunately for me, just like four years later in Sheffield, I had an up-close view of the terrible events that unfolded.

Lots of things went wrong in the build-up to the game. For starters, it should never have been played at this particular stadium, Brussels' Heysel Stadium, which was an antiquated athletics venue with crumbling terraces. It is a decision UEFA should regret. They got it wrong in my eyes and in many other people's eyes. There were serious questions to be asked about ticketing, segregation and security within the stadium too, although these were to come only later.

On the morning of the match, Joe Fagan had announced he was retiring from his position as manager and handing over the job to Kenny Dalglish, who would become player-manager. Joe was aged 64, but we were nevertheless all a bit surprised. Joe had been so successful in his two years as a manager and was such an integral part of the club, and we all thought he would stay in that role for longer.

When we arrived at the arena, the mood seemed fine. We were used to big matches and had run a gauntlet of hatred on previous European encounters, but there was none of that in the lead-up to this game and no sense of it on the way into Heysel.

Yet by the start of the warm-up, something palpable had changed inside the stadium. From the pitch I could see Juventus fans starting to throw things towards the Liverpool section. Then I looked down the other side and an apparently neutral section wasn't neutral at all, but full of Juventus fans. The only thing dividing this area of the stadium from Liverpool's section was a chicken-wire fence. Even chickens could jump over that particular fence. The fence did nothing to protect anyone. I could see it from the pitch, but the police didn't seem to be paying too much attention. It was very strange.

On our pre-match walkabout Steve Nicol and I had received a portent of what was to follow when we came within firing distance of some Juventus fans. A fusillade of concrete, stones and coins rained down upon us.

Skirmishes broke out on the terraces, with groups of supporters running at each other and pelting each other with stones and missiles. Heysel seemed to be turning into a war zone. Stones and bottles were flying through the air. Fights were breaking out in the stands. The police, it seemed, were nowhere to be seen.

Several times there were appeals over the loudspeakers for people to calm down. Joe Fagan was asked by UEFA to go out and talk to the Liverpool fans via the stadium tannoy. Phil Neal, captain that year, was asked to do the same. Both returned with horror and fright in their faces. Fagan dissolved into tears in the dressing room after seeing the hostile scenes in the stadium.

On the terraces there was a surge of Liverpool supporters towards the Juventus section. Panicked, the Italian supporters rushed away and in the scramble a wall collapsed.

Alan Kennedy, the coach John Bennison and myself were just going into the dressing room when we heard it collapse. We had the closest dressing room to where the fallen wall was, about 45 metres away, near the corner of the ground. When we were taken off the field there was a group of people asking for towels and water, so I ran into the changing room and got them. It was a terrible sight out there. I also helped someone to a doctor. We were told to stay in the dressing room, and people were coming in and asking us for water, so we'd get buckets of water and they'd take them back out.

We understood that something in the stadium had collapsed but had no real idea what was actually going on. We first heard it was in the main stand, where our wives, girlfriends and families were seated. Invariably the first things the players wanted to know was if their relatives were OK. John, Alan and I went back out and we could see that that stand was fine. There was a mix of relief that our loved ones seemed to be away from the worst of the trouble and horror at the unfolding situation.

From the tunnel, Joe Fagan asked us to return to the dressing room. We knew there were fatalities because the ambulances were arriving. We were getting lots of conflicting information: one official said that six people had died, but a Belgian policeman said it was more than forty and rising. A second Belgian policeman argued that no one really knew how many had died.

Some players immediately felt it was not right to play the final. Joe Fagan convinced us all that we had to, based on the information coming through from the authorities: that the violence might spread into town. On a personal level at the time, I thought it was the sensible thing to do but on reflection, the decision from the police to order the game to be played while victims lay dead in the parking lot was extremely insensitive.

To play a game when people are dying, how do you even begin to rationalise that? UEFA argued that they risked inflaming tensions and creating more violence by cancelling the final. At least with everyone in the stadium they could contain more trouble. To a certain degree I could understand their logic, but it disregarded the fact that people had gone to see a football match and had lost their lives.

The kick-off was delayed by seventy minutes and by the time the game started there was a collective state of shock, which soon gave way to an eerie calm.

When we walked out, surrounded by 58,000 spectators, they had moved people from the side that had collapsed. There was a gap from the main stand, then a tunnel and the collapsed wall. Behind there were ambulances and people lying on the ground. We went onto the field and I could still see the rescue teams to my right.

This was Juventus's third European Cup final. They were yet to win the competition, while we were the reigning champions, having won each of our four finals. A fifth would have been a spectacular achievement.

Even if I'd tried to block out what I'd witnessed, I was acutely aware of what had gone on. I picked up two knives not far from the goal that had been thrown onto the grass, embedded, about a foot long, and standing in the earth. I took those knives and put them behind the goal. That was when I saw him. On the running track behind my goal a white-haired man was sitting. I'll never forget his face. A Liverpool fan sitting on the place where the pole-vault would be, absolutely sobbing. Where did he come from? Photographers next to him were also sobbing, while the game was going on.

After only three minutes Gary Gillespie came on for Mark Lawrenson, who sustained a shoulder injury. After thirty minutes I saved a shot from Antonio Cabrini after he stormed forward from his left-back position. I quickly started a counter-attack where Stefano Tacconi saved Ronnie Whelan's shot. It was 0–0 at half-time. We were OK going into the dressing room. Fagan told us just to go out and play the same way.

In the second half the Polish striker Zbigniew Boniek made a run, Michel

Platini played a pass through and Gillespie took Boniek down outside the box, but his momentum took him into the area, where he fell. The referee, André Daina from Switzerland, blew the whistle and awarded a penalty. We didn't expect him to give a penalty because the point of contact was outside the box but Boniek's momentum took him in. I wonder whether the referee felt obliged to ensure Juventus won the game to avoid further problems.

Platini stepped up, I jumped to my left, and he put the ball away to my right: 1-0. I think that was the end of the game as a contest. None of the players wanted to play any more. With only sixteen minutes to play, Whelan was taken down in the penalty area, but Daina didn't give us a penalty. Nobody was in the mood for arguing too much.

The referee did his job to get the thing finished at ninety minutes, and that was it. We lost 1-0 to Platini's penalty.

I remember going into the dressing room afterwards and making sure our families were OK. We got changed straight away and left the ground as quickly as possible. We didn't hang around. There was a post-match banquet with some boozing back at the hotel but I didn't take part.

I went to meet my mother, who had seen me play for Liverpool for the first time, travelling from Africa with my stepfather. After the game she said she never wanted to go to another game ever, and she never did. For me, it was incredibly sad how she only watched my games on TV from then on.

TO SEE FOOTBALL BE REDUCED TO A TRAGEDY WHERE 39 PEOPLE lost their lives made me feel hollow. The youngest victim was only eleven years old. Heysel made me fall out of love with football and the resulting crisis of confidence made me question my future in the game.

We flew back to Liverpool, and were booked to go on holiday the next day to the Cayman Islands to see a friend, John Ray, who was originally from Blackpool and a Liverpool fan. I remember saying to Debbie on that trip, 'That's it, I'm not going to be a professional footballer any more.'

I didn't know what I'd do with my life, but to be involved in a team where some of our fans did such horrible things to other fans was horrifying, especially after my experiences in the Bush War. Football had been my escape. It helped me bury the memories from the bush, scenes I did not think I'd ever witness again.

You don't expect to experience death at a football match. I was adamant that I wanted to quit and my wife respected my decision. I am impulsive and perhaps had the Heysel disaster not come at the end of a season and there had been games to play I would have seen through my decision and gone back to Africa.

Instead I had time to reflect on my thoughts. We were in the Cayman Islands for two weeks, relaxing. I learned to scuba dive. John Ray came to me in the second week and said, 'Cayman Islands have got a game, a friendly against St Kitts at the weekend, but we haven't got a coach. Could you come and coach us?'

I agreed and helped the team to a 1–0 win. It reminded me that whether I decided to continue with football or not, the game would continue. I also realised that if I retired, the hooligans would win. I thought, *Nobody beats me; I'm not going to get beaten by these guys.* So I said to Debbie: 'I'm going to go back and play.'

Each player had his own set of circumstances which made it either more difficult or slightly easier to deal with. As captain, I think it hit Phil Neal the hardest. He was the club's most decorated player. He had played with a broken chin and a broken toe to appear in an incredible 417 consecutive games. To this day he is still on the top of that rank. Heysel was one of his final acts as a Liverpool player. The following December, Neal became the player-manager of Bolton Wanderers. Kenny Dalglish had been preferred to him for the same role at Liverpool in replacing Joe Fagan. It was a tough period for him.

For Joe Fagan, who had already announced his retirement, I think that it was hard to take too. He lived close to Anfield and he felt strongly that people living around him were at Heysel and had probably been a part of causing the tragedy. He thought he might have known them. I don't know if he did or not, and I'm not saying that he did, but it really hurt him.

I think everybody had wanted him to carry on and had Liverpool won the game maybe his decision to retire might have been reversed. But the timing of it, the way it happened, the sadness stopped him.

For me, Joe Fagan must be put up as one of the greatest managers of all time. In two years he won four trophies. Who else has achieved something similar? Anybody who knows football, knows that is an incredible achievement and he should be put up there as one of the best managers in the world.

*

FOLLOWING THE DISASTER, ENGLISH FOOTBALL CLUBS WERE withdrawn and then banned from competing in European competition for five years. Liverpool's ban extended into a sixth year. Many teams and players missed out because of this ban, including those at Liverpool and beyond who were in no way connected to the tragedy.

In all my years at Liverpool, the team around this period was at its strongest. I think every player that played in those games before and during that ban would think about what we could have achieved. It was a shame what fantastic players like John Barnes, Steve McMahon and Peter Beardsley missed out. Ronnie Whelan, Ian Rush, John Aldridge, Stevie Nicol and Ray Houghton were at their peak during the ban. We can only imagine what we might have achieved, how many more trophies we would have won, because in Kenny's first year taking over from Fagan we won a double. And surely, if that side were playing in Europe, we would have gone on to another final.

Are we still bitter? I can't speak for the other players, but they must have felt it just as much as I did. As players we were not responsible for what had happened. If they were going to punish us perhaps they should have made Liverpool play behind closed doors in Europe for a few seasons. Criminals are deemed innocent until proven guilty, but here everybody associated with Liverpool was found guilty by implication. We lost our impetus in European football. Had we not been banned, who knows how many more trophies we would have won?

The punishment after Heysel hit both Everton and us when we were performing at our peak, and the ban from European football put an extra strain on the relationship between the clubs. It was a difficult one. They were at their very best – they'd just won the league and their first European trophy, beating Rapid Vienna after a famous semi-final win over Bayern Munich. Then we went to Heysel and the disaster hit us. Everybody was blaming Liverpool fans for what happened, but Everton took the real brunt of it, because their European Cup adventure would never materialise.

Was it right to ban English football teams for that long? They said the English fans were the worst, but they weren't. There were hooligan factions in every major league in the world. That said, I think Heysel, along with the Bradford fire, in which 56 people had lost their lives at Valley Parade a few weeks earlier, were wake-up calls. There was previously a belief that football tragedies didn't happen in Britain, they happened around the world, in places that I knew like South Africa and Zimbabwe. Unfortunately it would take another horrible tragedy for the British authorities to fully get to grips with stadium safety.

AS Roma supporters stoned our bus before the European Cup final in 1984, and they stoned it afterwards when we came out with the trophy. They didn't get any ban. I've got no doubt hooliganism in England wasn't any worse than in other countries. The Italian fans are even today famous for trouble. They didn't get any sanctions after Heysel, because they were the victims.

Some of the people that created trouble before the game were Liverpool fans, but it is my belief that the riot was started by outside factions. Liverpool supporters travelled all over Europe in this era and, unlike other English clubs, such as Manchester United or Leeds – for whom trouble seemed to follow them around – they did not have a reputation for violence. My belief is that there were infiltrators from certain factions in London, wanting to get Liverpool out of Europe. They handed out pamphlets to people on the ferries coming across, boasting that Liverpool would be out of Europe in the coming seasons. They thought they were doing everybody a service because we were so dominant at that time.

The whole of that day in Brussels had been fantastic leading up to the final. Going to the stadium we saw red shirts playing against black and white shirts in the park, drinking together, playing football together, shaking hands, having a happy time.

Heysel proved to be worse than witnessing what I saw in the bush. These were grown men behaving like savages. My mother came over for the final on the ferry, and she was one of many who were handed pamphlets by the National Front, which basically said, 'Liverpool will not be in Europe again'. The NF saw Scousers as scroungers and envied Liverpool's success on the football field. She said that a lot of the people handing out pamphlets had Chelsea and Millwall tattoos on their arms.

People are still free now with blood on their hands. I later decided to try to find out for sure whether the NF were implicated in Heysel. I was depressed by what I'd seen and for a period obsessed with wanting to find out what had really happened. I travelled to one of their headquarters just outside Slough for a group meeting. They recognised me straight away but because I was a white guy from Rhodesia, they assumed that I was racist. So they welcomed me and I had a drink and tried to relax. One of the heads approached me and we got talking. I asked whether they knew anybody who was involved in Heysel and all of a sudden he went cold, said no, then walked off. He had sussed me and I decided it was best I leave for my own safety.

Unfortunately it backfired for them; the ban hurt the whole of the English league. We were banned for six years, the other English teams for five. They ultimately contributed to an injustice suffered by their own teams, because they couldn't play European football either.

MY MOTHER ONCE GAVE ME THE GOOD ADVICE OF REVISITING places where there have been difficulties or traumas to find peace. If you have experienced a tragedy, if you've had something bad done to you, go back and relive that at another time to heal those memories.

Ten or so years after the Heysel tragedy, I returned to Belgium with a BBC television crew to film a documentary. Though the stadium had been rebuilt, it was still an athletics stadium and still hosting football matches.

There was a plaque which said, 'We will always remember', but it did not include the names of the people who had died. There were other plaques, of course, like one to mark it as the venue where Sebastian Coe broke a world record in 1981, and the venue where Pelé had once played. But 1985? It was as if nothing had really happened in that year. It made me angry because something did happen and it was dreadful. History is not all about glory. History is about learning from mistakes, and few were bigger than the one at Heysel.

17

The Nature
of Goalkeeping

GOALKEEPING IS ABOUT MAKING A DECISION AND STICKING TO IT. Your positioning is vital, and you have to study the player on the ball: where is he shaping to kick it? What are his movements? Where is he looking? You must read the game. Instinctiveness comes into play when you're stopping shots on the line. In that moment you are not being calculating, it is purely down to the speed of your reactions. Saving a header from a corner is instinctive; reading the flight of a corner and coming to claim it is calculated.

Overall, I probably played in a more calculated manner. If you don't read the game well as a goalkeeper, you get too many nasty surprises.

As a goalkeeper you are not only the last line of defence, but you're also the first line of attack, and you have to think smart in how you choose to start the next one. If I saw a two-on-two situation developing upfield, I'd waste no time in kicking it up there to let them fight it out. Usually, one of the players doing that fighting on behalf of Liverpool was Ian Rush. I'd whistle as soon as I grabbed the ball and he knew what was coming. He'd prepare by walking to the touchline and bringing his marker with him, leaving a space in the centre. Then I'd release the ball in the space and inevitably he'd win the subsequent duel because of his speed and strength.

You analyse the danger, you see the run and the space, then act. I probably threw more than any other goalkeeper in the league in my time. Kicking wasn't really an option. We liked to play from the back as much as possible so most of the time I'd choose the shorter option. If Rush was available though, why not use him? You have to be streetwise.

Communication is also vital as a goalkeeper. You are the boss at the back and you need to like being a leader. Some are natural-born leaders, others grow into one. I was a leader in the army. From seventeen to nineteen I looked after people nearly twice my age at times; I had quite a range in my stick. From the age of seventeen I therefore knew I could lead. During my time as leader we only lost two people, while other sticks suffered many more casualties. Those two people lost their lives due to the circumstances – there was nothing we could have done.

There are physical hints at strong characters.

You have Neville Southall. And then you have Bobby Mimms. We knew Southall was a big, big character. We knew that we could go at Mimms. I think you can tell a lot about a goalkeeper by the strength of his hands. Ultimately, you need big hands and strong wrists to keep shots out. When you shake another goalkeeper's hand before the game and his handshake is weak, you begin to think about whether he has the strength behind him to parry a shot away. David Seaman had strong hands. Phil Parkes had strong hands. Tony Godden did not. Gary Bailey did not. Erik Thorstvedt did not. Bobby Mimms did not. Peter Schmeichel – you wouldn't know, because he didn't shake hands with anyone. I had to grab him on the pitch before a game at Old Trafford and he wasn't happy at all. It's fair to say, he had strong hands. Eye contact was important too. If another goalkeeper didn't look at you when shaking his hand, I interpreted that as him being a bit shy – let's have a go at him.

Goalkeepers in general are a different breed. Put simply, your job is to guard the goal. The penalty area – 18 yards long and 44 yards wide – is your domain. Nobody in your team, including your manager – unless he was a goalkeeper himself – can tell you what to do in that area. You have to stay 100 per cent in charge. Nobody can boss you around in there – you are the king of the box, the captain, nobody else. If you do your job in that area and prevent the ball going over the line, then you've done your job, full stop.

However, the king needs to be clear in his demands in his kingdom, making efficient communication critical. If the information you give to the people in front of you is correct, you will be OK. That's the power a good number one possesses.

As a goalkeeper you should try and catch the ball as often as possible. Punch it and give the opposition a chance? No. Make sure you hold on to it. I've seen goalkeepers who are brilliant, goalkeepers who love to fly, flick and punch the ball, but so many of them don't take hold of it. What's with the modern goalkeepers who don't like to catch the thing? If you catch the ball you have complete control, and you're not giving the opposition another chance. Get hold of the ball. Break your fingers when it hits you if you have to – you've still got the ball.

I was doing a week of training sessions with the goalkeepers at Melwood not too long ago. There they use the same balls as they do for the games. We practised holding on to the ball. A little while after, the goalkeeper I had trained with played a game at Anfield, and he didn't catch the ball like we practised. It was like he wanted to make everything he did in the game spectacular for the later television edit. Everything was punched out, and his legs were flipping everywhere. It was weird. I said to this goalkeeper afterwards, 'Listen, why can't you catch the ball?' 'This ball moves all over the place,' was his reply. I said, 'Well, I've been training with you the whole week with the same ball and you catch it during the training sessions, but this is in the game and now you're punching it – what's going on? It's the same ball.' They just want to show off.

Nowadays to be a top goalkeeper you have to have good feet. Can you play in a five-a-side without your hands? How good are you with the ball? The goalies that can play outfield are going places. The ones that are awkward with their feet won't make it to the top. They will be playing Championship and League One football. Can you run? You also have to be fit. You have to have explosive muscles, making gym work very important. Can you get to the top-left corner with your right hand rather than your left? You need to be flexible. I think yoga is very good for goalkeepers. Yoga, trampolining, table tennis – any of these sports.

In terms of your fitness as a goalkeeper there is a contradiction. You need to have explosive muscles yet be flexible at the same time. In other words, you need to be like a gymnast. If you're a gymnast, then you've got the perfect goalkeeper's body. You need to know how to fall and how to come down from a height without hurting yourself. You really can't teach that to a person who's never done it. It has to be taught to you as a child on a mat – can you jump from here and roll? Can you dive off the mat and then roll? It has to be taught at a very young age.

I would say the most important thing for a goalkeeper is his concentration. It's the brain that tells you what to do with your arms and your feet, and if you're not concentrating and if you're not sharp, then you'll be slow off the mark. Getting the people in front of you placed correctly is also vital, because their presence might mean you don't have to make the save at all; but when there is a save to be made, you have to be sharp. Your concentration has to be 100 per cent.

There are many ways to improve your concentration, like standing on one leg and juggling. Another common exercise is to stand on a half-round ball (a Bosu ball). While you concentrate on keeping your footing on this equipment, someone throws a ball for you to catch at the same time. Your mind has to concentrate on the unsteady surface you are balancing on and catching the ball at the same time. If you are the one doing the testing, ask him questions at the same time – test him at times tables. If he doesn't get the right answer, you know his mind is on other things. It's about kinetics. A lot of the German sides use kinetics in their coaching.

The key is all about being present in the moment. The lack of that presence is probably what is making a lot of people unhappy in life in general – most of the time they are living in the past or in the future, and rarely living in the moment. A goalkeeper has to be living in the moment, and if something bad happens, such as conceding a goal, he has to forget it and stay in the moment until the end of the game. Only after the whistle should you reflect on what happened during the game. As a goalkeeping coach that's when you give your assessment as well. If you've had a terrible day at work, like poor Loris Karius had in Kiev, it is highly important that the team around the goalkeeper assess what he did in the game. But only after.

What about mental strength? Some people say that goalkeepers are crazy. The legendary Arsenal stopper Bob Wilson even wrote a book on goalkeepers and goalkeeping called *You've Got to Be Crazy*. I subscribe to a different view. Goalkeepers aren't the only crazy ones, there are twenty outfield players that are lunatics in their own way as well. They are the ones chasing the same ball for ninety minutes, trying to score as many as they can and tiring themselves out in the process. We stay in our area, protect it and let the ball come to us. When we do have it, we throw it back out and get our teammates to fetch it – just like when you go and take a dog for a walk. You throw the ball and eventually it makes its way back to you. Sometimes you kick it further and then they chase it further. They're the crazy ones.

To be a good goalkeeper, you also need a high threshold for pain. If you struggle with pain, then I don't think you're going to be any good. If you go to the game and think, 'Oh, I really don't feel like this today, because there's a striker that's going to absolutely hammer me at the back post,' then forget it, don't even put the shirt on.

You have to have a high pain threshold – a pain barrier that you have to go through.

I have broken parts of my feet and my toes in a game before and played on as I simply hadn't noticed. Other than that, I have been very lucky. I only broke my ribs several times during my playing days, and my cheekbones playing for Southampton against my old bluenose friends, Everton. I also broke my right elbow once on an Easter Monday at Old Trafford. I have got a big scar there reminding me of a day in pain.

LEV YASHIN WAS MY FIRST HERO. HE USED TO CATCH THE MOST impossible shots. Pat Jennings, who played for Northern Ireland 119 times over 22 years and for both Spurs and Arsenal, was another of my heroes. He had shovels for hands, and so when he came for crosses he would be able to catch with just one of them. He is also a great person. Phil Parkes at West Ham (not the Wolves and Vancouver keeper) was also big enough to come for crosses and Neville Southall at Everton was probably the finest goalkeeper that never got the chance to play in a World Cup, because he played for Wales. He was heavy-set, but very strong. He could come for crosses, but he relied on his sharpness when he was in his six-yard box, and he was an extremely good goalkeeper. Dino Zoff was a fantastic goalkeeper for Italy because of the way that he played – he was excellent with his feet, not a necessity in his day. Anyone who plays in goal for Italy has got to be up there among the best. Internationally, I also have to mention Félix from Brazil as one of the best I have seen play, as well as Jan Tomaszewski of Poland, who almost single-handedly secured qualification for Poland at the 1974 World Cup at the expense of England. Tomaszewski had been branded a 'clown' by Brian Clough, so we had something in common.

There were some fairly good keepers around when I played, and especially in the English leagues. When you include keepers playing in a different era, there are a couple that have particularly caught my eye. Manuel Neuer has impressed me immensely with the way that he plays. His dominance and his presence are impressive. He plays well with his feet, and captaining both Bayern Munich and Germany says a lot about his leadership skills. The way he commands his area sets an example for his teammates. He will come back and be dominant again, even though Germany, who humiliated Brazil in the World Cup of 2014, surprisingly didn't make it past the group stages in Russia four years later.

In Italy, Gianluigi Buffon has been a magnificent goalkeeper, and with his 176 games for his country is the most-capped player for any European national team. His likely successor with Italy, Gianluigi Donnarumma, the youngster from Milan, is still only a teenager but looks like a very promising goalkeeper. They have let Buffon teach him in the national set-up, and therefore they shouldn't have to worry about the goalkeeping position for the next two decades.

If you have a look at Buffon, he has read the game perfectly way back from all those years ago when he first came into the Italian side. He made his debut in Serie A aged only seventeen in 1995 and his Italy debut at the age of nineteen. He still led Juventus in the season just gone at the age of forty.

The beauty of a goalkeeper is also the fact that you can make your game last for so much longer than everyone else. You can really mature with the game. Experience makes you build confidence and knowledge. But you've got to keep injury-free to last that long, so if you manage yourself well you can grow in the sport. You read the game a lot better when you are playing all the time and you're actually in the side year in, year out.

18

Winning Mentality

AS MUCH AS HEYSEL HAD BEEN HARD ON SO MANY OF US, BANNING us from playing in Europe certainly didn't take our motivation away on the pitch in the long run.

Appointing Kenny Dalglish, aged just 34, as our new manager was an absolutely brilliant move. His transformation from player to manager was seamless; it was the best move for the club and the way they handled it was perfect. Kenny stepped into the role very smoothly, and he had the likes of Ronnie Moran and Roy Evans to guide him – they were a fantastic trio.

It can't have been easy for Kenny coming in as manager, expected to maintain two decades of almost continual success at such a young age. He was still also, in 1985, a significant player for us and had played in most of our games during the ill-fated 1984/85 season. He made it clear that he had no plans to hang up his boots just yet, and wouldn't for another five years, although his time on the pitch diminished as he got older.

Where he succeeded as Liverpool manager was in breaking down some of the dressing room factions – and there were pockets within the dressing-room: the Scots, the Wirralites, the younger players – bringing in outstanding new players and retaining the best traditions of the Anfield Boot Room. It all seemed to come so easily to him. Before he was an unrelenting piss-taker and ruthless with the younger players, in particular. But when he became manager he realised that he had to change.

With me I felt at times that he could have protected me more from the criticism that came my way, but after a while I realised that he left me alone because he thought I had the mental strength to deal with it myself. That gave me a lot of confidence.

We had won the league four times in my first five years at the club, and inevitably in conversations about this period you are always asked what the secret was. I know for sure the answer is the camaraderie we had in the dressing room. Yes, we would fight for each other, but we would also help out the teammate who'd had a bad day at work. And yes, we would party together. The Scottish mafia – Kenny Dalglish, Alan Hansen, Graeme Souness – would party by themselves, but they'd party. Those from the Wirral would party among themselves as well, and then the rest would party as one. There were many parties. However, once we all came together at training we were expected to train well and seriously.

Another very important factor in Liverpool's success was the systematic research undertaken by the Boot Room, the homework they did on the players before they signed them. Good scouts helped pick the right characters for the team.

When I was playing at Crewe, I lived in the Royal Hotel and there were three of us together in the attic room. After about twelve games I kept noticing this fellow every Friday night in the hotel, and I had never seen him before. He'd wear a flat cap and sit in the bar. I used to have dinner in the dining room and he would come in and sit down and have a pint of lager. This was the night before the game, and then we'd all go to bed. Sometimes I'd leave the hotel and walk to the pub down the road for a nightcap. Eventually I would see the same fellow in the pub. The next day when we came down to the restaurant for our pre-match meal he would be there too, curiously looking at what we had to eat. I thought he was a bit odd.

I only found out in my third year at Liverpool who this person was – it was a Liverpool scout called Peter Dee. They sent him not to watch a game, but to watch how I conducted myself in the lead-up to one. They did their homework right from the start. They obviously saw me train as well, because the same chap with the flat cap was at a couple of my sessions. Crewe isn't far from Liverpool anyway, and it's a major station to change at.

I still see Peter Dee to this day, the undercover spy who gave my behaviour the thumbs-up. When I am back in Merseyside I go to Aughton, near Ormskirk, to visit him. He's a smashing old fellow who found a lot of the Liverpool players including Kenny Dalglish, Alan Kennedy, David Johnson and David Fairclough, and he's very good friends with Ron Yeats, who was Liverpool's chief scout for many years after his playing days.

Looking back, it is fascinating to read through what the coaching staff and the scouts at Liverpool logged: what kind of weather it was; how such-and-such had trained; how one player had an ankle problem. All this information was recorded in the books, so there must have been a ledger at training each day. This is what they did, and it was undeniably helpful when it came to picking the team. There were many parameters, and the analysis they did was very important to Liverpool's success.

Finally, the staff's constant work in keeping us grounded was a vital factor to our success. There was a clear message: everyone – from the manager and players to the cleaners and tea ladies – was equally important. The icing on the cake, of course, was how Ronnie Moran used to come in there with the medals in a cardboard box the summer after every season we won the league. That's about grounding; it brings you back down to earth. They used to say, 'Some people have got the grounding in them naturally or through their upbringing, some people haven't. Work out which one you are.' Then they would walk out. Everybody looked around in the room: 'Who has got it and who hasn't got it?'

IN LIVERPOOL'S MOST SUCCESSFUL YEARS, LOSING STILL DIDN'T come easy, but how we handled defeat depended on if it had come at home or away. Losing away from home, you could reflect on the defeat all the way back on the bus or train coming back. And if your assessment in your head was, 'OK, fine, maybe I did mess up, but I can live with myself tomorrow,' then you've assessed it right. If you cannot live with yourself the next day then you've done something wrong.

Bus journeys back, depending on where in the country it was, were often more about the guys getting together to decide where we were going that night to drink. When the bus 'had a breakdown' – or so we told our wives – we went to the nightclub. You'd sometimes get back home at 3 a.m.

Did we reflect? Yes. Some managers made us reflect. Did we regret losing? Absolutely, because playing for Liverpool in that era, we simply weren't used to it.

It was more important to have a drink after a defeat than a win. We would drink away the loss, and we didn't have so much after a win, because we were used to it. We drowned our sorrows rather than drank to our victory. In other words, we drank more when we lost than when we won. Personally – on a bus ride home from London – I would probably drink three beers if we won, whereas if we'd lost I'd have had a whole case, so twelve. That was the contrast. If we'd won we would be busy talking about what we did well, but if we lost you couldn't talk as much because everyone's heads were in different areas, analysing why it went wrong and who was to blame. Was it him or was it me? Everyone was thinking about their own things.

I remember a time coming back from Brighton on the bus. We had lost the game 2–0 in the FA Cup. In those days we didn't have a toilet on the bus. I was disgusted that this was the case, so I used to open up empty beer cans with a knife so the guys could pee in them. When they stood the can at the back and the bus braked, the cans would tip over and all the pee went down the front like a mini yellow River Mersey. Joe Fagan would say, 'Hey, that's disgusting,' and my response would be, 'Well, if you don't get us a bloody thing we can pee in, it will continue.'

On this occasion I brought a bucket with a lid and I put it at the back. The pee was filling up the bucket and by the time we were in the middle of London the bucket was full. I asked some of the guys to open the emergency door right at the back so I could throw it out, and I accidently hit a car as I did it. It landed on the front windscreen and so the driver couldn't see anything as the pee hit the window. He drove straight into a lamppost. However, our driver didn't see what had happened, so the bus carried on.

Liverpool soon got a letter, and Fagan questioned us on what had happened. We had to tell him that I'd thrown the urine in the bucket out of the door to prevent it rolling to the front of the bus like it had done previously. 'We didn't have a toilet, boss, and I brought a bucket. Maybe I should have got a bigger one, but I needed to throw that, so I threw it out and hit the car, and I didn't see what happened.' Paisley told us they wanted insurance money from us, but I think the club ended up settling the bill. One week later we had a bus with a toilet in it.

DISAPPOINTMENT WASN'T SOMETHING WE HAD TO TASTE IN Kenny's first season in charge. Unusually for us we started the 1985/86 season straight out of the blocks and by December had lost just a single league game. It was not us, nor Everton that season, however, that set the early pace. Manchester United won their first ten league games of the campaign, and their supporters were suddenly dreaming of a first league title in eighteen years. Nobody knew better than ourselves that nobody has won a league title in October. They of course fell away and Everton replaced them at the top of the league. By February it looked as if they would retain their title when their 2–0 win over us at Anfield put them eight points clear of us in third position.

In the eyes of the media and some fans too, there was a familiar figure at fault: me. The *Liverpool Echo's* Ken Rogers (an Evertonian, by the way) wrote the following under the headline 'Grobbelaar Blows It':

> *Hero or villain? Genius or clown? Will the real Bruce Grobbelaar please stand up. For 73 minutes the controversial keeper was in line for Liverpool's man-of-the-match award as the 134th Merseyside derby unfolded in dramatic fashion at Anfield. Then the Jekyll and Hyde streak that haunts him mercilessly returned.*

Kevin Ratcliffe's goal from 25 yards, Everton's first of the afternoon, had rolled along the floor before somehow squirming under me. I was out of position and should have saved it. Gary Lineker scored a second soon afterwards. And yes, as you probably could guess, it hurts a little extra making a massive error in a Merseyside derby. You sure can't hide in the city afterwards.

Yet it's not the defeat that matters, it's how you pick yourself up afterwards. The following Sunday we played Spurs at White Hart Lane. The game was heading for a 1–1 draw, which would have seen Everton extend their lead over us to ten points, when in the final minute Ian Rush scored a winner. That set in motion a run in which we won 34 points from 36 to secure the league title. Everton didn't really do anything wrong, they just couldn't live with our unrelenting winning habit. It was a brilliant recovery inspired by the decision of Kenny to reintroduce himself back into the team at the expense of Paul Walsh. With that, our play transformed. Ronnie Moran and Roy Evans convinced him to be a leader on the park again, and he was indeed a leader, but fundamentally it helped the structure of the team. Paul and Kenny were different players, with Paul preferring passes behind the defence and Kenny preferring them to feet. Kenny's return

That's me, bottom row second from right. [AUTHORS' COLLECTION]

Prepping for school with my kid brother. [AUTHORS' COLLECTION]

Mum and dad happily married. [AUTHORS' COLLECTION]

Dad looking less than happy with me. [AUTHORS' COLLECTION]

On patrol with my stick in the Bush War. [AUTHORS' COLLECTION]

Returning home, such a relief. [AUTHORS' COLLECTION]

Learning my trade at Matabeleland Highlanders as the only white player in the team. [AUTHORS' COLLECTION]

Honing my skills in the garden signing for Vancouver Whitecaps (below). [AUTHORS' COLLECTION]

The big jump to Liverpool, where handstands continued as a feature of my performance and winning trophies became a feature of life. [GETTY]

Racing cars at Silverstone with Alan Kennedy and Terry McDermott. [AUTHORS' COLLECTION]

Back in Zimbabwe, flying planes and standing in front of beautiful waterfalls. [AUTHORS' COLLECTION]

On tour with the Liverpool boys. Don't worry, Sammy Lee is wearing trunks… [AUTHORS' COLLECTION]

Enjoying a cup of tea with Phil Neal and Ronnie Whelan. [AUTHORS' COLLECTION]

They claim this is meant to revitalise your skin… [AUTHORS' COLLECTION]

Entering Dante's Inferno, otherwise known as Rome in May 1984 – a night that would define my sporting career. We would win on penalties and my 'spaghetti legs' would prove crucial. [ALL GETTY]

With the boys of the Boot Room: Joe Fagan, Roy Evans and the ferocious Ronnie Moran. [GETTY]

Winning the league at Chelsea and embracing first with Mark Lawrenson (above),
then with the rest of the lads (below). [GETTY/AUTHORS' COLLECTION]

After clashing with Jim Beglin in the FA Cup final, we would take the double. [GETTY]

My flamboyant side shining through once again, whether it be at the Milk Cup final or one of the legendary Christmas parties. They said I was a clown, so I became one. [ALL GETTY]

Hillsborough was followed by another FA Cup final win over Everton as well as Michael Thomas's injury time winner for Arsenal, which gave them the league title. [GETTY]

Liverpool's last league title in 1990. [GETTY]

Wearing a face mask would be the least of my problems at Southampton. [GETTY]

Passport problems denied me playing more games for Zimbabwe but beating Cameroon in a qualifier for the 1994 World Cup was one of the highlights. [GETTY]

Three court cases and football's trial of the century. [GETTY]

Back where it all began in Zimbabwe
at David Livingstone school. [AUTHORS' COLLECTION]

Coaching at Ottawa Fury. [AUTHORS' COLLECTION]

With my eldest daughters Tahli (left)
and Olivia (right) (Courtesy of Mary Evans).
[AUTHORS' COLLECTION]

At home in Newfoundland with my
second wife Karen and my daughter, Rotém.
[AUTHORS' COLLECTION]

allowed us to keep possession a lot more and from there we began to feel more comfortable again.

After securing the title with 1–0 victory over Chelsea in which Kenny – who else? – scored the winner, the following Saturday we had the chance to make it a league and FA Cup double. At the time only four other teams had managed this feat: Preston North End in 1888, Aston Villa in 1897, Tottenham in 1961 and Arsenal in 1971. Standing in our way were Everton – who else?

Everton enjoyed the early dominance in this game. They were slightly unlucky not to have an early penalty when Stevie Nicol tangled with Graeme Sharp, then took a first-half lead when Peter Reid struck a superb through ball. Lineker evaded the attention of Hansen and raced on to it. I surged out of my goal and blocked his initial shot, but the striker reacted quickest and struck the rebound past me. Everton were unequivocally on top, while we stood in disarray. The tension was high, and at one point I became involved in an alteration with Jim Beglin. The ball was rolling away from us and I said to him, 'Leave it, Jimmy.' He ignored me, put his foot on the ball and we both ended up running past it. Eventually I picked up the ball and said, 'Jimmy, can't you speak English?' 'I'm Irish,' he replied. I pushed him quite harshly in the shoulder, and I know he wanted to punch me back, and all the while a packed Wembley and the football world watched us boil over in anger. So I put the ball down and passed it to him, he gave it back to me and that was it, finished. Over.

Still Everton came at us and shortly after the interval Kevin Sheedy went close to doubling Everton's lead. It was against the run of play that Jan Molby latched on to Gary Stevens' aimless ball up the wing on the hour mark. The Dane played through Rush, who sidestepped Mimms and pulled Liverpool level. Rushie had scored in 121 previous Liverpool fixtures, of which we had lost none and drawn just 19. Suddenly, the momentum – if not history – was with us.

Moments later, a header from Sharp was tipped over by me. That was to be the closest Everton were to come to a winner. Six minutes after he had scored, Rush played in Molby, who turned the ball across the Everton goal. Kenny missed the chance, but the ball fell into the path of Craig Johnston at the far post, who touched home Liverpool's second. Six minutes from full time Whelan crossed for Rush to head home his second and kill off hopes of an Everton revival. We had won the first all-Mersey FA Cup final and become Double winners. Afterwards Jim Beglin and I clinked glasses and toasted our most successful ever domestic season.

*

WE NEVER TOOK OUR WINNING FOR GRANTED, BUT AT TIMES IT seemed almost habitual. Late in the following campaign it looked as if we would be champions yet again. A run of five successive league victories had, by March 1987, put us top of the First Division with less than ten games to go. And yet we let it slip, losing successive away games at Tottenham, Norwich City, Coventry and, crucially, at Manchester United.

Every time we dropped points, Everton picked them up. We still had a way back. On 25 April we had to face Everton at Anfield. If we beat them and they slipped up elsewhere we still had a chance. First though, five days earlier on the Easter bank holiday, we had to travel to Old Trafford. The day was to be a calamity for me and Liverpool.

The game was still goalless when United had a corner kick. Craig Johnston was on the post and I was close behind him. The header came from Norman Whiteside, the Northern Ireland midfielder, and I'd taken off and caught the ball in the top corner. I came down on Craig, who was underneath me, so I fell awkwardly on my elbow. You could hear the crunching sound, and I felt a sharp pain. If you imagine taking a hard-boiled egg and cutting the top off, that top part of the egg now moved inside my elbow. I was lying on the ground in agony when the so-called physiotherapist, Roy Evans, ran on with his wet sponge.

'What's the matter?' he asked.

'I think I've broken my elbow.' He got the water and the sponge, put it on my arm and said, 'Let me have a feel. Oh shit, try not to let the opposition know that you've broken it. There's eighteen minutes left, just try and hang in there.'

I got him to tape it up to hold things in place, and I played on.

I was our only goalkeeper in Manchester that day, so there was no one to replace me. In those days you didn't bring a backup goalkeeper to away games. John Wark was our only sub on the bench. The rest of the squad were playing in the reserve team against United that day as well. During those remaining eighteen minutes I had to make two one-on-one saves against Gordon Strachan. On the first occasion he broke through the lines and, given the state of my elbow, there was no way I was going to dive to the right. Instead I shimmied that way, so Gordon went to the left and I grabbed the ball from his feet. The second time I shimmied to the right again and thought, 'I'd better wait here a little bit.' Eventually I robbed it off him again as he went left again.

In the dying seconds of the game it was still 0–0 when a long ball came from their goalkeeper, Gary Walsh. I shouted to Alan Hansen, 'Jocky, leave it, it's going to bounce once, leave it!' What does he do? He tried to clear the ball. I don't think that he trusted me – maybe I'd done something wrong in training again and he wasn't talking to me. He hit this ball and it went straight to Peter Davenport. I was outside my six-yard box, and so Davenport hit a lob. I couldn't get my right arm up. I went after it with my left but the ball went in and we lost 1–0. If Alan had let the ball come bouncing to me I would have caught it, kicked it out and we would have drawn.

Bad news came from Goodison, where Everton had beaten Newcastle United 3–0. They were now almost totally out of reach, and although we beat them 3–1 the following Saturday they secured the title nine days later.

After the United game I was in great pain. I left the ground with my arm in a sling and needed an operation straight away. They wanted me to go to the hospital in Manchester. I told them not a chance. Imagine what could have happened to me lying in bed there with all the Mancs around me? When I was sleeping they would nick everything. Instead I went to a private practice called Park House in Crosby, and had my operation that night. Thinking I was safe there, I took my watch off and hung it up on the bar of the bed. However, when I came back from the operating theatre I looked at the bar and the watch had gone. Just my luck.

The injury made me miss the last four games of the season, and Mike Hooper took my place. I managed to regain it quite quickly, but in doing so I was playing with pins about ten centimetres long in my elbow. Every time I saved a shot I could hear a sound inside my elbow as one bone scraped another on the other side.

THAT SUMMER CHANGES CAME TO ANFIELD. A YEAR EARLIER IAN Rush had agreed to join Juventus for a British record fee of £3.2 million. The Italians had immediately loaned him back to Liverpool as they were limited in the number of foreigners they could play at any one time, and Rushie had had his best ever league season, scoring thirty First Division goals. But the end had finally come and he would be a huge loss.

In his place, Kenny spent big and he bought well. John Aldridge had already signed the previous spring and he added John Barnes and Peter Beardsley to the attack over the summer. From the outset we were almost unstoppable.

The addition of Barnes evolved Liverpool's play, Beardsley was the ideal replacement for Kenny, while Aldridge had a killer instinct. Before Barnes, you rarely saw a Liverpool player dribble with the ball. It was actively discouraged. 'Let the ball do the work.' When Jan Molby signed a few years earlier, he dribbled through midfield and smashed a shot in the top corner. Ronnie Moran was furious with him. With Barnes, it was slightly different because he operated in a different area of the field. Though dribbling incurred more risks, Barnes was usually found one-on-one with a full-back whereas in the centre of the pitch he would have had two, three or four opponents to dribble past. Barnes made Liverpool a more exciting team to watch.

It was a season where we lost only twice. One of those defeats was at Everton. I remember it well because I only lost three times at Goodison Park during my thirteen years at Liverpool.

This one had special significance because we were unbeaten in the league up to then and if we went one extra game without losing we'd surpass the 29-game unbeaten record from the start of a season set by Leeds over a decade earlier. Our only defeat all season had come the previous October to Everton in the League Cup.

The only goal of the game was scored when I came out to claim a corner early in the match, but dropped the ball and fell to the ground. It ran kindly to Wayne Clarke, who was lethal in front of goal, and he made no mistake in putting his side ahead. In scoring that goal, Wayne ensured that the record of Leeds remained intact – a Leeds team in which his brother Allan had led the forward line – and we had to settle for having equalled their feat.

That night, after making such a bad error in the derby, I made an even worse mistake by going out for a meal on Walton Breck Road in Anfield. Not the smart thing to do. I was sitting in a restaurant and there were a lot of Blues in there, and it's fair to say things got out of hand. I had a few choice words to say to this particular gentleman in his fifties who was out with his friends.

I had my baby daughter under the table, and things that they said to me weren't pleasant, so I told him where to go. Unfortunately, I said, 'Try walking a mile in my shoes before you open up your mouth.' He was sitting in a normal chair at the restaurant, and it was only when they were leaving and his friends brought the wheelchair from outside that I realised what I had said. When I found out he was disabled I immediately went over and apologised for the offence I had caused.

You have to be careful with your words in the heat of the moment.

I soon had a letter from the couple complaining about my behaviour, and I responded by apologising once more. However, if things are said out of context after a game, people shouldn't put you in such a position. He was the instigator of the abuse and I had merely responded.

We were almost unstoppable in the league in 1987/88, and although we lost again a fortnight later at Nottingham Forest we remained unbeaten for the rest of the season. In the return fixture with Forest at Anfield in front of the TV cameras we absolutely destroyed them 5-0. The watching Tom Finney declared it to be 'the finest exhibition I've seen the whole time I've played and watched the game. You couldn't see it bettered anywhere, not even in Brazil. The moves they put together were fantastic.' Ten days later Peter Beardsley's winner against Tottenham secured the title with four games to spare.

Everton dropped down to fourth position, while Manchester United finished the 1987/88 campaign as runners-up. This was Sir Alex Ferguson's second year at the club, and he was on his way to building the next generation of a club that would take over the throne from Liverpool and dominate English top-flight football in the years to come. But not yet. Still our city rivals were our toughest opponents. Both the red and blue sides of Merseyside feared no one at that stage. Together we sent the league title back and forth like a ping-pong ball, the rivalry intensifying.

At the time we were one of the best teams in Europe, but unable to play European football. It was a real shame Barnes, Aldridge and Beardsley missed out on the continental stage with such a strong team. But so did Everton too. As league champions in 1984/85, the stage was supposed to be set for them to play in the European Cup the following year. Instead, they were first in line to be punished after Heysel.

THE FOREST GAME AT ANFIELD WAS ACTUALLY THE THIRD TIME IN twelve days we had played Clough's team. In between the two league fixtures was an FA Cup semi-final at Hillsborough that we won 2-1 thanks to an Aldridge brace. That set up a final with Wimbledon, and set in motion my brief and inauspicious musical career.

Making the record 'The Anfield Rap' before the FA Cup final in 1988 was one of my funniest experiences at Liverpool. It was the worst rapping you've ever heard. Craig Johnston co-wrote it and we all took turns singing, dressed like rappers wearing caps back to front, sunglasses, tracksuits, with massive fake gold chains hanging around our necks, dancing and singing in front of this massive graffiti wall.

My bit went like this:

Well, I'm rapping now, I'm rapping for fun,
I'm your goalie, the number one.
You can take the mick, don't call me a clown,
Any more lip and you're going down.

The chorus was simple and catchy.

Walk on … walk on … with hope … in your heart … and you'll ne … ver
walk … alone

We were in the charts for ten weeks and reached number three at a time when the charts meant something. Craig made some money on that. Only two players never signed a contract – Mark Lawrenson and myself. The others were paid £250 each, but we wanted royalties. In the end we got nothing.

The rap was produced ahead of the final against Wimbledon. We had just won the league for the seventeenth time, and we were massive favourites to overcome a Wimbledon side who had finished sixth, then seventh in their first two seasons in the top flight. They had never won the FA Cup. In fact they had been non-league only a decade earlier.

But part of the beauty of football is that the unpredictable is possible and it creates some of the magic; the underdogs can actually win. However, it wasn't magical to us on this occasion. On a sunny day at Wembley in front of 98,203 people we lost 1–0 to Lawrie Sanchez's goal.

Who would I blame? I blame John Barnes. Just before half-time they got a free-kick. Dennis Wise took it and Sanchez headed the ball into the net behind me. An hour into the game we were awarded a penalty after a foul by Clive Goodyear on John Aldridge. Barnes had the ball in his hands, ready to take it. Aldridge said, 'I'm going to take it.' Aldridge went up, stutter-stepped, and the keeper Dave Beasant saved it. If Barnes had taken it, he would have scored. Though Aldridge was our penalty taker that season, Barnes's interference disturbed Aldridge's routine and gave an advantage to the goalkeeper. It would have been 1–1 and a different story. Barnes will probably blame me for not stopping their goal. Football is always a two-way street.

EARLY IN THE 1988/89 SEASON MIKE HOOPER GOT ANOTHER opportunity to take my place, and this time for a longer period. On 17 September 1988 we were playing Tottenham at home, and I just felt very, very cold, despite the time of year. It felt like I had a bad flu with a very high temperature. I was freezing when I came to the ground and so had a hot bath before the game to try and warm up. I got all my kit on and went out, and I was still cold. I had a pair of goalkeeping trousers on and another T-shirt to try and counter how I was feeling, and I tried to put it out of my mind.

This was the match where Tottenham's Chris Fairclough got sent off for hitting John Aldridge in the jaw, but they still held out for a draw with Terry Fenwick having equalised almost immediately after Peter Beardsley's goal.

I had friends from Belgium staying at the house that night so I took them home while I was still feeling frozen. The plan was to then take my guests and my wife out for dinner, but I felt awful and apologised for not being able to go out with them, which was a rare occasion, me missing out on a night out with friends.

I went up into the spare bedroom and I crept into bed, got warm, and when my wife came back she checked how I was doing. I didn't look too healthy and she said she was going to call an ambulance. I suggested she just went across the road to speak to the doctor who lived there, a friend of mine.

Soon enough he came over and confirmed I needed to get to a hospital. Next door to us was an old people's home; there were ambulances coming in and out of there all the time, so my doctor went round and asked where the next one was going. I was soon on my way to Arrowe Park Hospital.

At Arrowe Park they discovered I had viral meningitis, so they put me on various drips and isolated me from everybody. I had played in this condition, not knowing just how dangerous it could be to get meningitis.

Eventually I came out of isolation, but other patients found out I was in hospital, so they would come to my bed to ask for autographs, and invariably they would stay to chat. After ten days I started to feel a little bit better, so I discharged myself and went home. I could get better care at home, especially with the doctor across the road.

I lost four months of the season, which was very frustrating. I wanted to get back but Dalglish said no, he wanted to see me get stronger in training first. So I trained, and in the end he put me back in for a league match against Southampton on 21 January 1989. We won 2–0 and my longest absence in a Liverpool shirt was at an end.

19

Hillsborough

DESPITE BEING LAID LOW WITH MENINGITIS FOR A SIGNIFICANT chunk of the season and the events that would eventually cloud the campaign for eternity, the 1988/89 season was, for me, in football terms, the best time in a Liverpool shirt. The football that we played was breathtaking. We would blow our opponents away. We were forerunners of the brilliant brand of football Barcelona later played under Pep Guardiola. We would chase so hard to get the ball back, but when we got it we didn't panic. We passed it around at a rapid pace and always managed to keep hold of it. We made the opposition chase us because we passed the ball so easily, which soon tired them out.

Results-wise it was business as usual coming into April 1989. We still weren't allowed to compete in Europe, so instead focused on playing well in domestic cup competitions and the league, and embarked on what would become a 24-match unbeaten run.

Our run in the FA Cup was quite simple—on the way to the semi-final we beat Carlisle United, Millwall, Hull City and Brentford, all lower-league opposition. We were keen to see who we were to face in the last four. When playing a semi-final on a neutral ground prior to the final at Wembley, we often played at Aston Villa's Villa Park or Manchester City's Maine Road. This time, with Nottingham Forest our opponents, Sheffield Wednesday's Hillsborough was the venue of choice, as it had been a year earlier when we met them at the same stage. The other semi-finalists were Everton and Norwich City, and they would be playing at Villa Park.

On the Friday night before the semi-final, we travelled to Sheffield by bus.

We stayed in a hotel in town and had several hours to relax and prepare for the game. Ian Rush went for a haircut while Lee Chapman, the Nottingham Forest forward, came to see some of our players in the hotel. We had dinner together that night, the same old ritual. I stayed out of my room as long as possible as Stevie Nicol was in doing his usual thing, eating crisps and drinking beer. We were very relaxed and confident, not knowing what nightmares would unfold in front of us the following day. Those nightmares that still haunt me in my sleep.

The next morning we woke up to a beautiful, sunny, warm day. Mid-April at its best in England. 'Yeah,' we thought to ourselves, 'this is going to be a good day.' We couldn't have been more mistaken.

We went to the ground, got out of the bus and noticed that our fans were walking towards the Leppings Lane stand, not the Kop – the biggest terrace. Liverpool had more supporters and so this was unusual. Before the warm-up we went out to have a look at the pitch and saw pens three and four were filling up, while hardly anyone was in the pens to the side. I thought nothing of it at the time.

We got changed and came out on the pitch again, while more fans continued to come through the middle section. During the warm-up I saw the crowd spilling into these two sections, and still hardly anybody went in the other sections. *I'm sure that the authorities have got this under control*, I thought, as I headed back into the dressing room. Walking out for the 3 p.m. kick-off I noticed that some more fans were now in the other pens, but the two stands behind me in the Leppings Lane end were absolutely packed.

We kicked off. In the opening minutes Peter Beardsley hit the bar and there was a big collective scream from the crowd just behind me. When I was forced to retrieve the ball before taking a goal-kick a few moments later, that was when I saw the faces of the Liverpool fans being pushed up against the fence. The wire mesh was deep into their skin, and they were shouting, 'Please help us, Bruce!' They were in agony. The fence, cut into squares, was made out of hard metal mesh. I kicked the ball up the field and I also shouted to a policewoman at the gate. 'Excuse me, can you open up that gate. Can't you see that they're in distress?' There were these little doors in the fences you could open. She shouted back, 'I can't, we don't have the keys. One of the stewards has got the keys.' So I said, 'Find out which one has it, and open the gate!'

After five minutes the ball went over my bar again, and this time it landed in the pen. The ball came back out, but once again I could see and hear the distress of the people at the front. Their faces were pressed even harder towards the fence.

I shouted to the woman, 'Open the gate!' I retrieved the ball and went over to the left ready to take my kick. I looked over and finally they'd opened the gate. A major tragedy was unfolding and the referee stopped the game. It was 3:06 p.m.

I turned around and fans were spilling onto the pitch, some carrying bodies, and one said, 'There's only one ambulance! What can we do?' I said, 'Use the hoardings for stretchers,' because the advertising hoardings were just those V-shapes stuck together. That's what they did. They broke the advertising boards off to use them as stretchers and put bodies on them.

We were all in shock watching the tragic scenes unfold. Roy Evans came and dragged us off. I got my stuff out of the back of the goal and looked around from inside the goal, and I saw something that I don't want to see again, an image that still haunts me. People's eyes staring towards me from behind the fence; you could see them, but they were no longer looking, just staring out into the air.

Some came out onto the pitch crying from relief and fright, others came out of there and fainted. Fellow fans in the tier above lifted others up.

Behind the goal I recognised some of the young guys who had been screaming for help. One of them was Neil Hodgson, a 24-year-old lad from Anfield. He was in total shock after being squashed and was hyperventilating. His mate was badly injured.

The referee told all the players to go to the dressing room. Most of us sat there in silence, not knowing what to think or say. A Scouser came through and he said, 'You don't want to know how many bodies I've seen. It's like a war zone.'

Later, some of us went down the tunnel but were stopped from going any further. I saw all the people lying in front of Leppings Lane, line after line. We were told to get back in and have a shower because the bus was taking us home. We sat listening to the radio until the death toll reached number 40 in the reports.

Then we switched off the radio and sat in silence until we got back to Liverpool. Somehow I had to drive back to our home on the Wirral in this state of shock. I couldn't think clearly.

Janet Dean, the school lollipop lady on Heswall Road, was looking after our little girl. She was the mother of the referee Mike Dean and she used to babysit Tahli and Olivia and Stevie Nicol's daughter and son, Katy and Michael.

I came into the kitchen and Janet made us coffee. 'How did this all happen?' she asked.

'I don't know.' I had no words to describe what had happened. I walked her to the top of the hill on her way home. Coming back I couldn't sleep. I can't sleep at the best of times, but goodness me, this was different. I was thinking about what I could have done to help, what I couldn't have done, and what I should have done. Questions were constantly digging into my chain of thoughts as the number of lost ones kept rising. I had an eternal string of questions to myself as to what I could have done differently to save more lives.

There wasn't really anyone to talk to about these questions that built up guilt inside me. I had talks with my wife Debbie, but the feeling of sadness, emptiness and guilt wouldn't go away.

The news updates in the days to come would let us know that the youngest victim, who just came to support us but paid for it with his life, was only ten years old. His name was Jon-Paul Gilhooley, Steven Gerrard's cousin. Each of the victims had a story, a family; they left broken hearts. As details emerged of the lives they had left behind a bigger picture of the tragedy built up. There were families who had lost fathers, and parents who had lost children.

This was definitely one of the lowest points of my life. All the conversations I had with myself were to some extent damaging. You walk in circles, seeking answers, like a hamster going round on a wheel. You don't know who to turn to in order to stop these destructive internal conversations, or how to turn to someone when horrific things like this happen. All the while lurked the fear of something similar happening again in another of our games.

I walked down to the local store a few sleepless nights after the disaster, just to get out of the house and try to release some of my thoughts. The sight I caught of the front page of the *Sun* on display in the shop was shocking, extremely provocative and hurtful. Emblazoned across its front page was the headline 'The Truth' in which it alleged that our supporters stole the wallets of victims, urinated on them and attacked police officers trying to save lives. I knew that the reality was very different. I had seen myself people in severe shock or suffering injuries of their own trying to help the police, medics and stewards as much as they could. I was disgusted.

I thought the reporters who wrote the headlines and all the rubbish inside the paper were ignorant people. They don't know the anatomy of mankind. I've seen bodies that have just passed away. If there is liquid in them, they will urinate; the same happens with stools once the body is relaxed. So with them saying Liverpool fans are drunkards, Liverpool fans urinated on the dead and stole their wallets, I knew then that this paper was no good at all. They wanted sensationalism and to sell newspapers off the back of the biggest tragedy to ever hit British football and our city. It's the most despicable thing I've ever seen in a newspaper.

At the time I had a ghosted newspaper column with the *Sun*. Previously I hadn't thought too much about it; I was being paid to talk about my sport to a ghostwriter. Lots of players did it. That relationship came to an abrupt end after their lies. Who would want to be associated with the scum *Sun* after that? Not me. After they published their disgusting lies I called the editor Kelvin MacKenzie and quit my column on the spot.

Amazingly, given the rubbish and lies they had published about my club and my fans, there was incredulity at my decision to walk away. They don't have anyone saying no to them, they told me. I was in breach of contract. I told them I didn't care about any contract after what they'd written. They warned me that I would never write for another newspaper again. Actually, that's the first thing that I did: I wrote a piece for the *Daily Express* denouncing them.

The *Sun*, I realise now, had been doing it for years and years and years. They don't care whose reputation they imperil. If they want a good story they'll put it out there, even if they have to pay thousands for defamation further down the line. That's the way it has always been with them. The attitude comes from the highest person in that newspaper group, Rupert Murdoch.

This was an organisation that was a law unto itself and entirely lacking in self-awareness. The way they went about their business was disgusting. Not only were they ignorant enough not to understand the damage their lies did to a club and a city rocked to its core, but they couldn't understand why I wouldn't want to be part of it. There was no element of understanding; on the contrary, they were very angry that I was walking away. People didn't do that to the *Sun*.

I thought that at some point they would apologise for their lies, but they didn't. I realised from then that they would never apologise, not even after the court case with me years later. They're not a very apologetic newspaper, are they? This behaviour comes from the man at the top, Rupert Murdoch. Maybe he can allow behaviour like that over such a big football tragedy because he doesn't come from Britain. I do sometimes wonder what his forefathers did to end up in a convict colony like Australia.

*

THE CLUB OPENED UP ANFIELD FOR PEOPLE TO COME IN AND show support for the victims and their families and for people to have a place to grieve. The pitch turned into an ocean of flowers and scarves.

In the lounges we welcomed families who had lost their loved ones. The players and the Boot Room staff came and met the families. We also visited them in their homes and we went to show our support to injured supporters battling for their lives in the hospitals. What do you say to someone after something as horrible as this had torn their family apart, destroyed their health and left huge holes of grief?

Kenny made us go to counsel people, but in doing that we were also counselling ourselves. I was shattered as a human being, but it gave me strength. We'd knock on people's doors. People must realise the Hillsborough tragedy didn't just impact Liverpool Football Club; it hurt Evertonians and Tranmere Rovers fans too. It affected the whole of Merseyside. The father and mother might like Liverpool, but the son would like Everton or Tranmere. In Liverpool, families don't necessarily support the same football team.

I went to a family whose son had died, and the parents were Evertonians. I knocked on the door.

'Hello, my name is Bruce Grobbelaar,' I said.

'You killed my son.' The door got shut in my face. I knocked again. The door reopened. 'You killed my son; what do you want here?' And I said to them, 'I want to talk to you about that.' And I explained, 'Your son was coming to the semi-final for joy, not for a fight. He was coming to watch myself and my ten teammates play. He didn't know what was going to happen, and we certainly didn't know what was going to happen. So we didn't do anything wrong. We are all victims in this whole tragedy. The only common denominator that we had as players was that we played, and he came to watch us.'

Explaining the tragedy to so many families helped us. And Kenny and the club made sure there were players at the funerals for all the victims who lost their lives. Dalglish went to as many funerals as he could possibly manage to get to, as some of them were held at the same time. To the players he delegated between six and eight funerals each.

I went to eight.

The hardest one was probably the one in Aintree in a small traditional church near the racecourse, to honour and part with a boy, a teenager. In some of the funerals it was quiet mourning, but in this particular one the family were sobbing right the way through. It was just heartbreaking.

Debbie came with me to this one. It was incredibly difficult. Above the soft music, you could hear the sobbing. And then they played 'You'll Never Walk Alone'. At times like that you realise the song meant so much more than people will ever realise.

It was quite extreme and hard to go to that many funerals in such a short period. Almost all the churches were filled with people, because families, friends, neighbours from the whole street would come and say their goodbyes.

We honoured Kenny's wish for us to go and it meant a lot to the families that we did. Families acknowledged what we did and told us how much our football team meant to them. And they knew that they were not alone in their grief. They knew that Liverpool Football Club cared, because we really did.

Kenny and Marina Dalglish played remarkable roles in the weeks and months after the tragedy. What they did should never be forgotten. Kenny, in particular, shouldered so much of the burden and came into his own as a leader. He was selfless in providing support for the victims and their families, unified the players and club behind a common cause as well as serving as manager for the country's biggest football club. If it had not been for Kenny, I don't think the team would have played as well or been as ready for the rescheduled semi-final. I've said it many times, if people were getting knighthoods for things done in football, Kenny Dalglish should have been knighted a long time ago, because it was his and Marina's drive that saw us through this period.

Finally Kenny did get knighted in 2018. Not a day too early. The club also renamed the Centenary Stand to honour him before the start of the 2017/18 campaign, and I can't think of any Liverpool player who deserved such recognition more.

For three weeks after the tragedy our games were postponed. But we couldn't go without football forever, no matter how meaningless it felt while an entire city remained grieving and some of the victims continued fighting for their lives.

Once again I had to follow my mum's advice, to go back to the scene of disappointments in life. Football had disappointed us all, but facing it again helped healing – even though many of us didn't feel like playing. It's hard to describe how we did it. For us to overcome this huge burden that we carried, we picked it up and we played the semi-final against Nottingham Forest, and we came out the other side as victors.

That FA Cup semi-final was a game we just couldn't lose. When you get adversity in life you'll come out stronger, and this certainly happened. Because the grief took away so much energy not just from us, but also from the whole city.

Many of the families thanked us for getting back to playing, because the games gave them something else to think about for a little while. Plus it brought the Liverpool fans together and helped many get out of the house when the grief had a dark grip on them. Others sadly chose to never return to a football game ever again.

When we finally played the semi-final against Nottingham Forest on 7 May we won convincingly, and we beat them again in the league three days later to keep up our title challenge. That side of ours was phenomenal. We could pick up our pace, pass any team in the league off the park, and then we could actually play a little football; get behind the defence, do things. Kenny had us drilled very, very rigidly and athletically as well. We were special, but to come and be able to play like that after everything we and our supporters had been through was something else.

The semi-final victory set the stage for an all-Merseyside FA Cup final at Wembley; the second in three years.

HILLSBOROUGH UNITED THE CITY. IT UNITED EVERYBODY AS everyone in the city fought for justice. I can't think of any other cities that could have fought that long for justice, standing strong together.

In 2012, 23 years after the tragedy, the Hillsborough Independent Panel concluded its work after going through over 450,000 pages of documents and other material from the contributing organisations, including reports, minutes of meetings, transcripts, witness statements, letters and memos, and records of telephone calls.

The panel report found that as many as 60 per cent of the 96 could have been saved if they had been given oxygen and received life-saving help. The ambulances had been sent away, many of the supporters that tried to help were not allowed in the chaos and the stadium didn't have supplies of oxygen in their first-aid supplies.

There are a lot of things that you can say about it, but because of the pending trials of six people, it's very difficult for me to say what I really want to say at the time of publication. What I can say is that it's more than twenty years too late;

family members have passed away not even seeing the justice that they were campaigning for, for their loved ones.

I have a friend who has campaigned to get justice all these years. Her brother died at Hillsborough; and it has taken 28 years to get the tragedy investigated and for those responsible to be charged – that is longer than her brother was on this earth. And this could have been sorted out many years ago.

I STILL DREAM ABOUT THE HILLSBOROUGH TRAGEDY. NIGHTMARES haunt me. And sometimes my brain switches back on to that day, as if I see myself trying to relive it all over again. I ask myself again and again, 'Could I have helped those people any more? Could I have done life-saving CPR on someone?' And I tell my brain that I belonged to a team where we were told to get back into the dressing room. Everybody would say that they could have done more, but when they called off the game, we had to go in.

When I go past the Hillsborough memorial at Anfield I always stop and cross myself. I think they've got a nicer place for the memorial now in the new stand because you have more peace and space than when it was along Anfield Road. There are seats so you can go and sit down, and a lot of people do. I see people sit there before the games and there are a lot of people who go there to see what Anfield is all about, what the 96 mean to us, and what the fans meant to Liverpool Football Club. We remember the victims with their names and age, so people can come there, reflect and never forget them.

I am a friend of several of the survivors, like Neil Hodgson, the young man behind the goal on that dark day in Sheffield in 1989. We are very close. I always go and see him and his lovely family at Anfield when I am in Liverpool. Now he has a son who is a goalkeeper. He claims I saved his life and many more by getting the gates open when his mate was turning blue from a lack of oxygen.

I carry the 96 with me.

I love my sport and nowadays I play a lot of golf. I play with Titleist balls with the number 96 on, and my nickname, Jungleman. My trainers have got 96 on the strap. I wear 96 on my back in home games when I coach teams. I made a little flourish to it, so 96 looks like an emblem and where the 6 goes underneath the 9, they marry up in the middle. I sign my autographs with a 96 on them. The 96 will always be with me. I will never forget them.

20

Closure of a Painful Spring

THE FA CUP FINAL AT WEMBLEY ON 20 MAY 1989 WAS ONE OF THE most emotional and significant Merseyside derbies in history, played as it was against the backdrop of the Hillsborough disaster. The whole city was touched by grief, and some of our supporters were still in hospital battling for their lives. It was only five weeks after the tragedy at Sheffield. This was a game we simply played for all of the Hillsborough families.

For us to actually play against Everton in the FA Cup final this year was fitting for everybody in Merseyside, though at the time I thought the trophy should have been shared between Liverpool and Everton. It was only the second all-Merseyside FA Cup final in history. It needed to be us playing against each other, the Reds and the Blues of Liverpool, and thankfully it was.

Gerry Marsden came and sang 'You'll Never Walk Alone' before the game, and in that moment 82,000 Scousers in the stadium were singing, crying, wrapping arms around each other and lifting their scarves. They were Reds and Blues together. It's something that's quite unique to Liverpool: both sets of fans mingle more than they fight. Long may that continue. We wore black armbands and had a minute of silence before the referee started a testosterone rush of a game.

We had failed to win the FA Cup final the previous year, when John Aldridge missed his penalty against Wimbledon. He didn't take long to make up for that. Inside five minutes our top scorer had put the ball in the net.

But this was a game in which the substitutes would make history. Stuart McCall came on after 58 minutes and Ian Rush came on after 72 minutes. Up until the

89th minute we were winning 1–0 in a game that had been played at an incredibly high intensity, and Neville Southall had made a strong save in the second half from a John Barnes shot to prevent us from going two goals up.

But less than a minute before the full-time whistle McCall would equalise, paving the way for thirty minutes of extra time. I had originally saved the cross-shot that had come from Everton's right but I couldn't hold the ball and McCall tapped home. Wembley erupted, with many Evertonians running on to the pitch to celebrate.

Extra time was crazy, with three more goals scored in the first fifteen minutes. There could have had more. Five minutes into extra time, Steve Nicol angled a beautiful ball in to Rush on the edge of the Everton's six-yard box. Rush chested the ball with his back to the goal, span superbly away from his marker, Kevin Ratcliffe, and half-volleyed in: 2–1.

Seven minutes later Kevin Ratcliffe lofted a free-kick into our box, Alan Hansen headed it out, but once again the ball found McCall, who chested it and struck with a perfect, powerful volley. Impossible to save: 2–2.

We answered straight away: Whelan to McMahon, McMahon to Barnes, and Barnes to Rush with a delicious left-footed cross. Rush directed the ball expertly past Neville Southall with one of his rare headers, and we were back in front two minutes after they had equalised. Fantastic. We went on to finally win 3–2.

I walked up the stairs second after our captain, Ronnie Whelan, to massive cheers from the Reds. Her Royal Highness the Duchess of Kent presented us with the trophy, as she did on three occasions when I won with Liverpool at Wembley. In my career I also got to meet beautiful Princess Diana, who presented the cup twice, and both the Queen and Prince Philip who did so once each.

Everton contributed to a very good cup final that day, but it was one we simply couldn't lose.

AFTER THE CUP FINAL THERE WERE TWO GAMES STILL remaining in this extremely draining and emotional season. Because we had three weeks of games postponed after the disaster, we had a backlog of fixtures to catch up on. Between 3 May and 26 May we played eight times, including an FA Cup semi-final and FA Cup final. After our first league match back, an emotional goalless draw with Everton, we won our next four league games, moving three points clear at the top of the table after a 5-1 win over West Ham in the last of these four games, played three days after the Cup final. For our final match of the season we were welcoming our closest league rivals, Arsenal, to Anfield on Friday, 26 May 1989.

All the other teams had played all their games. Arsenal were second in the league, only three points behind us but four goals worse off; we only had to avoid defeat by two clear goals to win our eighteenth title.

The game was unusual as it was broadcast live by ITV. Twenty million viewers were eager to find out who would run off with the league title. Arsenal were in with a chance, but we were unbeaten in fifteen in the league at Anfield. This wasn't the first time the league winner would be decided on the final day of the season: Manchester City had beaten their city rivals Manchester United on the final weekend of the 1967/68 campaign, while Liverpool won by just one point over Queens Park Rangers in 1975/76. Later Blackburn Rovers would edge United in 1995 before United secured the title on the final day in 1998/99, as did Manchester City in a breathtaking finale in 2012. But what made this delayed game against Arsenal the most dramatic in the history of the English league was the fact that the two teams fighting for the league were facing each other – and doing so after all the other teams had played their matches. All eyes were on us.

Beforehand I asked a very good friend of Debbie and mine, an Arsenal fan named John Cook, who was a sergeant in the Surrey Constabulary, to visit and see the game live. It was done, of course, with the best of intentions. 'Hey, John, why don't you come and see a real team win this weekend? Don't bother to put your Arsenal top on because Liverpool are going to win the league.' He reluctantly came up with his wife, and would never regret it.

Before that game was the only time I heard Kenny as a manager say something negative in his team talk. He didn't demand that we win. 'If they score, don't worry, they need to get another one. You're at home.' The team talk should have been, 'It's your last game, show them what champions play like.' A last hurrah. If he had said that, everybody would have gone out and given their all to go and get a goal. My goodness. 'If they score don't worry, we've got another forty-five?' No, that was terrible. It was bizarre. Only he can answer why he said this but after the traumas of the previous months, maybe his judgement was a little bit off. It would end up as the most annoying game I ever have played.

At half-time, with the scores level at 0–0, we were still on course to retain the league title. We remained confident. We hadn't lost by two goals at Anfield since February 1986 and we were halfway there. Then, shortly after the break, Arsenal got a free-kick and it was floated into the area. We thought that it was offside or that Alan Smith had touched it with his arm, but he'd actually glanced the ball with his head, in off the post, to make it 1–0. We knew we were now level on points, but we still had the better goal difference. The clock ticked down. We had the league title in our pockets going into injury time. We were controlling the game until the last minute, the fatal last minute when we lost all control and the league with it. The narrowest of title wins for Arsenal could have been so easily avoided.

The ball was cleared to midfield and found its way to John Barnes on the right-hand side, by the corner of the Kop. All I saw was McMahon turning around, indicating by pointing his finger up: one minute left, guys. Then John did something that I can hardly describe and absolutely cannot understand.

Nine out of ten times in such a situation he would have just kept the ball in the corner to run down the clock, but I think he might have thought he was back in the Maracanã stadium in Brazil for a second. It was like he thought we needed to chase the game, when all he needed to do was to keep hold of the ball. He drifted past one man and tried to beat another, Kevin Richardson, and was duly dispossessed. Richardson played the ball back to goalkeeper John Lukic, who wasted no time in rolling it out to Lee Dixon, who stepped forward and lifted a ball into our half, where Alan Smith collected it and lofted it on to Michael Thomas. At this point, Alan Hansen was high enough up the pitch for a nosebleed. The ball went over his head and you could almost hear him saying, 'Aaaahh.' Oh dear. The race was on as Thomas went through, and everybody chased him. Stevie Nicol came across to try and atone for the errors others had made, but the ball rebounded off him instead, leaving Thomas through on goal.

There was only one area that I thought Thomas could put it, because by now Stevie was bearing down on him, trying to close the angle. I went down to my right, hoping he would cut off the left-hand side, but Thomas waited a second before chipping it over my left leg: Liverpool 0 Arsenal 2. It left the teams with the exact same goal difference, +37. Arsenal won it because they had scored more goals than us, scoring 73 and conceding 36 in that season. We had only let in 28 over the campaign but had scored just 65.

Going into the shower, I could hear their players celebrating wildly but I still didn't really know how they had won the league. You couldn't get a closer photo finish. Same points, same goal difference.

We had lost the game by the smallest margin possible. I felt absolutely sick. Everybody was shattered.

In the dressing room, I looked underneath the bench, and there were two cases of champagne. I took a bottle out, and it had 'League Winners 1989, Liverpool FC' on the labels – all of them. So I said to Kenny Dalglish, 'What's this?'

'Oh, those aren't ours now.'

'Well, Arsenal deserve it,' I said.

'Yeah, you can go and give them to them.'

I went to the players' lounge and got my friend John who had come up to watch on my invitation. I gave him one case of the champagne and I took the other and we went and knocked on the door of the away dressing room. George Graham opened it, and I said, 'Excuse me, George, well played, these are yours, sorry about the label. But here's a friend of mine, Sergeant John Cook, he's an Arsenal supporter, can he come in and drink this champagne with you?' John was invited in.

We were all dejected and it didn't help that we could hear them screaming and hollering in the dressing room next door. I went up to the players' lounge, met my wife and John's wife and sat waiting for her husband. Two hours later he came up with wet hair. When his wife questioned this, he revealed to us that he had been in the bath with the Arsenal team drinking the champagne I'd provided for them.

We were drained by the Hillsborough disaster. Witnessing it and then having such a close role in the mourning had taken so much energy from us, and in all of this we had to play so many games at the end of the season to catch up. The jar was empty. But saying that, we really lost the league in the first postponed game we played after the tragedy, against Everton. It felt like a friendly, a draw that united the city even stronger in the hardest days of returning to football.

But it still haunts me twofold – we should have won the league, we should have beaten Arsenal, as no one had managed to beat us since New Year's Day in the league, and it haunts me how I told my friend and Arsenal fan John Cook to come and watch a proper team play. You can only guess how many times that would be brought up again in the years to come.

21

The Last Title

THE BEST WAY TO SHAKE OFF ANY DISAPPOINTMENTS IN LIFE IS TO go back and face them, so after a summer break with the family to Portugal, we played Arsenal in the final of the four-team Makita International Tournament at Wembley – and lost again! Arsenal, it was clear, were going to be the team to beat for some years and their manager George Graham had built up a talented squad that was hard to break down.

We couldn't wait to try and take some revenge over Arsenal in the Charity Shield, though, and at Wembley Peter Beardsley scored the winner.

Ian Rush had returned from Italy the previous season, as he wasn't happy there. It was, he famously said, 'like being in a foreign country.' His return meant John Aldridge sat on the bench a lot more than he wanted, so Aldo sought new adventures in Spain where he became the first foreign player to join Real Sociedad. Mark Lawrenson had left the year before to become Oxford United manager, and although Gary Gillespie and Gary Ablett were both still at Anfield, Kenny sought someone with more experience. Glenn Hysén, a Swedish international and captain of all the teams he had played in, was bought to strengthen our defence and bring more leadership qualities to the team. Hysén seemed to be the one that could fill the role, and he came in very full of himself and did very well initially. He is a great character who I got on very well with right from the beginning.

Over the season we had some remarkable results, like beating Crystal Palace 9-0 in a game in which the eight different names on the scoresheet showed our dominance in all parts of the pitch. We also beat Chelsea away 5-2 and Coventry City away 6-1 in the last league game of the season. One of the most emotional games was when we returned to Hillsborough for the first time, seven months after the disaster, to play Sheffield Wednesday, a game we lost 2–0 for one of our only five defeats in the league that season.

The real disappointment was the FA Cup semi-final, in which we played Crystal Palace at Villa Park. In the league nobody could touch us and we were surfing towards an unprecedented second double after beating QPR in a replayed quarter-final at Anfield. Nobody gave Palace a chance, considering just months earlier we'd put nine past them without reply.

Yet the game was a calamity for us, full of uncharacteristic mistakes and confusion. It was one of the worst for the team that I can remember. I had several mix-ups with Alan Hansen. We led 1–0 at half-time, but then they equalised almost from the kick-off. Worse followed. I had told the defence to stay out of the box when Palace had a free-kick. When a delivery came in, they were on my six-yard box. So there was no way I could come out and they just dropped on top of me, I couldn't get anything and Mark Bright put Palace in front. Steve McMahon equalised and John Barnes's penalty seemed to have secured us a win when, late on, they attacked again. A long ball was pumped into my area and there in my six-yard box were my own players. I rose above them to punch the ball, but when it came back they were in the way and Andy Gray scrambled it over the line. The game went to extra time, and from a corner Palace bombarded us again. The ball was flicked on and Alan Pardew crashed a header past me to make it 4–3.

That was the final goal. I would voice my opinion. 'Who was it that dropped back? Why did you drop back? Are you completely crazy? Had you stayed there I would have been further out; that goal would never have happened.' We had big arguments in the dressing room. Things happen that way and those arguments made us better. We were allowed to express our opinion, and the coaches took notice of our input and used it in training. In those days we didn't have video analysts – but if you look at the YouTube clips from that Palace semi-final, it confirms my complaints: the players were right on top of my six-yard box. We all clashed together and the ball just fell, and got scooped over my head. If my defence had been ten yards further out I would have come and caught that cleanly by myself.

Nevertheless, we won the league title with two games to spare. We walked the lap of honour, and someone gave me a huge sombrero that ended up on my head during the celebrations. I was also given a tambourine. We have all been pictured wearing all kinds of silly hats in the heat and joy of victories. After winning the FA Cup final in 1986 Kenny looked like Super Mario with this huge red cap on. In the corner of the Anfield Road end I was carrying the trophy and I gave it to some youngsters and I got a camera and took a picture of them. Then I walked a little on my hands, as I always do when I am happy. I have had the pleasure of doing so many laps of honour with my Liverpool teammates in a stadium packed with happiness.

This feeling of happiness was the complete contrast of what happened at Hillsborough. We went through such highs and lows with Liverpool, such extremes. We won everything, but also at Heysel and Hillsborough, we experienced the very worst in football.

But this lap of honour in 1990 was extra-special. To see the joy back on people's faces and in the city and in the club after such a hard year. From winning the FA Cup and then the agonising defeat to Arsenal which cost us the league, to winning the league the following season again – these were dramatic swings, from being so low to reaching the dizzy heights of another league triumph. It underlined where Liverpool should be.

Little did we know then that this Championship triumph would be the last for our club. Winning had been so habitual. At that point I had won six league titles in my first nine years at the club. We were so used to winning trophies back then, if someone had told me the day Liverpool won the eighteenth league title, the record at the time, that it would take at least thirty years for the club to win it again, I would have thought that person was insane.

22

Kenny Resigns

THE 1989/90 SEASON HAD BEEN A YEAR OF RECOVERY FOLLOWING the traumas on and off the field of the previous twelve months. When pre-season training started in July 1990, the cardboard box full of Championship winners' medals was waiting for us in the dressing room to help ourselves again. There was no ceremony. There never was.

We were never ones to get complacent. The 1990/91 season started in blistering fashion for us, winning our opening eight league games. By new year we were in the position we knew so well: top. There had been the odd slip-up along the way against old rivals: a 3–1 defeat at Manchester United in the League Cup, a 3–0 loss at Highbury and an unexpected defeat to Crystal Palace just after Christmas, but we were unequivocally still the team to beat.

In the FA Cup we beat Blackburn Rovers and Brighton & Hove Albion after replays. That set up a fifth-round tie with Everton that has gone into the annals of FA Cup history. A 0–0 draw at Anfield forced a Goodison replay three days later, which many say was the greatest Merseyside derby of them all. On an evening of extraordinary passion and excitement, we went ahead four times, but on each occasion Everton pegged us back in the greatest Merseyside derby of them all. Everton had been in decline for a few years and Howard Kendall was in his second spell as manager after time in charge of Athletic Bilbao and Manchester City. By then we were easily the better side on paper but it was a derby game played at night, and with all the passion in the air you knew you couldn't go out and give anything less than everything you had. Everyone came off absolutely exhausted, but delighted to have been part of it. It was a full 120-minute derby scrap. We should have won, but we gave away soft goals. The discussions in the dressing room afterwards felt like an autopsy. Nobody in particular was to blame for the draw but collectively there was a feeling that everyone felt let down by one another.

No one saw what happened next coming. We had been told to get early into Anfield on the Friday. We were travelling down to Luton around 11am, as they played on a plastic pitch, and we wanted time to train and prepare before our game.

Kenny had us sitting down in the dressing room and he stood by the physiotherapist's table in the middle of the room, looking at the crowd. I was sitting on his right-hand side; Ronnie Moran was next to me and then all the other players were crowded around.

Kenny said, 'Listen, I have a little problem with someone here at the club, and it's not you guys. I've got to do something that I feel I have to do. It's someone at the club that I'm having a problem with, and I won't be your manager from now on – I'm resigning. So go forward and play your best football, but I won't be your manager any more.'

He turned and walked out of the dressing room, down the corridor.

We looked at each other in shock. Speechless. This had come from nowhere. We were leading the league, only two and a half months before the end of the season. No one saw it coming.

About two minutes later Alan Hansen got up and walked down the corridor himself. He soon returned, stood right where Kenny had been standing and said, 'Right, apparently there's going to be an interim manager, and I'm going to tell you that it's me. Grobbelaar, you stay on your line, stop messing about in the goal and coming forty yards out onto the field. Nicol, stay out of the pubs and stop drinking so much. Barnes, come on, what are you eating? Get fit; get up and down the line.' He went right through the team, lambasting everybody. 'Moran, don't be so hard on the young players – lighten up.' On and on he went, until he wrapped everything up with an 'I'll see you', and off down the corridor he went again.

Three minutes later new footsteps came down the corridor. Hansen came back and sat in the right place this time, and the chairman Noel White walked in: 'Gentlemen, just to tell you we've been trying to persuade Kenny Dalglish to lead the team again but he's adamant that he doesn't want to. So we're going to have to put an interim manager in charge. And the interim manager is' – and we all looked at Alan Hansen – 'Ronnie Moran.'

We then got ready to leave for Luton. By then Kenny's resignation was public, with him saying he had left the club for personal reasons. Later he would say that managing Liverpool along with the unimaginable burden of the Hillsborough disaster had become too much for him to handle and that he needed a break from the game.

Nobody could concentrate in Ronnie Moran's first game as a manager. We all had so many questions unanswered. We lost 3–1.

The following midweek we had a second replay against Everton in the FA Cup. We lost that as well, 1-0, and followed it up with another defeat at the weekend, this time at home to Arsenal.

Before Kenny's resignation, we had only lost twice in the league that season. In the remaining weeks of the season we would end up losing six league games. Without Kenny it wasn't the same. Our King had gone. Ronnie Moran was a leader and at Liverpool there were lots of influential leaders, but there always needs to be a top man and Kenny was our head of state.

Arsenal would win the title, finishing seven points ahead of us. They lost just one game all season. We, by contrast, lost eight times.

MY OWN THEORY ON THE REAL REASON WHY KENNY LEFT WAS because he wanted to buy a player and the new chairman said no. Noel White had succeeded Sir John Smith a year earlier, because John had always said that if he got a knighthood he would step down as chairman, and when he was included in the 1989 honours list he was true to his word. His successor left us all a bit perplexed. He had been a business partner of the Manchester City chairman, Peter Swales, and had strong business connections in Cheshire, but a lot of us wondered what was he even doing at our club. He wasn't even from Liverpool.

My opinion as to why Kenny resigned is that he asked the chairman for some money to buy a player he was particularly keen on and was told no. He probably said to the chairman, 'I'm going to do something you might regret,' and his bluff was called and he was allowed to walk away.

Kenny returned to management in October 1991 and became Blackburn boss. At Ewood Park Kenny bought this very same player he had sought at Anfield.

It was a great investment and his goals would help win Blackburn the Premier League in 1995. The player? Kenny always liked Alan Shearer.

RONNIE MORAN HAD A COLD-SHOWER START, TAKING OVER WITH no notice. He was angry. My goodness, he was angry. And yet, I don't think he was given enough time as a manager.

We had heard rumours about Graeme Souness becoming Kenny's full-time successor, but there were always rumours at Anfield. Graeme had become Glasgow Rangers manager in 1986 and, with a team replete with some of the best English players of the era, had enjoyed remarkable success at Ibrox. As players we didn't know what was happening, but we had a hint that something was brewing when Alan Hansen told us, 'Ah, when Souey gets here, there won't be any messing about. It will be back to business.'

On 16 April 1991 Graeme Souness was announced as the new Liverpool manager, having signed a five-year contract. There were only five league games remaining and we were still in with a shout of the title. Personally, I wouldn't have appointed a new manager at that time of the season, because it undermined Ronnie Moran's authority with the team. For Ronnie to come second after a season like that is not too bad. In the previous ten seasons we'd never finished lower than second, so Ronnie maintained that record. Ronnie was Mr Liverpool anyway, so although many of us expected Alan Hansen to step up, he was happy to fill in when Kenny left and then step back down into his normal role when Souness took over.

Going from being led by the old characters in the game like Bob Paisley and Joe Fagan to being led by our old teammates was a big change, but Kenny and Souey approached the task very differently. Kenny learned over the first year to grow into his role. We didn't get criticised too much by Kenny until the second year. He didn't really want to stamp his authority that much because he was still very much a player with an active role in the team.

Souness, on the other hand, came in and was ruthless from the off, as if he were still playing even though he wasn't. He had been brutal as a player, and he was keeping this style as a manager. Souness ruled by fear. He actually changed the dynamics of Liverpool Football Club when he came in as manager. He ruled the team like he used to play, because he was a very dominant person on the park.

The presence of Souness was immense, and he tried to take that into his managerial career. It didn't really help him, because we had been used to coaches and managers that were very well rounded, coaches who knew how to speak to players.

After Souness took over as the manager of Liverpool FC, the war was on.

23

The Souness Battle

'BRUCE WOBBLER'. 'BRUCE BLUNDERS'. 'NEW YEAR WOBBLER'. 'High-flying Eagles' Ian Wright gets the better of Bruce Grovelling'.

The papers really loved me. Luckily I didn't read everything they wrote at the start of my Liverpool career. And ten years later, after Graeme Souness first took over as manager it felt like history was repeating itself.

Flipping through the newspaper collection from Liverpool fan Terance McPeake, who has collated my clippings over my career, shows how 1991 was a rollercoaster of a year for me. I went from 'Grob the King' and man of the match one week to having my head on the block and facing speculation that my Liverpool days were nearing an end the next: 'Grob smacked again'; 'Up for Grobs'; 'Brucie on course for Euro exit.' I fought back, of course: 'I'll play at forty,' I told one journalist – which I did, to be fair, just not at Liverpool.

There was a lot of speculation about which goalkeeper was going to come and take over from me when Souness became the manager: Chris Woods from his old club, Rangers, Tim Flowers from Southampton.

When we played against Southampton at home after that story, I put a bunch of flowers in the Kop end. As I shook Tim Flowers' hand before the game, I said, 'Tim, there's a bunch of flowers in the Kop end; those are the only flowers that are ever coming to Liverpool.'

Souness asked me at half-time what I had said to Flowers. He wasn't impressed.

*

AFTER DOMINATING FOR SO MANY SEASONS LIVERPOOL WERE spiralling downwards after the change of manager. Having narrowly missed out on the title in 1991 we plunged to sixth in the 1991/92 campaign, Souness's first full season in charge, and I wasn't afraid to publicly express my frustration about the sudden drop in performance.

I had played for Liverpool for ten years, and we'd had such brilliant managers, then all of a sudden we got Graeme Souness on board. At the beginning of the 1991/92 season, he decided he wanted to do everything the Italian way. Graeme had played at Sampdoria and at the time Serie A was considered the best league in the world. No more steak as pre-match meals for us and he wanted us all to go on high-altitude training to Italy for pre-season. I was in Zimbabwe with the national team at the time and got a phone call demanding my return from several thousand metres above sea level to 1,500 for altitude training. It made no sense.

In the summer of 1991, Souness oversaw a major reorganisation of the squad. The majority of the starting eleven when he took over were in or approaching their thirties: Ronnie Whelan, Steve Nicol and Ian Rush were all 29, Peter Beardsley and Steve MacMahon 30, while I was nearly 34. A few of us had our testimonials coming up, including me. However, we quickly understood Souness had an agenda to get rid of the older players to create a younger team, and I feared I would miss out on my big testimonial, which I was due in 1992.

We were well paid then, but it was nothing like today. A testimonial was considered among players as a pension.

Senior players like Beardsley, McMahon and Ray Houghton were all sold before he had players in place that could match their quality. Alan Hansen retired. Jocky probably knew that his mate's character as a player was completely different to how it was as a manager. Or perhaps it was too similar, perhaps that was what was really the problem. Maybe I should have taken some advice from him on how to react to Souness the manager. I never had the conversation with Jocky on why he retired when he did, but I wish I had.

In their places he bought Mark Wright, Rob Jones, Mark Walters and secured Dean Saunders for a British record fee of £2.9 million. Over time he would give youth players like Steve McManaman and, later, Robbie Fowler a chance in the first team. McManaman was nineteen when he started playing regularly, and

Fowler was still only eighteen when he got his debut; however, both played well from the beginning.

In December 1991, I was flabbergasted when Souness bought the man who only eighteen months earlier had wrecked the league title for us. Michael Thomas had fallen out with George Graham, his manager at Arsenal, so Souness got him as an early Christmas present.

These new players didn't really live up to the standards that he needed – or that we wanted and expected. He brought in a player of Mark Wright's calibre because Jocky left, but Mark was no Alan Hansen. It also caused problems in the dressing room. Mark Wright was to play with Glenn Hysén but ended up taking over from him as captain, putting the nose of his partner in the centre of defence out of joint. Hysén lost the best part of two seasons through minor injuries and not being preferred by Souness. His Liverpool career never fully recovered.

When Hysén got injured we got Torben Piechnik, and gee, that was a bit of a disaster in front of me because he wasn't a Liverpool-level centre-half. He was a good centre-half, and a Danish international, but nowhere near the required standard for Anfield.

They were difficult times. Years later Souness admitted that he got rid of too many experienced players too soon. I don't think he wanted the confrontation from those senior players. He was also trying to get me out at the time but it was proving too difficult. I wanted to stay playing for Liverpool and I wanted my testimonial.

IN THE 1991/92 SEASON WE WERE FINALLY BACK IN EUROPE AGAIN after the Heysel ban. It had been a long six years without the bonus of European competition. In the first round of the UEFA Cup we played Finland's Kuusysi Lahti and beat them 6–1 at Anfield. In the return game, they won 1–0. I was blamed for the defeat and, again, the media predicted my exit: 'Liverfool'. 'Sad Bruce flaps up thin air'. 'Liverpool boss saw a blunder from keeper Bruce Grobbelaar gift in the second half.' 'Bye bye Bruce'. 'Grobstop'. 'Bruce faces axe'.

Instead of defending me, the following weekend the manager dropped me for the visit to Manchester United. Souness was always one to look for a scapegoat. Unfortunately for him, my replacement Mike Hooper injured his Achilles tendon after only two games in goal. Souness didn't want to play me, yet Hooper was injured, like so many other players on the team. Our biggest star and best player John Barnes was out for most of the season. Molby, Rush, Wright and Whelan would follow. In my opinion it was Souness's training methods that backfired. We were overtraining and it created a succession of injury problems.

We struggled in the league for the first time in all my years at Anfield, but this was to become the new reality under Souness. Genoa knocked us out in the quarter-finals of the UEFA Cup and we ended 1991/92 sixth in the league. It might have been Souness's first full season as a manager but this was a team that hadn't finished lower than second since 1981. Our fans were not impressed, but what really kicked off the rage for many of them was the exclusive interview Souness did with the *Sun* from a hospital bed after his heart operation in the spring of 1992, an interview that came out on the day of the third anniversary of the Hillsborough disaster. It was a misjudgement from which his reputation would never really recover among Liverpool supporters.

In the FA Cup we had some luck. With the exception of Aston Villa, who we faced in the quarter-finals, we would reach the final against Second Division Sunderland without facing top-flight opponents. We ended up playing Portsmouth twice in the semi-finals, drawing 1–1 after extra time at Highbury, where Ronnie Whelan scored our goal. In the replay we drew 0–0 at Villa Park, which meant for the first time since my heroics in Rome eight years earlier that we had a penalty shootout to deal with. We won 3–1 on penalties and I saved two.

It was shortly after this victory that the *Sun* ran its interview with Souness. What on earth was he thinking? The players had long since stopped talking to the paper after its vicious lies about the Hillsborough disaster. While Graeme hadn't been at Liverpool in 1989 he knew full well the strength of feeling within the dressing room, the club and city about this tawdry newspaper. Despite giving some bullshit excuse about the timing of publication, the newspaper knew exactly what it was doing printing on the third anniversary. It was part of a long-standing vendetta against the club and its fans and a move designed to cause as much upset as possible. Unfortunately, as I was to find out, it wouldn't be the last time that the *Sun* would inflict its venom our way.

The new players didn't react as much to Souness giving an exclusive interview to the banned paper as some of the senior players, the local lads and the staff. Ronnie Moran, Roy Evans, Ronnie Whelan and myself were all utterly shocked. Some tried to give him the benefit of the doubt, citing the effect that the operation must have had on him. In his defence he was naïve, and he soon realised that what he did was very wrong.

Souness donated his fee from the tabloid to Alder Hey Hospital but by then the damage was done.

The doctors had strongly advised him not to go to the FA Cup final at Wembley on 9 May, because he wasn't strong enough after such a big heart operation. Ronnie Moran was still caretaker manager on the day of the final, as Souness had just come out of hospital. We didn't know if he was going to come to Wembley or not, but he did and it made quite an impression on the players seeing him come to the final in such a poor state to show his support. That motivated the likes of young Steve McManaman, who would end up as man of the match.

On my team, for my very last trophy, I had Rob Jones, David Burrows, Mark Wright, Steve Nicol, Steve McManaman, Michael Thomas, Jan Molby, Ray Houghton, Ian Rush and Dean Saunders. Mike Marsh and Mark Walters were the subs. Although they were in the Second Division, Sunderland had some decent players, like the former Everton midfielder Paul Bracewell, who had played against me in the 1986 and 1989 finals.

It was, nevertheless, a cagey first half. At the interval it was still 0–0, but Michael Thomas would score a fantastic goal soon after the restart. It came after brilliant work on the right by McManaman, whereupon Thomas collected the ball and from a very tight angle smashed it over the top of the Sunderland goalkeeper, Tony Norman, at the far post. I thought, *Well, if he can do that, thank you very much; maybe he can do something with Liverpool*. The true Gunner became a Scouser with just one shot. After that Sunderland were finished. Ian Rush scored on 68 minutes. There was no way back from that.

AT THE END OF HIS TROUBLED FIRST SEASON, SOUNESS CALLED ME in for a meeting.

'Bruce, I want you to be the number one,' he told me.

'You want me to have the number-one jersey?'

'Yes, you can keep the number-one jersey; but I'm bringing in a young goalkeeper from Watford, David James, and I think that you should teach him how to be a Liverpool keeper.'

'I get to start the season?'

'Yes, you get to start the season.'

The 1992/93 campaign started off with us playing in the Charity Shield against Leeds United. This could have been my last trophy but Eric Cantona, then still a Leeds centre-forward, was on fire, scoring a hat-trick in a game they won 4–3. David James was on the bench.

Our scheduled opening game in the new Premier League was against Nottingham Forest on 15 August 1992 at the City Ground. Earlier that year the Premier League had been created to maximise television revenue from the burgeoning satellite TV technologies, but the side effect was changing dates on the fixture list to be able to broadcast more games live. While the money would flow into the game in the years and decades that followed, unfortunately it was the beginning of the end of football as a game played at three o'clock on Saturday afternoons. Ours was just the first of thousands of matches that would be moved over the years to accommodate TV. The Premier League put the game back 24 hours to Sunday 16 August.

For me, this was a big problem. Zimbabwe were playing against South Africa on that Sunday in the Africa Cup of Nations, and it was a very historical game as it was South Africa's very first competitive fixture back in world football after the end of apartheid. With the release of Nelson Mandela from prison and democratic elections, FIFA had finally lifted their long-standing ban. Obviously I wanted to play in a game of such significance, and I had got a plan worked out: after the Liverpool game a helicopter was going to take me from the Midlands to Gatwick and I was going to get the Air Zimbabwe flight to Harare.

For me, there was an additional incentive. By playing in this game, I was offered the opportunity to get my Zimbabwean passport back. It had been taken away from me after I published my first book, *More Than Somewhat*, in 1985 when I called the freedom fighters in the Bush War 'guerillas' rather than 'freedom fighters'. Robert Mugabe hadn't liked that, and as a result confiscated my Zimbabwean passport, since when I'd travelled around on my South African passport. However, the Zimbabwean authorities had been concerned that with the return of South Africa to international football I would go and play for the country of my birth not realising the rules in place then that if you had played for one country, you could not then play for another country later.

I was ready for the match and ready to get my passport back and then they went and changed the Liverpool game to the Sunday. There was only one game in which

I planned on playing, and it wasn't at the City Ground. The week before the Forest game, Souness came to me and said, 'What are you going to do about Zimbabwe? Our fixture has been changed to Sunday.'

I replied, 'I know that you've asked me to be number one, I am sorry, but I am going back to play for my country.'

'I thought you said you wanted to start?'

'Yes, I would have started if we'd played on the Saturday, and I would have flown over to play the game on the Sunday, but they changed it, and now I'm going to play my game in Zimbabwe, and play with the national team.'

This went down like a lead balloon.

Fifteen years after walking away from the Bush War, I found myself at the heart of a new conflict: between Graeme Souness and myself.

Since I was missing the Forest game I left for Zimbabwe on the Tuesday after the Charity Shield. I trained with my country on Wednesday and Thursday. My Zimbabwean passport, however, had still not been returned. Without it, I wouldn't be allowed to play. Friday came and there was more training, but still no documents and it was becoming a concern. Had I come all this way for no reason? Finally, on Saturday, with FIFA's match commissioner due to inspect our documentation, the passport finally arrived. At last I was ready to play for my country again. Peter Ndlovu scored twice as we beat South Africa 4-1. It was a big, big game for us.

Nowadays you can't really picture English football colliding with international duty, but back then different confederations adhered to different calendars and their international breaks didn't always fall into line with those in other confederations. Though the Africa Cup of Nations has always been in winter – and it wasn't a competition Zimbabwe qualified for always anyway – friendlies and qualifying matches in Africa, for example, were consistently played in different weeks to those in Europe, sometimes at random. It was only later that FIFA brought some unity to the international calendar. Moreover, back then clubs had first call on their players, which really meant that I was taking a stand against Liverpool.

Souness didn't like that I missed the Liverpool game one little bit.

Choosing my country over Liverpool in this game was the start of a war with my manager. They lost 1-0 in the opening game and I took the blame, despite being more than 6,000 miles away. Instead I was a spectator for the following ten matches. David James played but he was not a success. He conceded twenty goals in his first eleven appearances, including four at Aston Villa and four against Chesterfield in the League Cup at Anfield.

After the Chesterfield debacle Souness put me back in goal again, but it was short-lived. I played another eight games, but then he dropped me again, with David James and then Mike Hooper taking my place.

It did bug me, as I knew clearly that I had more experience and was a better goalkeeper than either, but I was still left out of the team. David James had all the attributes to become a fantastic goalkeeper but plunging him into the side at that time when the team was in transition was not the right decision. The Liverpool goalkeeper position is a tricky one to adjust to at the best of times.

My absence from the first team was my punishment for choosing Zimbabwe over Liverpool. I questioned it, but who's to question the boss? Souness thought that James was better than me at the time until he found out that we were languishing somewhere in mid-table. And when I played we started going up; and then I went back to play for my country again and he didn't like it, so out I went again into another spell in the cold. It was in and out. At that time he had three goalkeepers and he was juggling.

Mike Hooper was respectful; he knew his limits. David James didn't know his limits, and got the nickname 'Calamity James' from the fans. Had James had the right experience in front of him maybe his path would have been different. Instead, Liverpool's defence was changing constantly as well and this meant there was nobody there with the sort of authority to instil the discipline that was needed to round his game off. On reflection, I have some sympathy for him because without Hansen and Lawrenson and then a team of winners in midfield and attack, maybe I wouldn't have survived when I started out. Ultimately, it takes a smart manager to understand you don't change too much too soon, otherwise it becomes very difficult for players to settle and blend.

I also had my chances to leave, but bizarrely Souness put paid to that as well. Just after the start of the 1992/93 campaign, and shortly after losing my place in the team, I got an offer to go to Chelsea. At Melwood one morning Souness came and said, 'Ken Bates would like to see you down in Chelsea. I've agreed a figure for you for £650,000.'

This was huge. I was nearly 35 at this stage, and goalkeepers rarely commanded such big fees anyway. I caught the train down, got picked up by someone at

Chelsea and was taken straight to the chairman Ken Bates's office. Bates didn't waste any time laying down an offer: they would triple my wages, give me a great signing-on fee, as well as a house near their training ground.

'Mr Bates,' I told him, 'it's a great offer, but I'm going to have to talk it over with my wife.'

When I went back to Anfield and into training the following day Souness asked me how it went and if we had agreed on anything.

'I haven't agreed anything; I will let him know when I've had a discussion with my family and what we want,' I told him.

'Well, if you agree to go, the fee for Chelsea is going to change.'

'What do you mean?'

I don't know what was going through his mind or what was going to happen to the rest of the fee, but I didn't go to Chelsea. It was a very generous offer towards the end of my career. It would have been a good move to go to Chelsea in the 1992/93 season, especially since I was stuck with a manager that didn't want me and I would have played a lot longer in the Premier League. I never got bitter about the deal not going through. On cold reflection, after everything that had happened at Heysel, I wouldn't have liked to go to a team where I knew National Front members formed part of the club's support.

IT WASN'T LONG BEFORE THE CLUB VERSUS COUNTRY DISPUTE became an issue again. We had a World Cup qualifier with Angola in January 1993, but Souness asked me to come back, and said he was going to play me. This time I adhered to his wishes. As much as I loved playing for Zimbabwe, it was no fun on the sidelines at Anfield. Then, on the day of the game, he gave the team out: Mike Hooper in goal and David James on the bench. I didn't like that at all and asked him why he'd made me travel back only to leave me out.

By now, there was no chance of discussing concerns or frustrations with Souness. If you went to him and challenged his view, you'd be out of the team or further down the pecking order. This was another major cultural shift, because previously you were allowed to air your grievances, whereas now resentments were internalised and harboured. This was unhealthy for team spirit because nobody felt like they could be honest with one another, so problems didn't get sorted out.

*

I LEFT AGAIN AND RETURNED TO AFRICA. ZIMBABWE HAD ANOTHER World Cup qualifier, this time in Togo. If I wasn't going to play for Liverpool I would represent my country.

None of this, of course, helped my Liverpool career and I remained on the Anfield sidelines. I was shunned by the manager and there seemed little prospect of a return. Then in March 1993, I joined Stoke City on loan. They were then in the third tier – or Division Two as it had been renamed. For my part, I'd been out of the Liverpool team since the previous October and then waylaid having been hit on the head by a rock while playing for Zimbabwe against Egypt in Cairo in February. The ball had gone behind the goal and the ballboys had given up because all types of materials were raining down so I had no other option than to chance it myself. Bang!

The Stoke boss, Lou Macari, needed a goalkeeper to assist with their promotion push after his first choice, Ronnie Sinclair, had suffered a cruciate ligament rupture. It was very simple for me: Stoke presented the opportunity to play so I went.

I went straight into the team for my debut against Fulham, a match we won 1–0 thanks to Mark Stein's 72nd-minute penalty. There were three further games, including a derby win over Port Vale, a top-of-the-table clash and 'six pointer' that would eventually ensure Stoke emerged as champions. But then, just as abruptly as my Stoke loan spell started, so, a fortnight later, it ended.

The day after the Port Vale match I was at the Belfry playing golf with some friends and got a phone call from Ronnie Moran.

'Bruce, where are you?'

'I'm at the Belfry.'

'The boss wants you back here for training this morning.'

'Ronnie, it's April the first, I'm not falling for that one!' I said, and put the phone down.

The following morning, at seven-thirty, the phone went again. It was Ronnie, and he hadn't been joking.

'Get your arse back; I told you to get back yesterday, the boss wants you.'

Although Liverpool were thirteenth in the Premier League at the time, an unprecedentedly low position, Souness had no plans to change things around.

David James was staying in goal and he'd brought me back to sit on the bench. If I'd played another game for Stoke I would have gained another medal, because they were promoted as champions. I played the last game of the season for Liverpool, a 6–2 win over Spurs that saw us finish sixth, the highest position we'd held all season. Crystal Palace, who were relegated, finished just ten points below us. It was a long way from the Liverpool I'd once known.

AFTER THE 1992/93 SEASON ENDED DAVID RODWELL, A SOUTH African friend of mine, called. He owns Shoe City and asked if I could come out and play for his team, Cape Town Spurs. I was allowed to go and play three games in the off-season, so he signed me for those fixtures in the South African League.

Before the first game, a company for mobile phones offered me a contract while I was there, and they wanted to shoot an ad with me. I suggested I would put the cellphone in the back of the goal, and when we conceded our first corner, they should ring the phone, and film it. So we conceded a corner, and I heard the phone ring. I picked up the phone, 'Hello? Yes? Ah, Vodafone, just wait a minute, we're playing football now and they've got a corner, so can you hold on until I'm finished with this corner?' I put down the phone, corner came, I caught the ball, threw it out, then I picked up the phone again, 'Now, what do you want, Vodafone? And please don't disturb me while I'm playing a game of football.' That ended up as the ad on TV. It was done during the actual game, and the owner of the team didn't even know.

Then we went to Bloemfontein and played against Bloemfontein Celtics, followed by Kaizer Chiefs. In the three games I only let in one goal, against Kaizer Chiefs; we beat them 2–1. The other games we won 1–0 and 2–0.

AFTER THE 1992/93 SEASON ENDED DAVID RODWELL, A SOUTH

FEELING UNWANTED DEFINITELY AFFECTS THE CONFIDENCE OF A goalkeeper. And feeling unwanted under Souness did anything but boost my self-esteem. I have to admit there were times when it was getting harder to stay motivated. Ever since my testimonial in October 1992 our manager didn't even try to hide that he wanted me out. Souness's training methods left 23 players unfit to play three months into the new season.

The Chelsea offer was a reaction to Souness and me not getting on. And as much as I loved Liverpool, I was getting ready to move, as I wasn't in a happy place any more. After playing for the club for so long, and doing so well, being benched by an old teammate while Liverpool were in free fall as a club wasn't a good feeling. The old giant was falling behind the best teams and there were times when I felt totally helpless watching this decline.

Being dumped from the team and verbally bashed also started affecting my personal life. The bad feelings crept in there too. When I went home, my internal monologue went something like this: 'Oh, you're useless, no good to anybody any more.' This wasn't a good time in my life.

To build up the confidence of goalkeepers you instil assurance in them in training by praise. Too many goalkeeping coaches don't give praise when the goalkeeper has done something right. I've seen it time and time again. This was also my own experience with the goalkeeping coach that Graeme Souness brought in, Joe Corrigan. First of all, he was brought in because Souness had played for Sampdoria and at Sampdoria they had a goalkeeping coach. Again, we were subjected to the Italian way. I'd never had a goalkeeping coach before. His choice was Corrigan, a former Manchester City goalkeeper. I didn't rate him as a player and didn't rate him as a coach.

His methods amounted to smashing shots at the goalkeepers from ten yards and insisting we catch the ball. Previously, the goalkeepers had trained with the outfielders and this helped develop our understanding with the rest of the team. Suddenly, we were more isolated than ever. It didn't feel like Liverpool any more.

His style of goalkeeping had been the complete opposite to mine: he was physically big, six foot four – which at the time was considered tall – and never came out of his six-yard box. He was now going to teach someone who'd played 500 games for Liverpool how to play in goal? I said, 'This is rubbish. How can this man teach a Liverpool goalkeeper to play?'

As a coach he sure didn't praise me. And praise is very important in sports and in life in general; no matter how gifted you are at what you do. When you're praised you feel happy about yourself. When you don't get praise, when you are just being hammered, you feel dejected. In training if a goalkeeper lets one in on a particular drill, you repeat that drill, so you end on a good note; you don't end on something bad, before you move to the next drill. The likes of Ronnie Moran were the toughest of taskmasters, but they understood – in their way – the power of positive psychology.

Today this need for praise is more obvious than ever, because players are so public via social media. It's hard to imagine that Cristiano Ronaldo needs praise, but just look at all his postings on Instagram – he still needs to feel loved and confirmed as a person, just as we all do. All human beings are put together that way. It's very important as a coach not to have your players dejected when you're going into a game. Some managers let this happen, and it's heartbreaking for me to see that they do that. This is precisely what happened at Liverpool under Souness and his coaches. We were made to feel worthless at times.

And yet at other times, Souness could offer praise. I remember when I had a good game against Wimbledon in 1991. I was 34 years old, and after loads of questions about when I would be replaced, and some open criticism by Souness, he publicly came out in the media and said I was man of the match. A 0–0 draw at Selhurst Park was nothing to shout home about, but I came flying out of the dressing room.

The media loves the build-ups and the teardowns: 'Smashed and Grobbed' and 'Brilliant Brucie pulls out all the stops' were two of the headlines after that game. Instead of being robbed, the opposition was now being 'Grobbed' because I played so well.

*

THE 1992/93 SEASON WAS A DISASTER BY THE STANDARDS SET BY Liverpool over the previous three decades. Sixth place, a third-round FA Cup exit to Bolton, then a third-tier club, and out of Europe and the League Cup – previously staples of our glory years – by Christmas. Nor was there any European football to look forward to in the following campaign. For a period it looked as if Souness, and not me, might be the one to leave. The club's new chairman David Moores prevaricated over the manager's future – and then decided to stick with him.

As for me, I was stubborn, I wanted to stay. I wanted to become the goalkeeper with most appearances for the club in history. Ray Clemence had played 470 league games (665 games in total) and I was getting closer to his figures, while Elisha Scott in second place, with 430 league games (and 468 games in total) became reachable.

David James was injured and Mike Hooper was negotiating a move to Newcastle, so I started the 1993/94 season as first choice again. It began well, winning the first three games. Our new signing Nigel Clough scored four times in the opening four matches, and we took an early lead in the Premier League. But the old problems were still there. There was a lack of unity, too many of the senior players were left out or injured and there was an overall lack of quality from those brought in to replace them. In the first three weeks of September we lost to Coventry, lost to Blackburn, and worst of all we lost to Everton at Goodison.

That game was notorious for an altercation I had with Steve McManaman after conceding our first goal. McManaman was standing at the near post as we defended a corner, and as the ball swung in I shouted, 'Away!' He swung his left foot at the ball, but it only reached the edge of the eighteen-yard box. It also went straight to the Everton midfielder Mark Ward, who hit a half-volley straight into the back of the net. The person that I was actually after was the person trying to block that shot, Mark Walters, who had turned his back, as if he didn't want to get hit. I was that angry I went racing out of my goal, but I stopped when I got to McManaman. McManaman was standing in the wrong place at the wrong time, and I yelled, 'And you, when I shout away, get it away!' I grabbed his throat and there were some handbags. The referee came to McManaman and myself and was just about to send us both off. I turned around and said, 'Excuse me, sorry, we're on the same team, so you can't book us.' He got confused and let it go.

In the dressing room Souness did something he normally wouldn't do: he threw a boot at me. 'Don't ever do that again,' he said through gritted teeth.

I still hadn't calmed down by the end of the game though. 'Where's Walters?' I demanded, and I heard someone say, 'In the bath.' So I got my gear off and I raced in there and took his head, grabbing his hair and pulling him under the water. I actually sat on his head. I tried to drown him. I was that angry. My teammates pulled me off him and after a little bit of a tête à tête we calmed down eventually. We are very good friends now – on Facebook.

After that game there was a cull. Stevie Nicol, Ronnie Whelan and Walters were all dropped. Perhaps surprisingly, given what had happened between me and the manager, I kept my place. Afterwards the most significant change to our side was the addition a precocious eighteen-year-old from Toxteth whom Liverpool's supporters would come to know as 'God'. Robbie Fowler was included in a League Cup tie at Fulham and scored on his debut. In the second leg at Anfield a fortnight later he scored five times.

In my race to try to set an all-time record as a Liverpool goalkeeper I passed Elisha Scott's record of 430 league appearances in a 3–3 draw with Tottenham a week before Christmas 1993.

Yet not even God could save Souness. We remained entrenched in mid-table and when, in January 1994, we were beaten again at Anfield in the third round of the FA Cup by second-tier opponents – this time Bristol City – he finally resigned.

Souness was the best player I've ever played with, the best in the world for a time. For that I admired him. We were friendly as teammates – but perhaps not friends, for I don't think friends come easily to him and he often kept himself to himself as a player – and he was there the night I met my first wife Debbie.

But as a manager he was shit. I would tell him that to his face, but it doesn't mean I don't like him. Maybe today we would call him a visionary because he could see the way football was going, but the problem was he wanted too much change too soon. As a player he always demanded instant success and was intolerant of those that didn't provide it. As a manager you can't do that. You need patience, but Souness was impatient and it created so many bad feelings, which ultimately impacted on the team.

Now we get on well. We are older and wiser and have both had our bad times, so we have something in common again. As a manager, I never liked him, but he's not a bad lad.

*

I WAS NOW AGED 36 AND IN MY TWELFTH SEASON AT LIVERPOOL. I was fit and felt good. Liverpool weren't what they had once been, but I was playing and enjoying my football. In January 1994 Roy Evans was appointed as Souness's replacement. It was a return to the Boot Room traditions that had served Liverpool so well.

Roy is a nice guy. He was always the quiet one at Liverpool. A good coach, quiet, diligent; got on with his job in the Boot Room without a fuss. However, he should never have been appointed Liverpool manager; I think even he would probably acknowledge that now. He was an assistant manager or a coach – he was brilliant at both those roles – but he was too nice to be a manager.

My rapport with Roy was very good. He knew that I could do the job and I played a little bit more for him. But just a few weeks after his appointment my hamstring went in a game against Leeds and that was my season over. It happened in the second half when I raced out to clear a ball and it tore.

Little did I know then that it also spelled the end of my Liverpool career. Roy was so nice that he didn't even tell me he was going to give me a free transfer. It was the end of the 1993/94 season and we were both away playing at a golf tournament when I read about it in the newspaper. It was news to me. I asked Roy, 'When were you going to tell me?' He couldn't answer. I read him the newspaper reports and he told me it was true; I was free to leave Liverpool.

This really was the end of my time at Anfield. I needed another club. My contract was at an end. I was, for the first time in my life, technically unemployed, something my solicitor pointed out to a court that summer when I was up on a drink-drive charge.

MY LAST ACT AS A LIVERPOOL PLAYER WAS TO TAKE PART IN SOME end-of-season games in the country in which I was born.

Through my South African friend David Rodwell, the team was invited to play a couple of friendlies at the end of May 1994. This would lead to me finally meeting one of my true heroes in life, Nelson Mandela.

On 26 May 1994 we played Cape Town Spurs at Newlands Cricket Ground, a stone's throw from one of Mandela's residences. The President not only came to watch the game, but also joined us in the dressing room. John Barnes took the shirt off his back and presented it to Mandela, who duly put it on and we had photographs with him, then Barnes interviewed Mandela for television. So even Nelson Mandela was a Liverpool fan!

It was fantastic for Mandela to come into our dressing room. He loved football. He was a Mthatha Bush Bucks fan because that's where he was originally from – in Qunu in the Transkei. Later I would manage Mthatha Bucks. For me, he was just an incredible, incredible person. He was in prison on Robben Island for so long, under such tough circumstances. His cell was so little and he had nothing; it must have been so very hard being left in solitary confinement in such conditions.

Nowadays you can go and visit the old prison on Robben Island and see what a stark, harsh place it was; the former inmates will tell you what they had to do every day – go and break rocks, slate. Some people tried to swim across to Cape Town, and got attacked by sharks.

For Mandela to come out the other side after so many years in prison with no remorse, no hatred, and to govern South Africa through a period where it was getting a little bit hairy with friction between the whites and the blacks, and for him to actually stifle that and bring a measure of calm during that period, and be the father of the modern South Africa was incredible. I've got a picture of him made in nails hanging in our home, made by David Foster an artist who is a Liverpool fan, and it was given to us by our friends. Nelson Mandela is my South African wife's hero, and he is my wife's mother's hero, and mine as well. Against Cape Town Spurs I played the first half, David James played the second half. In a downpour of rain. We won 3–0. Still to this day, that match is the highest attendance at Newlands; around 59,000 in a stadium that only holds 29,000 for cricket. It was standing room only. That's how much pull we had. On 29 May we played against Kaizer Chiefs and drew 0–0 at the Ellis Park Stadium. It was my final game for Liverpool.

24

Southampton

EVEN THOUGH I'D WANTED TO LEAVE LIVERPOOL FOR A WHILE, when the moment of departure eventually arrived it was hard to take. Had Liverpool shown more of a commitment to keep me then it would have given me the confidence to back myself and stay. The offer of a one-year contract on reduced terms compared to other players felt like a slap in the face. A two-year extension may have made me feel a little differently even if I was being paid a fifth of what the Reds' top stars were on.

I considered my options.

I went off to Zimbabwe to play for my country, work on a safari business I was developing – of which more later – and contemplate my next move in football. There were a couple of short-term contracts, playing games in South Africa for Cape Town Spurs and in Malaysia with Selangor, which paid the bills over the summer, but I still wanted to play at as high a level as possible.

When the call came, it couldn't have been better. It was Alan Ball, a World Cup winner with England in 1966, a former teammate of mine at Vancouver Whitecaps, and now the manager of Southampton.

'Bruce, do you want to come and play with us?' he asked.

I left my holiday with the family quickly, and flew to Southampton, where I met the club's director of football, Lawrie McMenemy, and Ball. I signed a two-year deal with an option of a third year, and started life at The Dell. I didn't have any pre-season with them at all.

Although Liverpool had slid under Souness, there was still a significant gap in quality between what I'd left and what greeted me on the south coast. The Saints had only avoided relegation by a single point in each of the previous two campaigns and had found goals hard to come by after selling Alan Shearer to Blackburn Rovers for a British record fee in 1992. The money Southampton had received was spent on Kerry Dixon, David Speedie and Perry Groves, but the three forwards had managed just four goals between them in the 1992/93 season and they faced similar struggles during the subsequent campaign.

Ball had replaced Ian Branfoot midway through that season and built his team around Matt Le Tissier. This guy was a genius. He should have played for one of the biggest clubs in the country. Ability-wise and mentally, he was there right at the very top. He could have easily fitted into the system at Liverpool, where the club would have moulded him into a better player.

I respect why he didn't go elsewhere. He was very attached to Guernsey. His wife was from Guernsey and the only flight there was from Southampton on a Saturday night. It meant he could play home games and fly home for the evening at least every other week, coming back on Sunday.

I was to take the number-one shirt from Dave Beasant, who had played against me in the 1988 FA Cup final for Wimbledon. He had played for England too, as well as Chelsea and Newcastle. He'd moved to The Dell at the end of Ian Branfoot's reign and I think Alan Ball wanted to change things around so he asked me to play. This created a few natural competitive issues. As you can imagine, Dave wanted to play every week. Dave thought he should have been number one because he'd represented England.

Behind the scenes, the operation at Southampton was solid enough. Visiting teams found The Dell a nightmare of a venue because of its tight pitch, hemmed in by four small stands. It was a hostile place to go and even in Liverpool's glory era, results there were hard to come by. Unusually, as Southampton players we only saw The Dell on match days because all other daily activities took place at the training ground.

Above Alan Ball was Lawrie McMenemy, a figue who'd never played as a professional and had served in the Coldstream Guards before working his way up as a non-league coach to manage Southampton in the 1970s. He won them promotion from the Second Division as well as the FA Cup in 1976 and built up a really good team in the 1980s that briefly challenged Liverpool at the top of the First Division. He was back at Southampton as director of football. He was a very different character to Ball and his military background shone through.

Ball was a very nice man, a player's manager – the sort of manager that understood players because he'd been one himself. He afforded Le Tissier freedoms that other managers might not have, but he got the very best out of him. Similarly, he placed faith in me when other managers – Souness particularly – did not. There is a truth in football that players tend to like the managers that pick them every week and, under Ball, that was the case with me. Yet he was a thoroughly decent person as well. He stood by me when others would not have. This was just about to be tested.

25

The Sting

TUESDAY 8 NOVEMBER 1994. THE DAY MY WORLD COLLAPSED AND from which my reputation – no matter how many times I have proved the allegations to be untrue – has never fully recovered.

Days earlier, Southampton had drawn 3–3 at Manchester City to continue the club's stellar start to the season under Alan Ball's management and I was preparing to fly to Harare for a crucial Africa Cup of Nations qualifying match against Zaire.

I'd had an earlier meeting at Gatwick with some Sky TV producers who wanted to talk to me about presenting a cookery programme. The concept was taking a yacht around the Solent and each week I would cook for different celebrity guests. But those plans would be rudely laid to waste.

I walked into the North Terminal at Gatwick Airport with my driver, friend and confidant Tony Milligan. Tony was a retired police officer from the dogs unit and I got to know him from his years standing on duty by the tunnel entrance at Anfield. After he retired from the police force he came to work for me; I knew him as Moany Tilligan or Spike; he was someone I trusted implicitly. It was here that I was confronted by two newspaper journalists.

'Bruce Grobbelaar? Guy Patrick and John Troup from the *Sun* newspaper, sir.'

I nodded; it wasn't unusual to be approached by journalists, although they didn't normally hunt in packs. It soon became apparent why.

'We have a series of grave allegations which the paper intends on publishing tomorrow. We wondered if we could have two minutes with...'

We walked over to the side of the terminal building.

'It sounds awful, but you threw a Premier League match last season.

You received £40,000.'

'We've got it on tape...'

I sat down bewildered, punch drunk, almost. The allegations were so incredible as to be incomprehensible. The picture of me sat down looking forlorn on a bench in Gatwick Airport would be carried around the world in the days that followed.

'I didn't,' I said.

One of them showed me a picture of me apparently receiving an envelope full of money.

'I didn't...'

'We've got it on tape...'

I regained my composure briefly and told them that if they put that in the paper they would be sued. So, they phoned through to the editor, Stuart Higgins, and put me on the phone to him.

'Listen, I've got two of your reporters here. They've put to me allegations that I received money for throwing games. I've never attempted to throw a game in my life. The money that they're talking about in large quantities last season, that a certain person said I received, was my own testimonial money.'

'The £40,000?'

'I've said to them that if you run the story it'll destroy my marriage, it'll probably destroy my career...'

'Can I ask you, sir – I've got to ask you directly – did you ever accept cash to lose games?'

'No, I've never...'

I never had any inkling that this was going to happen, but I knew straight away that it was a sting. And I knew exactly who had done it. I knew that the story originated from my former business partner and I told Stuart Higgins just that. And knowing what I knew about my erstwhile business partner I had to stop his vicious fantasies getting into the public realm.

I was leaving for Africa that evening, Tuesday 8 November, to play in an important international match for my country. I knew then that I couldn't go, at least not that night, that I had to get back to my family and advisors and head this off.

After the initial confrontation with the *Sun* journalists, others had seemingly got word that something was afoot and the Air Zimbabwe desk was suddenly crawling with journalists all trying to get on the same flight as me. I knew that some of them were likely to be already booked through to Harare.

I had to think carefully and quickly about what to do. I told Tony, 'I'm going to check in as normal, but I want Air Zimbabwe to get me a vehicle to collect me on the runway and get me out of the airport and back up to Liverpool.'

So that's what I did. I phoned my wife to warn her what was about to happen, but the reporters had already gotten to our home on the Wirral. They'd timed it to the exact moment.

Her response had been to close the door in their faces. She didn't panic, but she was understandably upset.

'Chris Vincent is behind this,' I said. 'I'm coming to Liverpool to sort this out.'

THE ORIGINS OF THE CASE AGAINST ME WERE A MIXTURE OF fantasy, vindictiveness, poor judgement on my part and the willingness of an insidious media empire to try and bring me down. It was a perfect storm and I found myself in the eye of it.

In October 1992 I had celebrated eleven years as Liverpool goalkeeper with a testimonial match against Everton. The game – and everything around it, dinners, golf days, public speaking – earned me a significant amount of money. At the time, payments from testimonials were tax-free. I was 35 years old and thinking forward to my life after playing. I had a pot of money and wanted to invest not just in my family's future, but to reconnect with Africa too. South Africa had not long come out of apartheid and the time seemed right. My children were born in Liverpool and I wanted them to have something to go back to in Africa. I had told them all about Zimbabwe and South Africa, the wildlife and the people there, but it was not the same as having a physical connection with the country.

South African wineries was one area I was looking to invest in. My cousin Archie put in a lot of research into this possibility and he found a 300-acre vineyard in the Paarl wine region.

Debbie, however, didn't think it was a good investment. 'What do you know about wine?' she asked. 'You know nothing about wine, Bruce.' My view was that you didn't have to know anything about wine as long as you had the right people in the right jobs running the place, but my wife was adamant that this was a bad idea. 'You know nothing about wine, why would you go into wineries?' she kept saying.

I didn't agree with her, but it cast enough doubt in my mind and I passed on the sale. Instead, the famous golfer, David Frost, bought it and started producing acclaimed Cabernet Sauvignon from his vineyard. With hindsight these could have been Bruce Grobbelaar wines. It was a fateful decision. If I had bought it my life would have been very different. Perhaps today I would be enjoying my own wine and the travesty that subsequently unfolded would never have happened. Perhaps if I had bought the Paarl vineyard the incoming nightmare may never have unfurled.

Around the same time I first fell in with a fellow Zimbabwean expat, named Chris Vincent. It was a chance encounter and, having been so careful over the prospective investment in the Paarl vineyard, I was reckless to the point of stupidity over my initial – and subsequent – dealings with him. Looking back now I can only ascribe this as a reaction to the disappointment of missing out on the vineyard.

It was July 1992 when I was first approached by Vincent. I was in Harkers, a wine bar in Chester. People came up to me all of the time; it was one of the by-products of fame and of playing for the biggest football club in Europe. I was used to it, but Vincent grabbed my attention straight away, and it wasn't only his accent.

'I don't know if you remember me, but I was in the army. You took over from 2RAR [the Second Battalion, Rhodesian African Rifles] in the Rhodesian War. It was Christmas Eve 1976 at Chipinge.'

My ears pricked up. I was, of course, in the Five Independent Company, which is a mobile unit, the only independent unit in the whole of the Rhodesian War. And we were Fireforce and we were the first to come and take over from 2RAR so they could go on leave. We did indeed take over the Fireforce in that era in Chipinge. There was a captain there in Chipinge but I didn't know what his surname was. I believed what I heard when he told me it was him: Captain Vincent.

Immediately there was a natural chemistry and kinship because of our shared heritage. We were fellow countrymen. We had fought on the same side in the war. We had common experience with Rhodesia's black African population – he through the regiment he fought in, I through my football. We had apparently come into contact with each other during the war. At that time I didn't have anyone else like that in my life: I lived in England, my wife was English, as were most of my friends. Rhodesia, in 1992, was part of a different world.

Chris was blond, slightly balding, tanned, diminutive in stature but very charismatic. In Rhodesia we came from very different backgrounds. While mine was very working-class, he came from a wealthy and well-known family; his father Norman, originally from Northern Ireland, worked as an executive in the sugar industry; his brother Keith was a lion-hunter.

We shared stories of the old country and as the drinks flowed he started singing the 2RAR song – 'Sweet Banana' – and I joined in.

A, B, C, D, E Headquarters, I will buy you a sweet banana
A, B, C, D, E Headquarters, I will buy you a sweet banana
Banana, Banana, Banana, I will buy you a sweet banana
Shield, spear and knobkerrie, soldiers in war and peace
In war she fights with bravery, I will buy you a sweet banana
One Two and the Depot RAR-O, I will buy you a sweet banana
One Two and the Depot RAR-O, I will buy you a sweet banana
Banana, Banana, Banana, I will buy you a sweet banana
Shield, spear and knobkerrie, soldiers in war and peace
In war she fights with bravery, I will buy you a sweet banana
Rhodesia, Burma, Egypt ne Malaya takarwa tika kunda
Rhodesia, Burma, Egypt ne Malaya takarwa tika kunda
Muhondo, Muhondo, Muhondo Inorwa no kushinga
Nhowo pfumo netsvimbo ndiyo RAR-O
Muhondo ne runyararo ndichakutengera sweet banana
A, B, C, D Support Headquarters, ndidzo ndichapedza hondo dzoze
A, B, C, D Support Headquarters, ndidzo ndichapedza hondo dzoze
Banana, Banana, Banana, ndichakutengera sweet banana
Nhowo pfomo netsvimbo ndiyo RAR-O
Muhondo ne runyararo ndichakutengera sweet banana

After a while Vincent took out some photographs, maps and documents and told me about his plans for creating a safari camp in the old country. It was a reserve game some 130 kilometres from Victoria Falls. There would be lodges, different chalets, along with all sorts of plains animals – impala, kudu, sable antelope, wildebeest and giraffes. It would be a high-end operation: a chef would be on hand 24 hours a day to tend to every need of our guests. It sounded perfect in so many ways.

And then came the killer question: did I want to be part of it?

'When do you need a decision?' I asked him.

'By the time you've finished your beer.'

I swilled it down and said, 'Yes.'

The next morning I met him at Manchester Airport and gave him a cheque for £5,000. It was the first in a series of errors that would have catastrophic consequences for me.

AS A FOOTBALLER YOU LIVE IN A WORLD OF HANGERS-ON. SOME JUST want to be seen with someone famous; others want money, or connections within the game. I was acutely conscious of that and over the years had seen off dozens of them. On this occasion, however, I let my guard down.

If you met Vincent in his prime he was very, very convincing. Straight away Debbie was suspicious of him, but – largely because of our shared heritage – I was blind to his ways. Experience tells me you should go with a woman's intuition on these things. Debbie used to get angry at his presence, feeling he was taking over our lives. A man can't see the damage until it happens, but she had him figured out from the outset. She said later that she was upset at a change she noticed in me. She said I put on a macho image, as if I was in the bush; that I'd talk in the jargon of the army. I started smoking again and drank more.

Vincent's plans were tantalising. For me it was about having a foothold in my homeland, of opening Africa up to my girls and to the rest of the world. But there was a promise of riches too. 'We stand to make a great deal of money from this, Bruce,' he had told me that first, fateful night in Harkers.

Vincent claimed that he had agreed deals to buy packages of land from Charles Davy. Davy was a very prominent wildlife activist in Zimbabwe, whose daughter Chelsy was later the long-term girlfriend of Prince Harry. Charles was Vincent's hero; he'd worked for him for a year and wanted to be like him and emulate what he'd done in conservation work. To create an environment for the animals in the camp. Now Davy was giving him – us – a way in.

There was 27,000 acres near Victoria Falls and another 15,000 acres further south. There was also meant to be an eight-bedroomed luxury tourist boat, the Catalina. Davy wanted £2 million. The agreements and financing for the deals were in place for these purchases – some Welsh property developers had agreed to put in £6.5 million – but Vincent needed £20,000 until this part of the transaction cleared, which is why he came to me. For that I would get a 10 per stake in Vincent's company, Savannah Management. It seemed too good to be true. It was, of course, too good to be true.

I put my money in, but the money from the Welsh developers never materialised and by early 1993 we were looking at alternative plans. Not that I was asking too many questions at this stage.

Vincent had, by then, inveigled himself in my life. He infiltrated my family. He was always there: at the games, on the golf course, in bars when I was socialising, at my home. I was complicit in this, of course; he was there because I let him – I was bloody stupid – and when Debbie was away I'd get the babysitter to stay over and go out drinking and golfing with him.

In Zimbabwe, when we travelled for business, we would go out drinking in Victoria Falls. We hung out in hotel bars, but while I would have a fair few beers or smoke 'n diesels, he would drink wildly. That wasn't for me, however; I was still a professional athlete and in all the places I ever went to all through my life I was always in control of my faculties. Often I would leave him and head back to camp; sometimes he would stay out all night.

On reflection it was all a ploy to gain my confidence, to bring me onside. There were elements of our relationship that were later exaggerated by Vincent in court and in the interviews he sold to the press. If you read some of the things he said you'd have thought we were closer than brothers. But that was never the case – at least from my perspective. Maybe he had it in his head that we were like that; only he can possibly say. Later John Fashanu joked that he was in love with me: but who knows what he really felt. Maybe he was – who knows? Later, when things fell apart, I would tell the court that we had been 'embarrassingly close'. That was probably as accurate a summation as you could have.

We were also partners in a business that we believed was going to grow. It was a dream that – because I didn't appreciate that it had no foundations – was one I felt was worth pursuing. To own and be able to share with people a corner of African paradise, who wouldn't want to be part of that? Little did I know at the time that it was caked in fantasy.

By early 1993, with the Welsh investors now consigned to the past, Vincent had come up with a new plan. This time he went to a Zimbabwean landowner and businessman called Neil Hewlett, who had bought land adjacent to one of the sites he had sought from Davey. The deal was that Hewlett would build a luxury lodge on the land and our company, which had now been renamed the Mondoro Wildlife Corporation – Mondoro is Shona for 'spirit of the lion' – would lease it from him for £10,000 per month while we raised the money to buy the 14,000-acre site from him outright. There were four thatched-roofed, white-walled guest cottages grouped around a central reception and dining area. The interiors were simply but tastefully decorated. There was a swimming pool shaded by tall trees. The site was called Acacia Palm Lodge.

Hewlett was someone from the outset that I found honest and businesslike. The lease-back solution, which had been his idea, was a practical solution to get us up and running as a business. A going concern would hold greater interest for other partners than proposals on paper. When I went to see it for myself, although Acacia Palm Lodge site lacked big beasts like elephants and lions, it was incredibly beautiful and I didn't think we'd have any issues attracting the sort of high-end visitors that would make it a profitable and worthwhile venture. It was the foothold back in the old country that I dreamed about. And at the same time, Chris was an enthusiastic and convincing salesman for my dreams. If only he could get me to sign another cheque to help get Acacia Lodge off the ground...

Of course, I gave him what he asked for and increased my stake in Mondoro. Preparations began in earnest. Acacia Palm Lodge would open in May 1994.

I WENT BACK TO ENGLAND TO RESUME MY PLAYING CAREER. IT WAS the 1993/94 season, and I was approaching the end at Liverpool.

In Zimbabwe, Chris Vincent stayed on to work as manager for the new camp, but we needed someone else to front it. A friend of mine, Peta Bala'c, a South African goalkeeper now living near Chester, had a daughter, Bernice, who was at a loose end, having left a job with Marks and Spencer. I think a switch to Africa was as eye-catching to her for the same reasons as I saw it as an attractive proposition for my daughters: a reconnection with her family's home continent and a place for adventure. And so I offered her a job working as a meet-and-greet at the camp and she flew out to join Vincent in March 1994. The Zimbabwean bush was a long way and far removed from a retail role in the UK and so I gave Peta my word that I'd look out for her.

By the time the camp opened I unexpectedly had more time on my hands than normal. An injury sustained while kicking a ball away against Leeds United in February 1994 had brought my season and, as it would turn out, my Liverpool career to an end.

It was during this time that the first seeds of doubt in my mind were sown about Chris Vincent. I had an inkling that perhaps he wasn't everything he said he was when I was passed a copy of Andre Dennison's *War Diaries*. Dennison had been the mastermind of 2RAR in the Rhodesian War and for me this was a compelling read. But in the book there was a reference to a Lieutenant Vincent beginning active service in 1978. Was it the same Lieutenant Vincent who had spun me that story in the Chester wine bar about my unit taking over from his in Chipinge at Christmas 1976? If it was, I certainly had questions to ask him.

I let that one go at the time, but over the spring of 1994 as the camp neared its opening date there were some concerns as to whether Vincent was going to be able to deliver all of the investor money he said he had been promised. There was toing and froing with other investors and long-awaited promises hadn't materialised. This was money that was essential to the camp's operations.

The sense that all was not as it should be heightened when I headed out to Zimbabwe at the end of the 1993/94 season with my family and Steve Nicol and his family. The tension between Neil Hewlett and Chris Vincent was palpable. Almost as soon as I arrived at Acacia Lodge Hewlett started attacking Vincent and his running of the camp. Neil felt that Vincent's outlook was naïve: Chris wanted the camp run to a very high standard and to be profitable within a couple of months, whereas Neil's experience told him it would take a couple of years to reach that position. Chris held his own, but soon lost his cool and I had to physically restrain him at one point.

Did Hewlett implant the idea in my mind that Vincent wasn't up to it? Probably not at that stage. It was a family trip, the mood was relaxed and at night we sat around the fire singing songs and drinking beers. As well as Debbie and the girls, my mother had joined us. A few days later we hosted the Jungleman golf tournament to raise funds to send a Zimbabwean team to the Special Olympics. More friends from Europe flew over, including Russell Osman, the former Ipswich player. The tournament, like our holiday, was a great success enjoyed in the sort of convivial atmosphere I had hoped would permeate Acacia Lodge.

If only it was just a holiday place, but the reality was that Mondoro was a going business concern and an important part of my plans for life after football.

The business side of things was clearly the cause of much tension. There were increasing arguments between Chris and his brother, Keith. There had been a row at the Jungleman golf tournament that I had walked in on. On seeing me, Keith had warned his brother, 'That's it, that's the end of it,' before storming off to join his wife. Chris had joined me afterwards and I'd asked him about it, but he brushed the incident aside. Nevertheless, it fed my perception that something was not right.

Looking back, I think it might have been because of a putative deal with Steve Boler. Steve was a Cheshire millionaire who had made his fortune in the kitchen business and was a major shareholder at Manchester City. Conservationism was a passion of his and he was looking for local partners in a game reserve. There was talk of him putting more than £6 million into investments such as our camp, and he was also talking with Charles Davy at the time – including our camp. Because he was British he needed local partners to get around rules on foreign ownership.

For him to join us as a partner would have been good, but the camp didn't need that sort of money. I asked Vincent what was going to happen to the rest of the money and he told me we were to split it. I was flabbergasted. The camp itself was only worth several hundred thousand, and the upgrades would probably have only cost another million to make it one of the best safari camps in all of Africa.

'Hang on a minute,' I said, 'You can't tell Steve Boler to put six million pounds into the camp and pocket four million of it. He's not stupid; he's going to want to know what has happened to the rest of his money. If you rip him off like that you'll end up in the Manchester Ship Canal with concrete slippers.'

When I got back to England, I stopped Steve's son from giving us the cheque. Mondoro needed investment but not of that magnitude nor to suit the agenda of Chris Vincent. Did this help sow the seeds of a rift between Keith and Chris, and Chris and myself? I don't know, but I didn't want any part in such underhand tactics.

Debbie, meanwhile, had caught wind of the magnitude of my financial involvement in Mondoro and, given that she had two years earlier pulled the plug on my interest in the vineyard, was not happy. Vincent was not someone she either liked or trusted. When she received a call from Neil Hewlett in July asking her to ask me why a payment on a safari truck Mondoro had bought from him hadn't been made, she was as angry as I was bewildered. Where had the money gone?

I was in Cape Town at the time guesting for Cape Town Spurs, where I played three games, keeping clean sheets in all of them. There were times when I was struggling to keep up with the drama in the bush but it was now clear to me that something was very badly wrong. This was a time when mobile phones were still in their infancy and the internet was not something many people used. The world, frankly, was not as well connected a place as it is now. I did, however, speak to Neil Hewlett and I could detect the urgency in his voice.

'Bruce, is there any chance of you coming to see the camp and for us to have a meeting?'

'What's the matter, Neil?'

'You've fallen behind on your payments.'

'What do you mean? I'm fully up to date with my investments in Mondoro.'

'How much money do you think you have paid?'

I told him the amount.

'Have you got any evidence of that?'

'Yes, I can bring it.'

'Bruce, I haven't received anything; I've received £8,000: £2,000 and then another payment taking it up to £10,000 – and that's the total sum that I've received from you guys taking over the camp.'

What had happened to the money? I had to find out and I could only do it in person.

On 2 August 1994 I flew in to Harare and then on to Victoria Falls. I'd been in Kuala Lumpur playing in a tournament for the Malaysian team, Selangor. My contract with Liverpool had come to an end and I was using the time before my transfer to Southampton completed to earn some appearance money by playing overseas.

When I arrived in the hire car, Bernice was shocked to see me. 'What are you doing here, Bruce?' she asked.

'Where's Chris?'

'He hasn't come back from town yet.'

Neil Hewlett had warned me that things had gotten so bad that I needed to protect myself; that Vincent had been using company accounts to run up all sorts of debts. So I headed back into Victoria Falls and went around all the local businesses settling and closing all of the company accounts the camp had: petrol, groceries, everything; I made sure that it was left at zero. After that I went around the casinos and closed the accounts that he had opened up, and even his brother's account too. Talking to the locals, I could see what had happened: he'd spent his days – and my money – being the main man in town. I made sure that nobody was to extend any form of credit to our company, Mondoro.

Back at the camp, Neil Hewlett and I compared our bank accounts. The transfers from mine to an account controlled by Vincent were clear, so too was the conspicuous lack of activity in terms of payments from this account to Neil's. All my worst fears were confirmed. I told him that I had drafted a letter resigning our lease and would sign it in front of him and others that evening. The mood was brusque but businesslike; I think Neil could see that I had been wronged. And then I waited for Vincent.

He turned up at the camp in his Land Rover around lunchtime.

'Bernice! Get me a beer!' he yelled by way of announcing his arrival.

'OK,' Bernice told him, 'but there's someone on the veranda to see you.'

Vincent walked on the veranda and there has never been anyone more shocked to see me than then. 'Bruce, what are you doing here?' he asked.

'I've just been to see Neil Hewlett.'

'Don't believe Hewlett,' he said immediately, without asking me what we had discussed. 'He's a lying, cheating, sonofabitch. He's on my back all the time about this camp. I'm running it to the best of my ability.'

'That's interesting,' I said coolly. 'And what happened to the money that's supposed to have been paid to Neil Hewlett?'

'No, he's got it!'

'I'm just going to tell you that there's a meeting tonight at Neil Hewlett's place,' I said, and then I went on my way.

Later that day I returned to the camp. At the bottom end of the property Neil had a small lodge, where we were all to meet. I was there early. Hewlett's wife arrived, as did Maureen, Keith Vincent's wife. Keith was a partner in the business and was away hunting, which was why Maureen joined us. Bernice joined myself, Neil Hewlett and his wife. And then we waited for Chris to come in.

He was late; he had no regard for meeting times – he never did. Straight away, Neil Hewlett went for him: 'Did you tell Bruce Grobbelaar that I was a lying, cheating sonofabitch?' Vincent couldn't answer so Neil repeated the question. 'Did you tell Bruce Grobbelaar that I was a lying, cheating sonofabitch? You better answer me.' Then he put on a Dictaphone. 'Did you say that to Bruce Grobbelaar?' he asked again.

Meekly, Vincent was left with no option but to admit that he had said it.

'Oh, I'm the lying, cheating sonofabitch?' said Hewlett. 'Here's my ledgers; you paid me this amount of money, £2,000 and then it went up to £10,000; here's Bruce Grobbelaar's withdrawals from his bank, paid into your bank here in the country. Where's it all gone?'

He couldn't answer.

At this point I stood up and said, 'Neil, that's it. I've got all the evidence. I know that there's the biggest conman I've ever seen and I'm sorry that I'm going to have to close this camp; I'm no longer putting any more money into the camp. Unless you get the money in a certain amount of time, which I know will never happen, I'm closing the camp. Here's my resignation, could you witness it please.' I signed it, gave him a copy, gave all the copies out, kept a copy; I resigned from the company that night. No further money went in.

Vincent tried to claim that Neil Hewlett had other expenses, that he had to fix boreholes and other things around the property. Neil showed me the money that was paid to fix those boreholes, not that it would have cost anything near what he claimed. Vincent showed me that he had paid some money, but it was all ledgered in different ways. The sums didn't add up.

So, the camp was closed and I bought a ticket for Bernice to go home the next night. The poor girl had been there for nearly a year, but had only been paid intermittently – usually when Vincent had had a win in the casino – but even after everything that happened Vincent didn't want to let her leave.

'You've got to stay here with me,' he told her, but I couldn't possibly let her stay. I'd promised her father I would look after her.

That night I stayed in town, while Vincent went on a drunken rampage around the camp, drinking beers and then shooting up the empty cans, shouting out my name as he did so. Bernice had been scared. The next day I went out to the camp, picked her up, flew back to Harare in the morning. But Vincent met us at the airport in Victoria Falls, and told her again that she couldn't go. He seemed increasingly desperate.

'Bernice is my responsibility. I am taking her back to England,' I told him. 'She has got family to go to.' As a man of my word, who had promised her parents I would look after her, I couldn't possibly leave her. So I took her to Harare for the connecting flight and waited around at a friend's house because the plane was going to be leaving later that evening.

When we checked in at the airport, guess who arrived? Vincent had driven from Victoria Falls to Harare, which takes eight hours. But this time he had not come for Bernice, he had come for me. As he confronted me, Bernice pleaded with him to stop. He looked me in the eye and warned me: 'This is not over.'

26

Vincent

WHEN I TRAVELLED THE LONG JOURNEY BACK TO ENGLAND WITH Bernice, it was clear that something had gone on between the two of them. Out there in the remoteness of the bush close friendships are often formed, but it seemed to me to be something more than that. Bernice was young and impressionable and Vincent could be charismatic, larger than life, persuasive and sometimes overbearing. It turned out that my impressions weren't misplaced: their friendship had occasionally evolved into something more, although Bernice was keen to emphasise that Vincent wasn't her boyfriend and never had been. For Chris Vincent, however, Bernice was his new obsession.

Vincent was a supreme narcissist. He built up imagined wrongs and always portrayed himself as the victim. There was no sense of proportion or rationality. I didn't really appreciate it at the time, but his sense of self-entitlement knew no bounds. I was later told a story about him encountering one of the Welsh property developers in a pub in Chester shortly after they backed out of their finance deal with Mondoro. When the businessman approached Vincent to say hello, Vincent told him he had nothing to say to him. Twenty minutes later they encountered each other again and when Vincent was greeted again something in him snapped. He went for the businessman, grabbing his windpipe and nearly throttling him before being dragged off by four other people. Vincent later admitted that he would have killed him if left to his own devices. This poor guy's only offence – other than passing the time of day – was his failure to raise millions of pounds at the height of a recession for a pipe dream deep in the African bush. For that he nearly paid with his life.

Now, imagine how Chris Vincent felt about me? I'd done nothing wrong except bankroll him for a couple of years, but in his mind he nursed a litany of grievances. He had nothing left: no money (and none of mine, either), his family had disowned him, his business dreams had collapsed and died, and now I had taken away the woman he had an unrequited love affair with. Later he told a journalist that he had homicidal thoughts at this time. It was inevitable that he was bent on vengeance.

But how would he extract his revenge on me?

Violence? Slander? Or something else?

*

THREE MONTHS AFTER THAT CONFRONTATION IN ZIMBABWE I found out in the departures hall of Gatwick Airport just what Christopher Vincent had in store for me.

I knew, I just knew, from the moment those journalists approached me, that he was behind it.

But the magnitude of what I was to face didn't immediately strike home. What I did know, however, was that I had to get back up to the north-west to be with my family, advisors and lawyers and take whatever action I could to stop these malicious untruths spreading. It was like being confronted with a cancer: you knew it could spread with deadly intent, or be blasted away with whatever medicine you could give it.

At the same time, I also had my duties as a footballer to fulfil; an important game for my country to play in a few days' time. I even had the team's kit with me. At the time I sorted the kits out because I had access to suppliers that were not available in Africa. I also knew that if the funds went via Zimbabwe it would be stolen by the Mugabes. So I arranged a deal with NK Sports in Manchester. They used to give me three kits for every game, a white one, a yellow one and a green one, and I'd check them in with me. If I didn't turn up in Harare it would put a lot of people out; an entire nation.

Tony Milligan was by my side. I trusted him. He was my driver, but also my confidant and friend. He was coming with me to Zimbabwe, but I knew then that I wouldn't be able to go with him – at least not straight away. But we had to wrongfoot these reporters, who were hanging around us like a bad smell.

We came up with a plan. Tony had the kit for Zimbabwe. I was going to get on the plane with him as planned, and we went and checked in as normal. But I had no intention of taking the long flight south. The check-in lady could see that something was up, and with the clock ticking down to departure she asked me, 'Bruce, what do you want to do?' With Tony I'd hit upon a ruse. I told her, 'Listen, check me in as if I'm going on the plane, and get me out into some sort of vehicle that I can get to Heathrow Airport.' She did just that. She was brilliant. Tony and I went on the plane as normal but halfway up the gangplank I went back down the stairs onto the tarmac. Tony went on to Zimbabwe with the kit, while I got into a police vehicle, which took me to Heathrow Airport. From there I boarded the flight from Heathrow to Manchester, got off at Manchester and a car took me straight to my lawyers, Cuff Roberts, in central Liverpool.

I'd wrong-footed the reporters, some of whom were now on the long, long flight to Harare, accompanying only Tony. Meanwhile, my lawyers and I went to war with the *Sun*.

My lawyer, Brian Canavan, got a judge to try and get an injunction out on the story to stop it being published. But the judge – while sympathetic – was realistic and said that it was probably too late in the day to do anything. I called my manager at Southampton Alan Ball and told him I'd done nothing wrong, but that he was going to read a story about me in the newspapers the next morning. 'I'll still be going to play for my country and I'll see you on Monday,' I promised.

Ball was brilliant. His response was simple and just what I needed: 'I'll see you on Monday.'

I was experiencing shock, but I never panicked. I knew what Chris Vincent's demeanour was. He had put it to me about the games that were later mentioned in the court cases, so I knew exactly what his objective was. He had warned me, 'This is not over.' And it wasn't.

FROM THE BUST-UP IN ZIMBABWE AND THE END OF MONDORO TO a late-night session in Cuff Roberts' darkened office in Liverpool's Old Hall Street, trying to limit the damage he had somehow created, Chris Vincent and I had come a long way. But how had we got to there in the space of three short months?

A week after our confrontation at Acacia Palm Lodge, Vincent had used a Mondoro cheque – which would bounce – to pay for a flight back to the UK. I think he still thought he could turn things around: find new investors for Mondoro, 'win' Bernice back, and get his own back on me. Nobody, however, was interested in putting bad money after good into his safari scheme. Bernice didn't want him. Which left me.

He was also, by his own admission, completely broke. He claimed later that he was unable to even feed himself. And so his desperation for cash or revenge or both drove him to the *Sun* newspaper.

Chris would have known that I had history with this particular newspaper. The 1980s were the highpoint of the British tabloids – or 'red-tops' as they were commonly known. While today print news media seems to be in terminal decline, back then millions woke to the *Daily Mirror*, the *Sun*, the *Daily Star*, *Today* or one of their Sunday sister titles delivered to their doorstep. The battles for circulation were ferocious. The papers paid well for celebrity backing, just as they did for stories of celebrity scandal. I had a column for the *Daily Mail* and then around 1986 I started to write for the *Sun*. As I've said already, I didn't think too much about it at the time. Lots of players did it.

That relationship came to an abrupt end in April 1989 after the Hillsborough disaster.

As disgust gave way to visceral anger in Merseyside and beyond, the *Sun's* circulation plummeted. The newspaper's executives tried desperately to regain their lost sales in the city – for instance, they ran a high-profile 'justice' campaign to ensure the juvenile killers of the Liverpool toddler Jamie Bulger were incarcerated for life – but they would lash out at those who got in their way too. I was to be one such victim.

In early September 1994, around five weeks after the collapse of Mondoro, Chris Vincent called the Wapping headquarters of the *Sun*. He told them he had a story involving international football players and bribery; he told them he was a close friend and associate of mine. Straight away the *Sun* sent a reporter named John Troup from their Manchester bureau to meet Vincent at his home in Chirk in North Wales. Vincent told him he needed cash immediately before he would talk. The *Sun* were more than willing to hand over payment for his 'story' and they signed a letter of agreement on the spot. It's not clear if they ever did any due diligence into him at all. And then Vincent began sharing his vengeful fantasies.

His story went like this. With the Wimbledon centre-forward John Fashanu I had been involved with a Far Eastern gambling syndicate whose aim was to fix the results of football matches. He claimed that I had been paid £40,000 in cash by Fashanu to throw a game for Liverpool against Newcastle United in November

1993, following Newcastle's 3–0 win. He further alleged that I had tried to throw games against Manchester United and Norwich City but had been unable to do so. Other people that I knew were implicated in this nexus of lies and fantasy. It was unimaginable, ludicrous garbage. Lies. The *Sun* nevertheless handed over an initial payment of £150.

Vincent had a significant problem that even the *Sun* and its disgusting journalistic methods had no way around: he could not stand any of this up. Of course he couldn't, because it was fantasy. Rubbish. So he hit upon a ruse. He would get me to incriminate myself by getting me to talk on tape about my so-called crimes. He would do this by inventing a fake gambling syndicate – similar to the one he had already invented in his initial pitch – and implicate me in its workings. After all, he told the *Sun*, if I could be 'bribed' by one set of 'criminals', why not another?

The *Sun* were inevitably ecstatic about this entrapment plan. Not only would they get the juiciest tabloid scandal of the decade across their front page, they would strike out at the only columnist to have ever walked away from them. Not only that, they'd strike at the heart of a city that shunned and reviled them. All they needed was for Chris Vincent to make contact with me and their wicked plan could be set in motion.

27

Tapped

I WAS AT THE SOUTHAMPTON HILTON WHEN A FAMILIAR NUMBER appeared on my phone. It was September 1994, weeks after my move to the south coast, and I was still finding my feet. The Hilton was a temporary residence as I looked for a flat. Debbie and the girls had remained in Heswall.

The number was Vincent's. Like a fool, I took the call.

'Hey, Bruce, I'm back in town.' I said nothing. 'Let me start by saying how sorry I am that it didn't work out with Mondoro, but I'm determined to pay every penny back to you, and I have a new venture...'

On and on he went with his salesman's patter. If you didn't know all his dark secrets and the way he was you'd almost be taken in by it. He had a charm, a way of talking that would suck anyone in. This time I was under no illusions that he was up to no good, but I was curious. Very curious. Perhaps that is just an inherent part of a conman's *modus operandi*: offer the victim something they really want. Who wouldn't be curious when someone was offering you a way back to tens of thousands of pounds that had been lost?

I wanted to get to the bottom of what he was up to. I adopted the role of Inspector Clouseau. I wanted to find out what this scheme was; and expose Vincent's lies. It was a game of double-bluff worthy of a John le Carré novel. Every venture he had been involved in was built on fantasy and other people's money. If others were to be embroiled in one of his mad schemes, maybe I could warn them too, as I had Steve Boler. I was naïve, yes. I was wrong, sometimes. But I thought I had enough experience from my war days to get the information and then to go to the police.

This was to be my undoing – the biggest bloody mistake of my life. It was a far bigger mistake than parting with money to Vincent in the first place; he could only spend that. This time he wasn't after money, he wanted to do to me what he believed I had done to him and destroy me as a man. In his tiny mind he blamed me for losing his family, the love of his life (although it was largely unrequited) and his dreams of becoming a conservationist big shot (which were mostly delusional). His vengeance would wreak a truly terrible effect on my life.

I agreed to meet him. Southampton were playing Tottenham a few days later and I arranged to meet him at my hotel – the Swallow Hotel at Waltham Abbey – just off the M25. He was the same as ever, reckless and charming. If he showed repentance he was never very convincing that he meant it. He could probably see that I was very guarded and if you listen to the recordings he was secretly making for the *Sun* newspaper at the time, then that mostly shows through. The fact that he was miked up didn't stop him asking me to lend him money after everything that had happened. He was skint and his family had rejected him, he said. I refused.

'What do you want, Chris?' I asked him at one point, slightly exasperated that we were going around in circles.

'I want to get you your money back,' he said.

'How are you going to manage that?'

'I have this new venture...' he said.

'I know that,' I said, cutting across him. 'Tell me what it's about.'

And so, in his roundabout way, he did. There were businessmen he had met at Chester Races who bet heavily on football, he said. They're looking for someone to fix results so they can win large amounts of money. They'd like you to be part of it.

At this stage I nearly choked on my drink. I should have walked out there and then, but I didn't. I didn't want to say anything or challenge him in anyway, because I wanted to know what would happen next. Some could say that I was falling for the confidence trickster's routine again, but I really wasn't; I just wanted to know what he was up to and who was behind it. I was too bloody curious for my own good. What I didn't know was that this and all our other conversations were being recorded by the *Sun*.

I accept that this might sound hard for the reader to believe. It was a challenge two decades ago to convince a jury that was what I was up to. But those who know and knew me recognised that insatiable, unpredictable curiosity within me. There was also an element of my African upbringing at play: that I had been taught to be self-reliant and work problems out for myself. Sometimes these character traits manifested themselves in ways that some would consider strange or unnecessary.

For example, there was a regular correspondent to the Liverpool *Football Echo's* letters page in the 1980s who was fixated with me, slating me week after week. I didn't know who he was and he didn't have the guts to put his name to his criticism, other than by signing off 'the Yankee Bar' – a drinkery by Lime Street station. So, from time to time, after a home match I would head down there to seek him out, so that I could challenge him – or her.

'Did you write to the *Football Echo* about me?' I'd ask groups of people.

No one ever admitted to being the Yankee Bar scribe. Some people respected me for coming down to face my antagonist, but most considered it unorthodox or eccentric. That was just me, however. Later I tried to track down National Front members who I felt were responsible for Heysel. If you knew me you'd understand; perhaps if you don't, by reading this book, you'll have an understanding of the unorthodox logic that sometimes governs my mind.

Whenever we met, it was always Chris Vincent driving the conversation. In court we would listen to the covert recordings he made of these times and it was two men trying to entrap each other: he to get his thirty pieces of silver from the *Sun*; me to find out what the hell he was up to. In my guarded way I'd just go along with him without ever committing to his crazy schemes, searching, always searching for what he was up to and who was behind him.

He would ask me to pick games to lose, but my response was always the same: I'm not picking any game.

If you look at the five games that were supposedly under suspicion – Liverpool against Norwich, Manchester United and Newcastle, as well as Southampton versus Coventry and Manchester City – I was only on the losing side for the Newcastle match, which – if you believe these fantasies – must make me among the worst match-fixers in football history.

The *Sun* set Vincent up at the De Vere Grand Harbour Hotel in Southampton. He was equipped with an expenses tab while they put a team of their best spooks and journalists to spy on us. They specialised in honeytraps and the high-profile victims of theirs and their sister paper the *News of the World* included the broadcaster Frank Bough, whose predilection for S&M they 'exposed', and Jeffrey Archer, who they showed making a £2,000 payment to a prostitute. Vincent's room was bugged and had been fitted with secret cameras.

I don't know how long they had been staked out before they got me in the door, but I remember the date because it was my 37th birthday: Thursday 6 October 1994. Why did I go and meet him? Boredom mostly, but more than anything else a desire to see what the hell he was up to.

I headed over to the hotel in late afternoon following a round of golf and we shared a couple of spook 'n' diesels before playing a few frames of snooker. All of our conversations were being recorded by the *Sun*, but these guys were so on their game that they never captured any of our conversations. The tapes either ran out or the radio frequencies wouldn't reach their recording devices.

Just by coincidence it was during this time that I was meant to have made my most startling 'confessions' to Vincent. I was meant to have confessed to letting in a goal for Southampton in a 'fixed' match against Coventry (a game that we won 3–1), taken a phone call from one of my so-called co-conspirators (something that phone records never verified), and discussed the activities of another 'corrupt' player. And yet, despite wiring up Vincent and the hotel like the FBI on an undercover swoop against the mob, they somehow didn't capture any of this compelling 'evidence' on tape. Isn't that an unfortunate coincidence?

Vincent then lured me to his hotel room on the pretext that he had some papers relating to Mondoro that needed to be signed. His real reason – and unbeknown to me – was that the *Sun* had a secret camera there, and he had two grand in his safe as part of the entrapment plot. Like a fool, I followed him; followed him towards my doom.

In Vincent's room the talk soon switched from Mondoro to my family to his harebrained match-fixing scheme. I'll admit my interest was piqued; not because I had any interest in corrupting my sport, but because I wanted to know what he was up to and who was behind him. As I've said many times before, I understand why people find that logic difficult to understand, but that's just how my mind works: I'm innately curious. I was also naïve to the point of stupidity: instead of doing my self-styled Inspector Clouseau I should have just gone to the real police there and then.

But I didn't. When Vincent started talking about his new match-fixer friends from Chester Races, I started concocting my own stories to suck him in. I insinuated that match-fixing was part and parcel of football. I claimed that I'd lost £125,000 while playing for Liverpool against Manchester United because

I'd made two 'blinding saves'. I mentioned a couple of games when we hadn't lost. 'The thing is,' I said at one point, 'I don't like to lose. It's instinct...'

Vincent was evidently sensing the kill, but the grim irony was that at the same time I thought I was luring him into revealing more about his scheme and who was really behind it. Armed with that info I would have gone to the police. Little could I have imagined it was a second-rate tabloid newspaper pulling his strings.

'They're prepared to give you two grand every two weeks on the basis that you pick one game,' he said of his syndicate pals.

'What's two grand?' I asked.

'It's two grand every two weeks until you pick a game, and if you dip in [lose] on that game – a hundred Gs,' Vincent said, before going into more details about his imaginary associates and how the scheme would work.

I thought I had him at this point; that he was about to reveal who these scoundrels were. Furnished with that information I could then go to the law. Vincent, however, had similar ideas about me; only he would go running to the *Sun*.

I tried to find out more about his friends – he said they were called 'Richard' and 'Guy' – and who else was in on the racket. He suggested meeting his associates, but I told him I wasn't interested. Then he suddenly produced an envelope, which he said contained £2,000, to show they were 'serious'. At this stage I think the magnitude of what I'd got myself involved in struck home. Honeytrap or not, I couldn't take that sort of cash. I didn't trust Vincent at all. I didn't know what he was doing, but the notion that this was all a big set-up was suddenly all too apparent.

I lectured Vincent on the dangers betting on football posed. The Swindon Town manager Lou Macari, who I later played under at Stoke, had been fined and banned for betting against his own team. I didn't take the money. In fact, Vincent kept it for himself.

I saw Vincent again a couple of weeks later. Far from being spooked by the appearance of cash, he had only piqued my interest in his scheme. My inner Clouseau had convinced me that I was on the verge of uncovering a huge match-fixing scam in English football. I still needed to find out more before I could take it to the authorities, and I thought I could do this by suckering him in.

My interrogations of his syndicate and his methods continued. Speaking of his imaginary plan, he said, 'I see it as a way of giving you back the cash you put into the business.' I tried to unravel the syndicate members' identities – Vincent gave me a few more details; one was a Hong Kong property developer, he said, and he mentioned Sporting Index, which had introduced spread betting into Britain – and their methods. Likewise the small matter of getting significant amounts of cash into the country. But I was always wary, always careful not to get taken in. He talked in huge numbers – £100,000 – but I held back. 'It's too dangerous,' I told him. If he was setting me up I couldn't incriminate myself, despite my own ulterior motives. In fact I didn't; I was very careful, despite all of Vincent's best efforts to snare me. Yet again, the most telling piece of 'evidence' that he supplied against me – he claimed that I said, 'I'll do the Liverpool game at Liverpool' – was not corroborated by any taped evidence.

There was one final meeting with Vincent on 3 November. This time it was at a serviced apartment on Grosvenor Square in Southampton. He said that he had got a new job and had been given a company flat. Of course, it was nothing of the sort. It was laden with hidden microphones and cameras. It was to be the scene of the final betrayal, where they would film me taking an envelope with £2,000 cash in it – a package, you must remember, I had refused to accept on two previous occasions.

When we entered his apartment, he handed me the envelope.

'There you are, sir,' he said. 'I've just been carrying it around the fucking countryside.'

I took the envelope and threw it on the sofa.

Vincent started ranting and raving: about Mondoro, his family, the Rhodesian War, Zimbabwe, me, everything. He was on edge, swearing with every second word. I tried to get him to calm down. 'You're starting a new life now,' I said, referring to his 'new job', which like everything about him was a sham.

He went back to the subject of money and he said he was due to pick up another couple of grand from his syndicate the following week. 'Do you want me to drop it off at the airport?' he asked. I ignored him and talked about something else.

We were going for dinner at an Italian restaurant in Brockenhurst, near where I had a flat at the time in Lymington. Vincent gave me the envelope and I put it in the pocket of my jacket. He gestured or said that he had no jacket of his own. That was the moment that would be captured on film and shown around the world. The part that wasn't was when I put the envelope in the glove compartment of his hire car the minute I sat down in the front passenger seat.

The dinner was unremarkable, I don't remember anything about it. But Vincent subsequently claimed I received a call from a match-fixing syndicate and agreed that Southampton were going to lose 1–0 to Manchester City that weekend. For that, I was allegedly going to be paid 'small money – £25,000'. Again, phone records did not verify that; nor did Vincent's covert recordings – despite his being wired up like Donnie Brasco. Nor did what unfolded the following Saturday – a 3–3 draw.

MY LAWYERS WORKED HARD THAT FIRST NIGHT AFTER THE journalists approached me at the airport, but were realistic about what they could do. We warned the *Sun* that if they published their match-fixing fantasy we would issue a lawsuit immediately, suing for defamation of character. But the cat was out of the bag and TV and radio started reporting on the story overnight.

At the same time I was aware of the possible implications of an unsuccessful action, that in the *Sun's* proprietor Rupert Murdoch I was effectively up against the most powerful media mogul in the world and that his News International Group had a way of inveigling and wheedling its influence in every aspect of British society, whether it was with politicians, the judiciary, or simply the minds of its readers. Whatever was going to happen this wasn't going to go away quickly and without a fight, and I was duty bound to protect my family and the assets we owned. I signed everything over to my wife – everything – so I owned nothing as an individual and if I failed in my legal challenges they would be unable to pursue me for costs. Even if I lost my reputation at least the properties we owned would be safe.

The next morning, devastating headlines landed on a million doormats.

GROBBELAAR TOOK BRIBES TO FIX GAMES

The story, at first sight, was dreadful. Its first paragraph read: 'Soccer star Bruce Grobbelaar is exposed by the *Sun* today for taking massive bribes to throw key matches.' On page 2 of the same issue its headline read: 'GROB: I let in 3 goals and picked up £40,000'. Over subsequent pages was a litany of innuendo, malicious falsehoods and lies, which continued for the next week. They came from hours of transcripts provided from covert recordings made by Vincent, who had been paid by the *Sun* to spy on me.

Vincent spoke out in the *Sun*, portraying himself as some sort of paradigm of virtue. We had been 'best friends', he claimed. 'We had so many good times and so many great parties – he was a great bloke to have a beer with.' He felt 'very sad' looking back on what had since happened but 'even sadder for all the Liverpool fans who idolised him for years and worshipped his every step'. He added: 'I feel saddest of all for Bruce's wife and family because they are all innocent in this.' Was the conman repentant already?

On the Thursday I flew out to Zimbabwe. The story by then was leading every news bulletin and newspaper in the country. Press were camped outside my house. Journalists were speculatively booking on every flight to Harare, knowing that I intended on playing for my country. I was booked into Seat 1A, my barrister, Brian Canavan, 1B; but I was smuggled aboard the flight ahead of boarding and allowed to hide in the cockpit. When journalists came aboard there was much kerfuffle as they searched the plane for me. Some didn't know whether to stay on board and take the long trip to Africa or wait behind.

As the plane started taxiing I emerged from the cockpit and went to my seat. There was more jostling for position among the journalists, but a stewardess came to my rescue.

'You put that camera away. This is now Zimbabwean soil and I want you to leave our boy alone. You leave him alone and you'll be OK.'

That was the sort of spirit that kept me going. People from the old country were unstinting in their support for me. They knew me, they idolised me, they trusted me, they knew my integrity.

Journalists who had already reached Zimbabwe were finding that out for themselves. 'He's like the grandfather of the nation and he's played his heart out for Zimbabwe,' Michael, an office worker, told the *Guardian's* correspondent. 'We were just one match short of qualifying for the World Cup against Egypt. You should have seen him. There is no way he didn't go for that ball.'

Further support came from the Zimbabwe Football Association (ZIFA). While I was up in the air, a spokesman told the reporters who had been ringing the phone off the hook: 'If he is courageous enough to come here the least we can do is to let him play. These are only allegations. You are supposed to live in the civilised world yet he is being executed without a trial.' Within an hour of landing the Zimbabwe FA's technical director had offered me the job of coaching the country's Olympic team, which I accepted.

When we landed I was the centre of attention again and I gave a short statement as we waited for our bags. 'Good morning! Welcome to Zimbabwe, my country. I've done nothing wrong. I'm coming out to play a game. You're welcome to come and watch me. All the best!'

I went from the airport to the hotel, got changed and went straight to training. I could see already that local people were unstinting in their support as we drove in. Horns were honked, people waved and gave me the thumbs-up or shouted their support. When I joined up with my teammates they broke into spontaneous applause.

More backing came from my manager, the veteran German Rudi Gutendorf. 'I can't believe that Bruce has done anything that these allegations say he has done. To me, he is like Kevin Keegan [whom Gutendorf had managed at Hamburg] – a good, clean representative of the game in England.' He added: 'Already I can say he is the best goalkeeper I've ever worked with and I've worked with the lot, including Sepp Maier who won the World Cup with West Germany.'

In the afternoon I played golf at Warren Hills and the photographers were all hidden in the bushes taking pictures. At Saturday training the place was full of English journalists and so too was the game. Debbie had also flown out to support me and watched from the stands with Brian and Gordon Crawford, who we used to stay with when we were out there. They were among the only whites in the whole stadium. Zimbabwe's national team had never seen interest like it.

I always tried to be friendly and accessible to the journalists there. When I spoke to them I tried to focus on the match that we faced.

'I am ready to play and do the best I possibly can – as I always do,' I said. 'The pressure will not get to me. I do not feel under any more pressure than I usually do for big games.

'As you can expect, this has been really hard on my wife Debbie and the rest of the family. My wife is OK; I do not need to say how I feel. I've received great support, especially from Southampton, who are 100 per cent behind me. Talk about police action doesn't worry me because I refute the allegations. I'm here for the football. Others may be here for different reasons but I am here to play – and win – a very important game for my country.'

My hopes of a nice easy game after a gruelling week were not to be realised. Although 45,000 fans filled the stadium, many with banners bearing legends such as 'Bruce is innocent' and 'Screw The Sun', it was, nevertheless, a hostile environment and the Zaire coach would complain that his players were attacked and intimidated. Outside the ground Brian Canavan was mugged and robbed of his watch. Leo Mugabe, Robert Mugabe's nephew and the president of ZIFA, always sensing an opportunity for a quick buck, tried to charge British journalists $5,000 per man to see the game. They eventually settled on $500 between them all.

Adam Ndlovu, the elder brother of the Coventry striker Peter, gave us the lead just after half-time, but Menama Lukaku (the father of Romelu and Jordan Lukaku) equalised fifteen minutes later. The game was heading for a 1-1 draw when deep into stoppage time Peter Ndlovu was knocked down in the penalty area. Ignoring protests from the Zaire players, he calmly slotted home the spot-kick to give us the winner. With the final whistle all hell broke loose and the Zaire players chased the Zambian referee around the pitch. Seeing as there was no protection for him I ran across the pitch and intervened.

'Grobbelaar saved me,' said the match official, Christian Chikuka. 'I was being kicked and it was a dangerous situation. He rushed from his goal to assist me and I will always be grateful to him. I will be reporting everything to FIFA, including what Bruce Grobbelaar did for me.'

I travelled back that night on Air Zimbabwe, with Debbie and Brian, got back at 9am. and went straight to training at Southampton.

How do you focus? I knew I'd done nothing wrong. I tried to analyse exactly what Vincent had done, who he had been speaking to and what else he might say. But it was difficult. Every aspect of my life was suddenly under the most intense public scrutiny. Aspects of my private life were on the front page of some newspapers. Debbie and the girls had to run a gauntlet of tabloid photographers just to go to school or the shops. What I spent, what I wore, who I associated with; every part of my life was suddenly all tabloid fodder.

The worst part of it was probably a story the *News of the World* ran alleging that I'd been fornicating with other women, which was published while I was still in Zimbabwe. They were digging with information Vincent had given them. It's true that we were in the company of other women when we were out together, but a lot of it was just flirting and joking; the sort of harmless antics that might be fun at the time but could easily have been taken out of context when transcribed and put into a newspaper.

It was not the sort of thing anyone would want their wife to read, no matter how exaggerated and misconstrued it all was. When Debbie saw it after we returned from Zimbabwe she sat me down and made me read it while she looked over me. If I'm honest, it didn't look good at all. I told her that there was only one person there who I knew and I'd known her since before I'd met Debbie. When she calmed down she was OK with it – to a certain extent, anyway. My in-laws, Bernard and Heather, were great too, speaking to the press on the family's behalf and being generous in their portrayals of me as a husband, father and son-in-law.

At Southampton Alan Ball and Lawrie McMenemy were hugely supportive throughout this whole ordeal. McMenemy told reporters that his club was a family and when a family is in trouble it unites. Having missed the flight to Zimbabwe so I could sort my affairs out with my lawyer in Liverpool, they unquestioningly accepted that I had to do what I needed to do. When I got back to the south coast the next week I was called straight into their office.

'Did you do it?' they asked as one.

'No, I didn't,' I told them.

Six times back and forth this questioning went on. 'Did you do it?' 'No I didn't.'

'Right, you're going to be playing,' Ball finally told me. 'Get your head down and get on with it.' And that was that. They were great. It was just the sort of response I needed. They stuck with me the whole of that year, even when I was injured with a depressed cheekbone and had to wear a facial mask to protect my face.

Not many others were so forthright in their support. A lot of people I considered friends seemed to hedge their bets, not knowing what to believe. Little could they have known then that it would be another eight exhausting years before my name was finally cleared and they could step forward and call themselves my friend in public again. By that time I could count my true friends on one hand.

One person who was unstinting in his support was Alan Hansen. He had perhaps more at stake in terms of reputation than others, starting out as he was in what would be a highly successful career in punditry. 'At no time, not once, did I suspect he was deceiving Liverpool Football Club,' he said. 'No one else did, either. It was never a topic for consideration. He played under three of the shrewdest managers the British game has ever seen in Bob Paisley, Joe Fagan and Kenny Dalglish. If any one of them had the slightest doubts about him, if they suspected something was up, they would have had him through the doors, out and finished.'

Football was what I needed in this period. I knew I'd never done anything wrong, so that was paramount. Going out and playing: yes, you're going to get the chants, but I'd had it all my life. When you're out on the pitch you need to be the best you can. Our first game back against Arsenal, the away fans showered the field with fake £10 notes, but instead of the Queen's head there was mine. I could see the funny side of it, and filled my cap with the notes and beckoned to the supporters to throw more. Then they started singing to the tune of 'My Old Man's a Dustman':

> *Grobbelaar is dodgy,*
> *He wears a dodgy hat,*
> *And when he saw that forty grand,*
> *He said: 'I'm having that.'*

I played well. We won 1–0, our first win in ten matches, and at the end of the game, as I bowed to all four corners of the ground, even the Arsenal fans applauded me.

28

Arrested

AS INCONCEIVABLE AS IT FIRST SEEMED, THINGS SETTLED DOWN as the initial media furore subsided. I trained and played and got dog's abuse from visiting supporters, but that was OK – I was used to it. I had my own routine in Southampton and would commute up to the Wirral to see my family, or grab a few days' holiday as the school holidays allowed. I enjoyed playing under Alan Ball, and while The Dell was rather more basic than Anfield it had its charms.

I heard nothing from Chris Vincent, but through others was aware of what he was doing. The *Sun* – as was their way – discarded him as soon as the story left the front pages. When he went to their headquarters in Wapping and met the editor, Stuart Higgins, insisting on more money, a house and a car, his ridiculous demands were rejected. Things then turned nasty and when Vincent started making threats, Higgins had him turfed out by security guards. Cast out by the *Sun*, he went around other journalists hustling for cash in exchange for more fantasies about me.

I was also aware that Vincent was paranoid and would spread lies, trying to insinuate that I was violent or part of some sort of conspiracy to get at him. On one occasion I was apparently due into Gatwick Airport from Zimbabwe on an accompanying flight at the same time as him and he refused to leave the plane without an armed police escort. I didn't even know he was there, much less have a plan to attack someone in one of the most closely guarded sites in Britain! At no time have I ever threatened him. At the meeting at Hewlett's place I told him I didn't want to see him again and that if I did I might do something that I'd regret. But when we did meet again I'd calmed down a little. At no time did I ever pursue him. He was beaten up in a bar in Johannesburg but that was nothing to do with me.

All the while my lawyers prepared for the forthcoming libel trial, in which I was certain I'd not only clear my name but walk away with sizeable damages from the *Sun*.

There had been talk of police investigations but I wasn't really aware at the time that they were ongoing. I think I felt the allegations were so far-fetched, so patently ludicrous and the police so busy with genuine law and order issues that they would not take it up. Indeed the head of Hampshire CID told a TV reporter, 'He's on our doorstep. There's probably nothing in it, but I'll take a look.' So far, so non-committal.

I was aware, also, that I was being watched all the time.

Around this time I received a letter from Jimmy Smith, a former baseball player and football commentator who had fallen on hard times and, after being caught smuggling marijuana, was serving a stretch in Wormwood Scrubs. He wrote warning me about what the authorities would do, having spoken to a colleague in the underworld with police connections. I was paranoid enough to burn the letter after reading.

A few days later I had a mysterious phone call from a friend in South Africa.

'Brucester, can you go along to our golf club and pay my fees?'

'My golf club?'

'No, *our* golf club.'

I knew then that it was code for something else, so I drove down there and called him back from one of the payphones.

'What's going on?' I asked.

'Bruce, your phones are being tapped. If you listen when you pick up the phone when someone calls, you'll hear a click.'

The next time someone called me at home, I was first to the handset and I did indeed hear a click. Somebody called again soon after, and again there was a click. A third time, another click.

I surveyed our street and a white van that had previously escaped my notice was parked a little further up. I'd previously assumed it to be a works van of some description, but there were no works going on. The more I thought about it, the more I realised it had been there for a number of days, if not weeks. So I decided to take a look.

I walked along the street and rapped on the rear doors. There was a shuffle inside and I pulled them open. There, inside the van, were two guys and an array of electronic equipment, with headphones on. They were shocked at my discovery of them.

'Hello, fellas,' I said. 'You don't need to be sat out here listening in to my conversations. Why don't you come into my office and you can listen to an extension in the warmth.'

Fifteen minutes later the van was gone. Who they were – journalists, police, private detectives – I'm not sure, but the clicking stopped.

Despite all this intrigue, it was nevertheless a surprise what happened next.

On Monday 13 March 1995 I was preparing for a midweek home match against West Ham. The previous weekend I had rented a little cottage just for the weekend as I had my former teammate, Brian Budd, visiting from Canada. Brian had been with me at Vancouver Whitecaps and was a well-known Canadian sports broadcaster, but was probably most famous as the three-times champion on the TV series *World Superstars*. We'd spent the weekend playing pool and catching up and had been out for an Indian meal on the Sunday. On the Monday morning he was going to travel up by train from Southampton to Glasgow to catch up with Ally McCoist, a good mutual friend of ours.

Brian was an early starter and despite a heavy night on the beers was up at 5 a.m. to go for his daily run. He planned on catching his train an hour or so later and stuck his head around my door to tell me he was off for a jog before his long journey north. He went out, came back, showered and was off by 5:45 a.m.

Fifteen minutes later there was a knock at our door. Tony Milligan went to answer it. I thought perhaps Brian had forgotten something, but from my bed I could hear it was someone else.

'Bruce Grobbelaar, you are arrested. I am reading you your rights. Anything you say can be used as evidence against you in a court of law...'

At the end of it, Tony said, 'Do I look like Bruce Grobbelaar? I'll go and get him.'

Tony came into my room. 'It looks like you're in trouble.'

I put on my dressing gown and went to let the WPC and her colleagues in. She started to read me my rights again.

'Come in,' I said, 'I'll make you some tea.'

She explained that her colleagues were going to search my house. I explained that it wasn't mine, that I was only renting it for the weekend, but she wouldn't listen. I have no idea how they knew where I was or why they did not just go and search my own house.

'I'm sorry, Mr Grobbelaar, we will have to search your residence.'

'It's not my house,' I said. 'I'm just renting it for the weekend, I live up the road. I'll take you there now.'

But they weren't listening and once they'd drunk their tea they wasted four hours searching a place I had only stepped into for the first time 72 hours earlier. After that they took me to the cop shop and charged me and from there it was to the oldest police cell in Britain, in Southampton. Fifty-six hours later they released me, but the wheels were in motion towards a criminal trial.

The arrest had blindsided me. It was not something I had expected. My lawyers and I were making good progress in our libel action against the *Sun* and were putting together a strong case. They had warned me that if the police got any evidence against me there was always the risk of an arrest, but what did they have?

Some recordings of Vincent talking shit and me doing my Inspector Clouseau act? Was this enough for the CPS to build something more than a load of headlines?

Sat in a police cell on my own in Southampton, these thoughts went through my mind. Part of me started to doubt myself. What if I had done something wrong? But as hard as I tried I couldn't possibly imagine what that was, or how my behaviour could be interpreted as such.

When they let me out I realised that those dark thoughts that had briefly permeated my mind could be laid to rest. As well as myself, the Aston Villa and former Wimbledon centre-forward John Fashanu, the Wimbledon goalkeeper Hans Segers, and a Malaysian businessmen, Heng Suan Lim, who I knew as Richard Lim, had been arrested as my co-conspirators. I knew all of them – Segers and Fashanu I had played against many times – but the idea that we were involved in some sort of conspiracy to lose football matches together was beyond the realms of reality.

It was fantastical. Poor old Hans had nothing to do with anything. He was devastated, he was truly distraught. I honestly don't know what the rationale behind his arrest was, other than that he'd played for Wimbledon in a dramatic game at Everton on the last day of the 1993/94 season. Everton had gone into that game needing to better the results of various rivals at the bottom end of the Premier League table to stay up and had ultimately prevailed 3–2. I'm guessing that the police or CPS looked at that match, and thought, 'high-profile game, a huge amount resting on its outcome, a dramatic late win for Everton'. But to do so was like putting two and two together and coming up with twelve. If the game was fixed then why would Wimbledon go into a 2–0 lead? How could Segers have done anything to let in two of the Everton goals, a penalty and a second-half wonder goal by Barry Horne?

The evidence – if you could call it that – was a late bobbling winner from the Everton forward, Graham Stuart, which Segers misjudged and dived over. On *Match of the Day*, even commentator Barry Davies acknowledged, 'Hans Segers, to tell the truth, made a bit of a mess of that.' But I tell you something: to have gotten to that stage in a cauldron of noise and intimidation – the Wimbledon bus had been burnt-out the night before – and succeeded to throw a result would have required a huge and elaborate effort. And if Fashanu was his master co-conspirator, how was he co-ordinating things from his position in the Goodison stands, as he wasn't playing?

Fashanu and I were the two most prominent African footballers in England at the time. Although he was born in London and had played twice for England in the late 1980s, he identified as a Nigerian, the country of his father's birth, and expressed regret at having not chosen to represent the Super Eagles instead of England. His wife Melissa was of West African aristocracy and through her family and his own prominence he had become an influential figure in that part of the world. We had got together on a few occasions, once to discuss a charity football match to benefit the families of the Zambia national team, which had been wiped out in a plane crash in 1993. On another occasion we had discussed helping bring African footballers to play in Europe. Investment in Mondoro had also been briefly discussed but had never come to anything because Vincent had never produced a business plan.

Richard Lim was a young businessman, who was well connected among the elites of Malaysia. 'Dato' is the honorific title given to such people. I was first introduced to him because he was well connected with clothing manufacturers in the Far East and getting kit for the Zimbabwe national team was always a challenge. ZIFA never had any money and this was a time before sportswear manufacturers saw the benefit of endorsement deals with smaller footballing nations. Remember too that the world was a much bigger place in the early 1990s. Now if you wanted to find a clothes manufacturer you'd just go online. Then you'd have to know someone who could act as an intermediary or make an introduction. Richard had those connections. He was someone who could help.

Richard would also occasionally pay for tips on football. I had a similar arrangement with the Norwegian newspaper *Dagbladet* and I was always very clear that I couldn't ever do this for my own club as FA rules on betting – as limited as they were at the time – forbade it. Again, you have to view this through the context of the time. Now, in the internet age, a plethora of information is available, not just in terms of team news, but data, statistics and form. Back then, particularly if you were outside the UK, there was very limited information for followers of football. Rightly or wrongly, I viewed this work as a form of punditry. If people happened to bet on it, then so be it. Besides the Grand National or when I play golf with my mates I'm not a gambler and take no interest in it.

As players we had very limited knowledge of how football in some countries was undermined by match-fixing. Typically it is done through a mixture of blackmail and coercion, where fixers prey on underpaid – or unpaid – and vulnerable players. I didn't know this world existed, and it certainly wasn't like that in England. In Richard's home country of Malaysia, this unfortunately was – and still is – the case, but I had little true understanding of it then, even if I did play a couple of exhibition matches there in the summer of 1994.

With *Dagbladet* I had a regular deal to provide tips. With Richard it was infrequent, three or four times. Should I have done it? There was nothing proscribing it at the time. Maybe I was naïve but I didn't see anything wrong with it then. Viewed now, in an age when the rules have changed to such an extent that footballers can no longer bet and someone like Joey Barton has seen his playing career ended because of it, of course I wouldn't have done it. Things have moved so far the other way these days, that if I'm working for Liverpool in pre-match hospitality I can't place a bet even if I wanted to.

When the police presented this case that I was part of some sort of wide-ranging criminal conspiracy with Richard, John and Hans I simply couldn't believe it. It was fantastical. The connections between us were so loose and disparate that even in the furthest reaches of my imagination I couldn't understand how they would or could construct a case against us. Sat in a police cell for such a long period of time, lots inevitably goes through your mind. But working out how they joined the dots together on this case was simply beyond me.

29

The Relief

FOR THE REST OF THE 1994/95 SEASON I HAD THIS POLICE investigation hanging over me. Southampton finished the season tenth. We'd drawn a lot of games, but it was a solid campaign in which I'd played thirty times – despite everything that had gone on and the injury to my cheekbone – and we finished ahead of the likes of Arsenal, Chelsea and Everton.

A lot of my time at Southampton was played against the backdrop of the growing media furore about the match-fixing accusations made against me. The club were great. They were unwavering in their support. Alan Ball believed me from the outset and my place in the first team was never under serious question. I sustained a nasty cheekbone injury and wore a mask to protect myself and still he played me. And why not? Southampton were enjoying their best season in a decade and I was playing my part in this renaissance.

Teammates in Britain are pretty harsh when it comes to taking the mickey. And yes, some of them took the mickey, as you'd expect. Iain Dowie, for example, stuck a wad of Monopoly money underneath my towel. He was trying to break the ice, though I did get a sense some of them thought I was guilty. One person that trusted me was Ken Monkou. He was very supportive. We'd drive to training together each day.

Matt Le Tissier and myself used to go training, and just to warm me up he used to fire shots at me. Le Tissier was the sort of player that could actually hit the ball anywhere he wanted to. On one occasion there were some photographers hiding in the bushes and you could see them. So he shouted to me and said, 'Bruce! Just listen.' He whacked this ball – crack! – against the camera. Ow! I ran around the goal and there was this bruised photographer in the bushes with a bashed-up camera, complaining and moaning about Le Tissier.

'Well, you shouldn't be there, should you?' I told him, barely able to contain my laughter. 'That's trespassing.'

Despite the uncertainty that came from the court case there were happy memories, good memories from this period. I had a flat in Lymington, down on the coast by the Solent, and it was by a marina. The fishing boats used to come to the dockside and there was a pub right underneath me; I was on the first floor. So I had a bucket with a rope and I used to drop the bucket and say to the barmaid, 'Two pints of lager, please,' and put the money in the bucket. And I used to pull it up and we would sit there watching the sun go down. That was a happy time. We eventually sold the house on the Wirral and had the family home in Sussex, which is my girls' family home now, just outside of Rudgwick, West Sussex, on the Surrey border. Bramley was the nearest big town. We had good times there as well, too.

We lost just twelve of our 42 games in the 1994/95 season. We drew too many matches and conceded too many goals, but we scored plenty too. Under Ball's guidance Le Tissier had emerged as one of the most exciting players in the Premier League. Since Alan's arrival he had scored 45 times in 64 games, but it wasn't just the number of goals he scored, it was the sheer variety; he could hit them from anywhere, including, on one occasion, directly from a corner.

And yet, despite this tangible progress, there was a sense that Southampton were a club that did things on the cheap. Alan had been hired from Exeter City rather than from another Premier League club and his managerial salary was correspondingly low – the lowest for a top-flight manager by some distance. Most other clubs would have rewarded him with a new contract for the inroads he'd made, but that wasn't the way at The Dell. Instead, when Manchester City made an approach Alan was allowed to hold talks about their managerial vacancy.

Much to my disappointment he accepted this position and Southampton pocketed a tidy compensation fee. There was no foresight. It was penny-pinching at its worst.

THE WORST THING ABOUT THE STILL-UNRESOLVED QUESTIONS against me was the effect on my family. You deal with any crisis you are posed with in life the best you can. There is no other way. You cannot just fold up and hope it goes away. But to see my children suffer at school, the strain Debbie was under and the effect it had on her parents was hard to take. I had a release in football, but Debbie – who was remarkably strong throughout – had no such escape. I tried as far as possible to hide Tahli and Olivia from what was happening, but it was impossible to avoid that sort of scrutiny. It hurt them more than it hurt me. They hated to hear people bad-mouthing their father.

At the start of July, shortly after the start of pre-season training, I had to report to a police station, as did Fashanu, Segers and Lim. No charges were brought. In the meantime my libel case against the *Sun* progressed and around the same time we served our formal reply to its defence.

And then, quite unexpectedly, three weeks after having left a police station without a charge, on Monday 24 July 1995 the four of us were called back and, along with Fashanu's wife, jointly charged with conspiracy and corruption. There had been no further questions, no follow-ups, just these charges. I was old and wise enough to expect anything at this stage – even the insanity of these allegations going all the way to a criminal court. The knowledge of the truth made me calm. I was also lucky that I was playing football at this time and that my anger came out on the football pitch.

But to my family it was a huge shock. Debbie was devastated. Until then she had believed absolutely in my innocence, but suddenly this cast some doubt in her mind.

IN ALAN BALL'S PLACE AT SOUTHAMPTON CAME DAVE MERRINGTON, who was appointed from within the club's own ranks. He was popular with the fans – many of whom were aghast at Ball's departure – but he was a cheap option as well. He did not have the profile of Alan Ball – a tremendous World Cup-winning footballer. Dave's career began and pretty much ended at Burnley in the early 1970s where he'd played fewer than a hundred league games. He'd moved around as a coach but management is a bit different and following the progression made under Alan Ball, we slipped backwards the next season.

Merrington wasn't given much money to strengthen the team and basically had to work with the players that he'd inherited. One of the most significant changes he made was to replace me in the team with Dave Beasant.

The 1995/96 season was a real slog and I could only watch on from the bench as we laboured around the bottom end of the Premier League. Le Tissier's goalscoring touch eluded him and he managed just seven all campaign. By Christmas we had recorded only four victories; between late November and late March we won just once . Relegation became a real possibility.

In the end Merrington briefly reinstated me to the team and we went on something of a run, winning three of our last six games, drawing another one. We beat the champions-elect Manchester United in the famous game where Alex Ferguson demanded they be allowed to change their shirts at half-time, because – he said – the players could not see each other in their grey away shirts. We still won that one, 3-1. Eventually it was all enough – just about – to stay up on goal difference. In all we'd won just nine games all season and earned only 38 points.

Ironically, we stayed up at the expense of Ball's Manchester City team. Going into the last game of the season we needed to match or better City's result against Liverpool when we faced Wimbledon at The Dell. Neither Wimbledon nor Liverpool – who had an FA Cup final against Manchester United the following week – had anything to play for, but it was a tense day. We got word at half-time that Liverpool had taken a 2-0 lead, while we were drawing 0-0, but it was still tight. Then came news that City had pulled it back to 2-2. We were still staying up, but a goal against us, or another City goal, would send us down. What do you do in a situation like that? Stick or twist? Panic was setting in. I don't think Dave Merrington really knew what to do. In the end we were saved by false rumours that swirled around Maine Road that we'd fallen behind. Thinking that it would mean they'd stay up, Ball told his players to keep the ball in the corners to waste time and see the clock down. Fortunately for us, our game ended in a draw and City's attacking impetus and – ultimately – top-flight status died.

Southampton were saved, but it wasn't enough for Merrington, who was fired.

Despite the disappointing campaign, I was happy at Southampton and wanted to exercise my option for a third season, which would have taken me up almost until my fortieth birthday. The club had been loyal to me and, despite struggles on and off the field, I liked living on the south coast. But when Merrington's successor was named I knew that wasn't to be an option. The man who was to replace him was Graeme Souness.

Graeme was succinct and to the point when I met him to discuss my contract.

'I'd like to exercise my option for a third year,' I told him.

'We'd like to exercise *our* option to release you,' he told me.

And so, I was on the lookout for a new club again.

30

Hinterlands

THE ONGOING COURT CASE AND WHAT WERE STILL UNRESOLVED allegations against me had certainly affected my reputation in football. Besides the jibes of fans, I'd found former friends and teammates reticent to be associated with me – at least until I'd cleared my name. The belief that there is no smoke without fire permeated the game.

This became even clearer to me when I searched for a new club over the summer of 1996. I knew, even at the age of nearly 39, that I could still do a job at the highest level or at a big club. And yet, as I went on my holidays to Zimbabwe the phone remained mostly silent. The bigger clubs clearly didn't want to take the risk of being associated with someone who had these allegations hanging over them and who *might* face jail time. I could understand that attitude because football is a conservative game and, faced with controversy, the natural inclination of people is to sit on the fence. That's just the way it is and I considered it their loss.

There was a call from Neil Warnock, the manager of Second Division Plymouth Argyle. Life in the third tier of English football didn't really appeal – I still thought I was capable of playing higher up – and despite Neil's implorations that I was the only keeper for Home Park I was non-commital. He knew my pedigree; he knew what I was about and he was dogged in his pursuit of me. I was initially undecided and told him I'd think about it while I was away.

As I was nearing the end of our family holiday in Zimbabwe, all of a sudden and completely out of the blue I got a phone call from Alan Ball.

'Bruce, I need a new goalkeeper,' he told me. 'I've got this German – Eike Immel – and he can't catch flies in a sugar bowl. He can't catch anything because he punches everything that comes at him. So can you come to Manchester City?'

I was delighted. Although City had dropped down a level they were still a huge club with great fans. I'd be back in the north-west, where we'd lived for so many years, and working with Alan for a third time.

'Can you get to Manchester by tomorrow, ten o'clock?'

I jumped on the next plane out of Zimbabwe and got to Gatwick Airport at six the next morning, then caught a flight that got me to Manchester at half-nine.

Alan was waiting for me, but the news wasn't good.

'You've been blackballed,' he told me.

'I've been what?' I asked.

'Someone on the board has said no. I'm sorry. They're not allowing me to sign you.'

Ball left and I was alone in Manchester Airport, still without a club, having flown overnight across the world in the expectation that I'd find one. And I was thinking, *What the bloody hell am I going to do now?*

So I phoned Neil Warnock, the only person who'd come for me in the first place.

'Neil, do you still want a goalkeeper?' I asked.

'Yes! Please get to Bristol by two o'clock because we've got to sign this and get it through to the FA by three o'clock.'

'No problem.' I hired a car there and then, drove straight down to Bristol and we signed the papers immediately and sent them through to the FA. By late afternoon I was a Plymouth Argyle player.

'You're now Plymouth Argyle's new player,' Neil told me. 'You're coming through to Plymouth with me today, I'm going to put you up in my home, you get some sleep, and we've got a game tomorrow. Pre-season. Have you got boots?'

'Don't worry, I've got my boots,' I told him.

What he didn't tell me then was who Plymouth's opponents were the next day: Manchester City in a friendly. Not only that, but we beat them 1–0.

After the game I went through to the directors' lounge, walked straight up to Alan Ball and shook his hand, saying, 'Alan Ball, that's for you not signing me yesterday.'

Then I turned to the City director Steve Boler. If you recall, Boler had wanted to put £6 million of his own money into Mondoro a few years earlier, but I had stopped the cheque going in because I knew that Chris Vincent was going to take all that money. Despite that good turn, Boler hadn't felt able to put his name to my signing at City; the association with the ongoing court case was apparently too reputationally damaging to the club. 'That's for you,' I said, pointing outside to the scoreboard. It was the best feeling, having my football do the talking – even if it was only a friendly.

My time at Plymouth was enjoyable. The commute was a bit of a stretch – it was three hours from Surrey to Devon – but my friend Harry Weir, who I'd lived with years earlier when I was in Durban, was now living in Torquay, which is just up the road, and I would stop with him and his wife Anita. Mondays and Tuesdays Neil Warnock would let me stay at home. It was four days on, three days off.

Warnock was a fine manager to work for. Players that play for him tend to like him. Those up against him tend not to like him. That's the way he is. I think he's one of the best managers outside of the top flight and that history has been unkind to him. He's achieved eight promotions in his career but for whatever reason whenever he's reached the Premier League, chairman have sacked him. My view: he's often taken clubs that have no right to be competing in the Premier League in the first place into the promised land. Maybe the jump has been too big for the club more than it has been for Mr Warnock.

Back at Plymouth all those years ago, things weren't going so well on the pitch and after a run of four league wins in five months the chairman, Dan McCauley, fired Warnock and appointed his long-term assistant, Mick Jones, in his place at the start of February.

We would finish the season nineteenth, but were never seriously under threat of relegation. The most notable moment of an otherwise forgettable season was the so-called Battle of Saltergate, when we faced Chesterfield at their home ground. Despite having Ronnie Mauge dismissed in the first half for a high, two-footed tackle, we were leading 2–1 with minutes to go when Chesterfield's Darren Carr, challenging for a cross, caught me with his elbow. While I was flat out, down on the ground, a complete melee broke out involving all nineteen outfield players. There was boxing all around me. When order was restored four players – Chesterfield's Carr and Kevin Davies and Plymouth's Tony James and Richard Logan – were sent off, a record for the Football League. The referee lost control and proceeded to book just about everyone else, including myself – and I was the victim! I was suffering with concussion and played out a dazed final two minutes in front of a makeshift 3–3–1 line-up.

31

Football's Trial of the Century?

THE FIVE OF US HAD TO WAIT FOR A FURTHER EIGHTEEN MONTHS before our trial was finally heard. It was January 1997, 26 months after the *Sun's* initial allegations, but a lifetime in football. My top-flight career had come to an end. Hans Segers had also seen his career in the Premier League finish, while John Fashanu had retired from the game altogether.

I think the fact that I was now at Plymouth rather than still in the top flight or further up the league ladder was reflective of the stigma now attached to my name. Bigger clubs didn't want to take a chance on me in case the allegations might have turned out to be true. I get it: if I was the owner of a team with a player I liked having that hanging over them, I might be reluctant to take them on. It was their loss in the beginning. I could have gone to Manchester City, but I didn't because I was blackballed by the chairman. I went to Plymouth because Neil Warnock was dogged enough to see down such resistance from the boardroom. I went with Neil to Oldham and Bury later on because he could see my qualities as a footballer and as a person. He saw a winner.

The case should never have gone to court. It was lunacy. There was no evidence other than the honeytrap put together by the *Sun* and their conman acolyte, Chris Vincent. Virtually everything hung on the veracity of his evidence, but even the prosecution couldn't hide their distaste.

'Most, if not all of you, will have little sympathy for Mr Vincent,' said the Crown's QC, David Calvert-Smith, in his opening remarks. 'His decision to expose Mr Grobbelaar was the result of a business quarrel, not a desire to prevent corruption. His decision to expose Mr Grobbelaar through the *Sun*, rather than going to a police station, was the result of a desire to enrich himself and no doubt he hopes to be paid more.'

Vincent, said Calvert-Smith, had done 'nothing' to stop the so-called corruption I was accused of and was 'happy to benefit from its proceeds'. Moreover, Vincent had also 'recently been charged with a serious offence' himself. This is yet another reason to ask yourselves, he said, 'before we accept what this witness says, we have to look at it very carefully'.

This came from the prosecution!

Later, the judge would describe Vincent as 'a thoroughly dishonest conman.' But the reputation of the Crown's star witness was even at this stage shot to pieces. He had been declared bankrupt on 21 March 1995 with debts of £98,820.97, but worse was to follow. In September 1996, as we awaited trial, Vincent had approached John Fashanu, asking for £500,000. In return he would not give evidence in the forthcoming trial but would go, in his words, 'where Jesus couldn't find me'. Fashanu's representative, who fielded the call, had the common sense to record the approach and go straight to the police. At a second meeting a few days later Vincent asked for £300,000 within earshot of a police officer. He was charged with attempting to pervert the course of justice and remanded in custody in Winchester Prison. The irony of this whole sorry saga was that the man who had invented the whole affair – the 'whistleblower' – would be the only one to spend any time in prison.

I had only been in a courtroom once before, when I was twelve years old and accused of stealing stuff out of a shop. It's not nice to be accused of anything in such an environment, even if you are adamant about your own innocence. Little could I have known then that over the next five years it would become a home from home of sorts.

The *Sun* dubbed the case the 'trial of the century' and was in no doubt that the Crown would get a conviction. I knew I was innocent, but it wasn't me who needed convincing – rather the twelve men and women of the jury. However, having seen my own defence demolish the *Sun's* lawyers in the libel case – which was now adjourned pending the outcome of the criminal trial – I had no doubt that we had a very good chance.

The two strands of the Crown's case could be summarised as follows. They had evidence of large sums of money being transferred from the Far East to unrelated bank accounts controlled by John Fashanu and Richard Lim. They also had the dossier of taped evidence relating to the *Sun's* entrapment of me. What the prosecution had to do was join up the dots and show that the Far East money was used for the purposes of match-fixing. Yet the transfers paid to Lim and Fashanu had nothing to do with me; and nothing as far as anyone could tell to do with football. Both men had significant business interests of their own which these monies probably related to. The only cash that I'd received from either man was for a handful of betting tips I'd naïvely given Lim.

In the absence of hard evidence of a criminal conspiracy the prosecution had two strategies they used. One was an emotional argument – that we had 'defiled' English football and 'betrayed' generations of children who lionised us as heroes. This was spurious because we were all innocent. The other was the 'evidence' from Vincent, whom the prosecution had described from the outset as someone with whom the jury should have 'little sympathy' and who had tried to 'enrich himself' by bringing me down. It was all just so absurd that it had got that far.

In fact, in their case against the other three men, the prosecution acknowledged that 'We don't have a Vincent figure'. They had payments, telephone records and matches that Wimbledon had lost but nothing else. 'Can you draw the inference that the money, the telephone calls and the matches are linked?' the prosecuting barrister asked the jury.

It didn't take long for the other defendants' barristers to dismantle their arguments. Ron Atkinson, Fashanu's manager at Aston Villa, appeared as a character witness and spoke glowingly of the player, as he did me. The only other witness to a cash payment Fashanu had supposedly given me utterly rejected any possibility of such a transaction taking place. Fashanu and Lim's business interests and overseas partners were explained to the court, likewise Fashanu's business relationship with Segers. These included investment in airport duty-free stores, the renovation and resale of repossessed properties and trading in used cars. There was also the forecasting of football matches, but other than possibly contravening FA rules there was nothing untoward in what they had done. Nor could the prosecution demonstrate that there was.

Then they turned to me. They questioned me about my links to John Fashanu and Richard Lim, which I've already outlined, and then Chris Vincent. The whole sorry Mondoro affair was raked over again and then it came to the events of autumn 1994.

'He came out with a blinder, as I say. He said he had met some people at Chester

Races that liked to bet on sure-fire runners, and he wanted to know if I was interested in throwing games for them,' I told the court of that first fateful meeting after we had returned from Zimbabwe. 'It was the first time I'd ever heard it mentioned. I said, "You must be daft. Nobody could throw a game. No one person."'

What followed was rather harder to explain. We met subsequently in Southampton and Vincent had told me he could get my money back if I was interested in throwing games. How to explain my Inspector Clouseau routine? I told the court: 'I thought I'd go along with it and see what his reaction would be, let him talk, let me find out what I can. He said, "Aah, I'm sure you must have tried to throw games." I thought, why not agree? He mentioned the Newcastle game. I said I might have.'

I was honest about my own stupidity to the court. I couldn't say anything else except the truth, no matter how unlikely it might have seemed to the jury. 'I tried to gain his confidence,' I said. This was true, but it was hard to rationalise. Ultimately my plan to entrap him didn't work; his did.

The prosecution played video tapes of parts of the games in question to try and show my guilt. In the Manchester United game, about which I'd bluffed about losing £125,000, they showed footage of me looking downhearted at the end.

'Is that the face of a man who has just lost a lot of money, Mr Grobbelaar?' the prosecution barrister asked.

'That's the face of a man who has let in three goals against one of their biggest rivals,' I replied.

A lot of the prosecution's so-called evidence was phone records. Who had phoned who and when. The reality was that the calls could have been and often were about anything and the prosecution were trying to draw inferences based on their timings around games. They had no idea what the calls were about and I usually couldn't remember – they were, after all, three or four years old – although I'm sure about one thing: they weren't and never were about match-fixing.

There were, nevertheless, moments that I'm sure raised a few eyebrows. There was the revelation, for example, that I kept £25,000 in my sock drawer, which to a lot of people was an improbable amount of money. But football at the time was a cash business. I had the cash because when you go out to Africa you have to pay cash and are yourself paid in cash. You speak at a dinner, you are paid in cash. My deals with football boot and glove manufacturers were always given to me half by cash, half by cheque; that's just the way things were done in those days.

So money accumulated over months and years. My sock drawer was very deep! That's just the way the game worked then.

I also had a long and deeply held belief that you need to keep cash in case of an emergency, a habit that dated back to my youth. My first girlfriend's father owned Foyers Hotel, where I sometimes did shifts, and he gave me some very good advice: 'Don't trust the banks.' When I would come as a barman to cash up he'd direct me to a secret vault hidden behind a false bookcase. He'd learned himself the hard way when a bank had collapsed and he had lost everything and was forced to start up again. So, wherever I was and wherever I am, I always keep a supply of cash in case the unpredictable happens.

People in the game came forward to help me too. Alan Hansen and Bob Wilson, two of the most prominent TV experts at the time, appeared as witnesses on my behalf. While Jocky Hansen had been my captain, and I knew Bob Wilson's daughter – I had done charity events with her – I didn't know Bob. He was an invaluable witness, expertly analysing every goal or incident that was called into question, and explaining why bad defending or outstanding forward play had left me with little or no chance of making a save. Alan Ball and Gordon Banks spoke in my defence too. Alan I had played with and under – he described me as 'a model professional who never gave me an ounce of trouble' – and I had trained with Gordon at Stoke City when I was a Crewe player. The support of two World Cup winners added credibility and immediately cut above the innuendo and mud-slinging.

Credibility was what it boiled down to. Who to believe? Me and my admittedly far-fetched plot to draw in Vincent, or the prosecution and their messy and disparate case that relied heavily on coincidence, emotional argument and the testimony of a man who had no standing. The prosecution were under no illusions about Vincent. 'Almost every uncomplimentary adjective under the sun has been used to describe him,' the prosecution QC said when summing up to the jury. 'Your task is to look at his evidence and decide whether or not it is safe to convict upon it.'

The jury went to consider their verdict on the morning of Monday 28 February 1997. We were called back at 3:50 that afternoon. I stood to attention alongside the four other defendants – to learn that the jury needed more time to study the secret videos.

We were called back again at 2:15 the following afternoon. Again, we were told, that the jury was still deliberating. This was agonising, but I had faith that they would do the right thing.

At 4 p.m. on Tuesday we were called back again. The jury had failed to reach a verdict and, the foreman added, there was no chance to reach an agreement. After weeks of hearings and years of preparations we would have to come back in a few months' time and have a new jury hear our case.

WHEN WE REASSEMBLED FOR THE RETRIAL IN WINCHESTER AT THE start of June 1997, the newspapers and the TV people drew analogies with a cup replay. Except in a replay tactics and line-ups differ and the tempo changes and an outcome; you wouldn't expect a replay to be the same kick by kick, tackle by tackle – for that is essentially what played out in Winchester Crown Court. It was more like a film showing to a different cinema audience.

That said, a few things differed. Media interest wasn't quite so intense this time. There were fewer journalists and public interest seemed to have diminished. That didn't stop some members of the jury from the first trial showing up in Winchester in order to lend me and the others their support, before being swiftly dispatched by the police as their presence was inappropriate. I had no knowledge of it at the time, but maybe it showed that some of them saw the first result as a travesty of justice and that the case should never have reached in court in the first place, never mind for a second time.

There was a slight change in attack by the prosecution too. This time they said they weren't going to attempt to prove I deliberately tried letting a goal in, which was an unusual tactic. 'You allege that he accepted money to throw matches, but you are not actually alleging that he actually threw a match,' pondered the judge. 'If one makes a corrupt agreement, how can one do that unless one intends to throw a match?'

The judge nitpicked his way through the trial, spotting gap after gap in the prosecution's case. 'What is your allegation? What are you saying? What is your case?' he asked the prosecution counsel after one particularly tortuously put-together point. It might as well have been the motto for the entire case.

Either way, the judge had a way of cutting through the absurdity of what we faced that probably worked in our favour. He also had a way of giving the case its proper perspective. 'No one has been killed, no one injured, no one raped or assaulted,' he said when summing up. 'No child has been violated and no one has been robbed. Nevertheless, the charges are serious, both for the defendants and for the honour and reputation of English football.'

He also had no time for Vincent and made that clear to the jury. 'You must be very careful indeed with Vincent,' he told them. 'If ever there was a man to distrust you may think it was him. You should think long and hard before accepting a word he says unless it is supported by someone else. You should consider the case without placing any reliance at all on anything Vincent has said, where that stands alone. People like that have only themselves to blame if their defence is disregarded.'

In total the judge spent three days summing up. The retrial had gone on for 42 days. When the jury were sent to deliberate we expected a quick verdict. The jury were sent out on Friday afternoon and we knew a verdict was unlikely before the weekend. Monday came and went, so did Tuesday. Then Wednesday.

On Thursday came a development. The jury had been poring over the tape in the hotel room in which I'd walked off with the £2,000 in cash (which had then been deposited in the car's glove compartment). It turned out that the transcript had been mistranscribed. A jury member had pointed out that it was I who had refused to take the money. According to their analysis the transcript went like this and not the other way around:

> Vincent: *'Do you want to carry this [the envelope containing money]?'*
> Me: *'No, no, no… that's yours.'*
> Vincent: *'I don't have a jacket – you carry it.'*

That was, of course, my recollection. The judge summoned me to his chambers and I put him right. The point of deliberation was surely critical to the case. Had they known this at the time it would surely never have gone to trial. How it had been overlooked in the years of scrutiny that had followed I'm not sure. But it had. When it was put to the prosecution that there had been a misinterpretation they had come back and said that the juror was 'very probably' correct.

Finally, on the Thursday afternoon, a week since they'd been dispatched, the jury returned their verdicts. They had deliberated for 26 hours and 20 minutes.

The foreman rose and the judge asked if the jury had reached a verdict in the case of Richard Lim on Count One. They had, and it was unanimous – not guilty.

Next was John Fashanu: not guilty.

Then Hans Segers: not guilty.

Count Two: Had the jury reached a verdict on Richard Lim? They had, unanimously. Not guilty.

John Fashanu? Not guilty.

And then it was my turn. I stood upright, trying not to betray any hint of nerves. And then I heard the words 'Not guilty' and breathed a huge sigh of relief.

Yet my ordeal still wasn't over for I still had one more count against me.

The jury foreman rose, and announced the verdict... No decision yet.

The other three were discharged and went to enjoy their freedom, while I was led back down to the cells. I wasn't really locked up, but I was kept away from anyone else and not permitted outside the court. Debbie had to bring me food and sustenance from outside.

We returned to court the next morning and went over the formalities before the judge again dispatched the jury and I was sent back to the cells. My only recollection of that day – Friday 8 August 1997 – was Debbie bringing me and my defence team a Chinese takeaway at lunchtime. Was this the last supper? Shortly after the lunchbreak ended I was asked to return to the dock.

'How do you find?' the judge asked the foreman of the jury. I stood bolt upright, impassive.

'Hung jury.'

After that he turned to them and said, 'After seeing what has been presented to you and you not grasping the whole situation I can only say, Bruce Grobbelaar, you are free to go.'

32

Journeyman

AT THE END OF THE 1996/97 SEASON MY CONTRACT AT HOME PARK wasn't renewed and I found myself clubless again, although not for long. Oxford United, who were a level above Plymouth in the Football League First Division, came in for me, and I gladly signed with their manager Denis Smith. I'd barely agreed the deal when a phone call came in from my agent. There had been another offer – this one from the Premier League. Sheffield Wednesday wanted me as back-up for their goalkeeper Kevin Pressman.

It wasn't an offer I was going to turn down, but – even though I'd arrived on a free transfer – there was the complication of the contract I'd just signed.

'Don't worry,' said my agent, 'I'll fix it.'

He called up the Wednesday manager David Pleat and told him that the fee was £30,000. For a Premier League club that was small change, but we all did nicely out of my week's stay at the Manor Ground. I got £10,000, my agent got £10,000 and Oxford got the other ten grand.

I was eight months at Sheffield Wednesday and didn't play a single first-team game, but it was a very important time for me. Being at Hillsborough and part of that club enabled me to get rid of the demons that I had faced ever since the dreadful tragedy there in 1989. We trained just behind the stadium, so had to walk past Leppings Lane to reach some training fields at the back. We did the walk quite often, which was good for me. At first it was very hard, but you slowly get used to seeing and feeling, and just remembering. And then when the games were played, you looked over and it was totally different because they had taken the high fences away. Over time I got rid of my fears of that place, while training and playing for Sheffield Wednesday.

Big changes were afoot at Hillsborough and my contract was not going to be renewed at the end of the 1997/98 season. I'd already taken my leave by then and joined Oldham on a short-term deal towards the end of the campaign. I was reunited with Neil Warnock but it was a short-lived stay for both of us; I played four times but Neil and I left after failing to reach the Division Two play-offs. Oldham were good enough to play a level higher, but I'd arrived too late in the campaign to effect any change.

The next season – 1998/99 – I was nearing my 41st birthday and was now firmly cast in the role of a football nomad, a time of weekly contracts and upheaval. I always wanted to play and was never afraid to work, so I was fine with all of that. At the start of the season I played some games for Chesham United in the Isthmian League. They were managed by the former Spurs and Rangers defender Graham Roberts and although it was a long way from the Premier League, crowds were usually up into four figures. But when Neil Warnock came calling again I couldn't resist.

This time we met up at Bury, who were then in the First Division, and I found myself as cover for Dean Kiely and alongside a young Paddy Kenny. Bury was a surprisingly rough place. It is near to Manchester and so I found the town centre off-limits at night time. The supporters only seemed to be interested in turning up to fight rather than lend their support. My friend Neville Southall had encountered something similar when he'd played there at the start of his career in the early 1980s; then the supporters had jeered him from behind the goal because he'd supplanted a crowd favourite. It showed how much they knew, because he'd go on to be one of the best goalkeepers in the world a few years later.

I played one game, a narrow defeat at Birmingham City in September. I joined Lincoln City in December on a one-month deal. I played twice: a 0-0 draw versus Colchester United and a 4-1 defeat to Wycombe Wanderers. That was my 867th and last professional appearance in English football, though a year or so later I signed week's contract with semi-professional Northwich Victoria from the Conference and played in an FA Cup final qualifying round match against Hednesford Town, a 2-2 draw

Whatever the level I played at I went out to win. I was philosophical about playing for Bury and Lincoln and Chesham and everywhere else at the end of my career, because although I'd known such great heights, I'd never forgotten the humble circumstances in which I'd started my playing career in South Africa. It didn't bother me if I was playing in front of 100,000 people for Liverpool or one man and his dog for Chesham, I always took great professional pride in pulling on whatever shirt I was contracted to wear and my motivation always remained the same: to win.

33

Groundhog Day

JULY 1999. GROUNDHOG DAY. THE CASE WAS TO BE HEARD ALL OVER again – this time as I sought reparations from the *Sun* newspaper. The libel case that I had instigated nearly five years earlier had finally come to court.

The *Sun* had the legendary QC George Carman representing them but, as entertaining as he probably was to the judge and the handful of journalists still following the case, he was always up against it. Two courts had already found there was no case for me to answer. Chris Vincent had been shown repeatedly to be utterly unreliable, a liar. Tellingly, Carman never called on him as a witness. He was, said Carman, 'a wholly unreliable witness'. He nevertheless used the secret tapes Vincent had made in his case against me.

'Was it not the case that the "real" Bruce Grobbelaar was to be heard on those tapes?' he pondered at one stage.

'The real Bruce Grobbelaar is not on that tape,' I replied. 'He's right here.'

The jury found in my favour and awarded me £85,000 damages. Not that I got to see any of that money, for the *Sun* immediately appealed the verdict.

That meant another court case, another eighteen months' wait. It felt at times that I lived in limbo, that no matter what happened I couldn't have my name cleared. I was now living in South Africa, coaching and managing, but still this great pall hung over me.

Then, on 18 January 2001, the Appeal Court verdict came through. Quite unbelievably it found in favour of the *Sun*. I was staggered. This had been Carman's final case before his death a fortnight before the verdict was published and I have no idea what dark magic he cast on the Law Lords, but Lords Justice Brown and

Parker dismissed my version of events. Lord Justice Jonathan Parker said that the jury's verdict was a 'miscarriage of justice'. Lord Justice Simon Brown – who was years later censured for plagiarism and 'thoroughly bad practice' in relation to one of his cases – said that it had been an 'affront to justice'. It was a devastating moment.

In legal terms it was an historic moment too: never before in legal history had a libel verdict been quashed by the appeal court. This, decreed legal experts, was 'amazing' – particularly when the victim was a tabloid newspaper. The veteran libel lawyer Peter Carter-Ruck described the verdict as 'astonishing'. 'In my experience, which goes back sixty years, I've never known a case where this has happened,' he said.

I found it astounding that having proved my innocence in three separate courtrooms that the Appeal Court could overthrow those decisions. Not only did it leave me facing financial ruin, as I was now liable for £1.5 million in costs, but my reputation was trashed once again.

The *Sun* could barely contain its delight. Its staff bragged how they were going to take my family home off me. On its front page it ran the headline: 'Crook, Cheat, Liar, Traitor'.

THERE WAS ONE MORE AVENUE AVAILABLE TO ME. THE HOUSE OF Lords could overturn the Appeal Court verdict. My legal team were in no doubt that we had a very strong case. And so they filed our papers and we waited.

Finally, in October 2002 – eight years after the initial sting, and more than three years since my libel victory – the verdict came through. They quashed the Appeal Court's verdict. My name was finally cleared.

Yet in financial terms it was a Pyrrhic victory. My Clouseau act had come back to haunt me. Although my reputation had previously been 'unblemished' and there was no question that I had been defamed and libelled, the judges claimed I had acted in a way on those tapes 'in a way in which no decent or honest footballer would act'. Given that behaviour – and I should be clear that they didn't say I'd done anything wrong – it would be an 'affront to justice' if they made the *Sun* pay me damages. As such they reduced my award to a 'derisory amount': £1. To award me anything else, they said, 'would be an affront to sport, public justice and public policy'.

The reaction of the judge was deeply disappointing, but I was phlegmatic about the award. The £85,000 I'd never seen anyway. It would have been nice because I could have taken my girls on holiday, and what can you do with a pound? I couldn't even buy myself a beer with it.

Because I was still liable for all the legal costs, I went into bankruptcy to protect myself, my family and the assets I had left. I did not know how much the legal costs would take from me. Reputationally bankruptcy is a horrible thing, whether you're a famous footballer or not. It affects the way people think about you.

Being a footballer, you are well paid. You have lots of disposable income. It supported a great lifestyle. I travelled a lot. I had nice clothes and enjoyed luxuries. But I was always well grounded; I knew where I'd come from and what I'd started with, which was nothing. I never forgot that back at the start of my careeer I'd scraped together enough to be able to play for Durban City and lived in a room in a friend's garden while sending money back for a baby that wasn't my own. I'd lived life the hard way, as well as very nicely. Had I not then things may have ultimately been much harder for me.

I'm glad that I did it because at the end it saved a lot. It saved my family but not myself. My marriage with Debbie finally collapsed and she was left with everything – all my assets had been signed over to her. Life gets a bit tetchy, but you move on. Life throws you many curves, but you've got to adapt or you die.

AFTER THE CHAOS HAD SUBSIDED I HEARD BITS AND PIECES ABOUT Chris Vincent from time to time. Although he never stood trial in the end for perverting the course of justice, he didn't seem to have changed much. There was the time he was kicked out of Kenya having been arrested for absconding from a hotel where he'd racked up a $10,000 bill. A Hollywood film studio was supposed to be interested in making a film about what had happened – with Mel Gibson playing Vincent! – but like so much else, this was fantasy. He appeared in a TV documentary about people who had lost all their wealth, which was ironic because he didn't have a fortune of his own to lose – just mine.

I encountered Vincent just once in all these years. It was a brief, tense encounter in the corridors of the High Court where we unexpectedly came face to face with no one else there. I said, 'If you want to finish it. Get a gun, I'll get mine, and come back to Zim, in the bush. Pick a date, we'll both get dropped off at a certain place, and we'll come and find each other and we'll sort this out once and for all.' He turned around and walked away.

That meeting never took place. I've moved on since then and I hope he has too. I don't know where he is and I don't have any aspirations to try and find him. Wherever he is in the world then good luck to him.

However, I don't forgive Vincent and I certainly don't feel sorry for him. But after all these years I do try and understand the chaos and avarice that culminated in him emptying my bank account and then wreaking his terrible vengeance upon me.

When I was discharged from the military I went straight into football. They say that nothing ever matches the adrenaline and thrill of playing in front of 40,000 people every week, but those that believe that have never been in the jungle with opposition soldiers wanting to take your life. When you fight a war like I did danger is omnipresent; if you take the wrong step or if you let your concentration lapse then you are dead. In football if you make a mistake – and I sometimes did – there is always next week or next season. In the jungle there are no second chances.

Nothing could ever replace that thrill of war or the camaraderie of having men living through the same extreme circumstances, but football at least filled some of the void. I went from one extreme place to another. Without it taking up my life I have no doubt that I'd have struggled to adjust to civilian life, that left to dwell on my experiences I would probably have suffered from some form of post-traumatic stress disorder. In fact I'm certain I wouldn't be here today without something so all-consuming to take my mind off the war days. Any free time we had during the war was spent under a haze of marijuana or alcohol. You just wanted to get smashed so that you could forget. I was lucky that I had sport to retreat to when the fighting was over.

I have no idea if Vincent suffered from PTSD symptoms, but he certainly struggled to settle down after fighting in the Bush War. I am told that even while still serving in the armed forces he nearly killed himself after overturning a two-and-a-half ton truck while drunk, having driven it down the wrong side of a highway and over the tops of two roundabouts. He walked away needing forty stitches, having lost four teeth and damaged his knee.

After the war he followed his father into the sugar business in Zimbabwe and then South Africa. He worked for a business consultancy in Johannesburg. He returned to Zimbabwe and worked for nine months in the safari business with

Charles Davy. He went from one job to another.

Others who knew him would speak of his grand business promises and even grander spending. 'Vincent was always dreaming, always talking big, talking about millions rather than more realistic sums,' one of his schoolfriends told the *Daily Star* when the allegations first surfaced. In one of his pitches he claimed that he would turn a £15,000 investment into 'a million in no time'.

Then he came to Wales in the late 1980s and worked for a chipboard manufacturer, by his own account a well-paid job with good prospects; but he was unable to stick with that either. His wife left him and he fell out with the company directors. He started his own company, Nationwide Boards, and employed 32 people in the town of Chirk. He was supposedly backed by a Welsh Office grant, but no such grant was ever paid. The company failed to pay its wages before Christmas 1991 and staff members were forced to bang on the door of his flat demanding their money. But it was all to no avail. The company was wound up at Wrexham County Court in April 1992 with debts of £200,000.

It was then that Vincent started pursuing the safari dream again. He was, my QC Rodney Klevan said, a 'serpent who slithers forward to his riches'. Which is where I came in.

He was bad with money, a spendthrift, extravagantly generous as soon as he had money in his account – usually my money over those years – until it ran out. Even when he was selling stories about me and making thousands at a time, the money was lavished on holidays and gifts for Bernice, but when it ran out he claimed to those who had by then fallen for his ways that he was left without anything to even feed himself with.

At the same time, I wasn't the only victim of his vindictiveness and fantasy. In 1995 he gave a statement to Hampshire Police alleging that Neil Hewlett had captured three poachers on the estate and executed them. The notion was preposterous, another of Vincent's fantasies. We didn't have anything for the poachers to come and shoot: we didn't have rhino, we didn't have buffalo, we didn't have elephants or lions. It was a load of rubbish; embellishment and lies and a waste of everyone's time as well. Hampshire Police liased with Zimbabwean police, who searched the camp. But of course they found nothing, for there was nothing there to find. There never was.

34

From Darkness into Light

THE COURT CASES WERE VERY DAMAGING. THE NEWS COVERAGE fell hard on my girls. My oldest child, Tahli, was in secondary school by then and mature enough to appreciate what the accusations really meant for the family. The long battle left me in some dark places. Ultimately, it resulted in Debbie and me splitting up. Even before the final verdicts, things with Debbie weren't sitting right. I accept that the pressure on her must have been enormous. We separated.

By the end of the case I had taken a job in South Africa as a coach of Supersport United, living with my youngest daughter Olivia, who was at the start of her teenage years. Olivia and I lived in a beautiful place called Dainfern Country Club, a golf estate just outside Johannesburg. I was working in Pretoria, the next city along the motorway. Over that eighteen-month period – whenever I was away with Supersport – Olivia was looked after by a Zimbabwean maid. I also had my cousin Archie living just around the corner.

Debbie would come out and visit us. We had arrived at an amicable agreement over the kids and Tahli remained with her in England. Unfortunately, having signed over more or less everything to Debbie to protect some assets in the process of bankruptcy, Debbie decided to keep what had been given to her. Since 2001, we haven't spoken. It took six years to reach a divorce settlement – another long battle with many hurdles.

I WAS STARTING FROM SCRATCH. I NEEDED TO MAKE MONEY. I wasn't worried about a career. I was worried about having the financial stability to provide for my children as well as myself.

I took a job coaching Hellenic FC in Cape Town. Hellenic was the oldest team in the South African League. They're sadly now defunct and disbanded, because the Greek owner died in an accident. He was from the Hadjidakis family; they owned 711 stores and franchises, around South Africa. Being there was a good experience. I helped out for six months and I saved them from relegation, despite being bottom when I joined with just four points from fourteen games. I won them their fifth point in my first game and we only lost one game in the second half of the season. I even played in goal for the last game of the season, against Kaiser Chiefs and I made history as the oldest player to have played in the top division in South Africa at 44 years of age – a record that got broken in 2013 by the goalie Andre Arendse. However, I had to substitute myself after 20 minutes when I cracked my ribs in a collision.

I felt totally empty, though. Olivia had gone to boarding school in the UK. I drank too much. I slipped deeply into a dark hole, often reflecting on what I was losing. I had gone through a lot. I had been let down. I had let people down. I was feeling sorry for myself. Until the divorce from Debbie had concluded, I didn't feel like I could move on. I was angry.

My fortune changed. My assistant at Hellenic supported Leeds United. They were playing Liverpool and so, one night – having won a game with Hellenic earlier in the day – we went down to a pub called the Kronenberg where they serve German-style beer.

I was sitting on a stool next to the bar when midway through the first half, I felt a tap on my shoulder. I turned around and a beautiful lady was standing there. Jeeez. She was gorgeous. Long, dark, wavy hair, decked out in Western Province rugby attire – scarf, hat, top. She said, 'You're in my seat. And what is that on the screen? That's not the national sport of South Africa.' And she shouted at the barman, 'Hey, what the hell is this?'

The barman pointed at me, 'Don't you know who that is?'

She shook her head and ordered, 'Get the rugby on!'

I looked at her and said, 'I'm sorry, I didn't see your name on the seat and the table, otherwise I wouldn't have sat here. Never mind, I'll take my stuff.' And I went to the other end of the bar while she and her friend sat down.

The seafood platter arrived, and unbeknown to me my assistant didn't like seafood. He ate the fish, but the prawns and mussels he didn't touch. It was a huge platter for two; I couldn't eat all of it, so I went back to the table to the girls. I said,

'I'm very sorry for upsetting you, but I'm going to be leaving now and I'd like to offer you this half of the platter.' They looked at each other and nodded yes.

They were both interns in Groote Schuur Hospital. Wavy-haired Karen was an anaesthetist and her friend Robin was a gynaecologist. They were not working for that much money as interns so they loved the good seafood. I said to Karen, 'I'd like to take your telephone number; I'm going to England now and I'll be back next week, and I know that your rugby team is going to be playing here next week and I'd like to come here and watch it with you, and pay for a meal.' She wrote her number down.

Returning from the UK the next weekend, I was quite excited, and I rang her up and arranged for a time and place for me to pick her up for the game the next day. I got the address, picked her up and we went to watch the rugby.

I've always said I fell in love with Karen's mind. She's incredibly bright. I know she was in a dark place as well when we first met; she had lost both her dad and her boyfriend through illness.

I went around the world – to Kuala Lumpur and Bangkok to play for the Liverpool Legends – and found out that she was graduating from medical school, and her mother Sylvia couldn't get to Durban for the graduation. So I flew from Bangkok all the way to Durban and I was there for her graduation as a surprise – and our relationship started from there.

Meeting Karen saved me from destruction. At that time I was living from pay cheque to pay cheque. I didn't have a home; I didn't have anything material. But Karen's support helped me focus on what was important. We both brought ourselves out of the dark into some light.

No meaningful relationship runs in a straight line. For a while, Karen and I decided that our separate lives made it impossible to continue seeing each other. I invested all of my energies in an anti-malaria programme. I had suffered a particularly nasty bout in South Africa after I had naively stopped taking medication to protect myself from the illness. My cousin Archie had taken me to hospital after I started suffering from malarial symptoms, which are similar to having a heavy flu, but the blood tests repeatedly came up negative. Only for the intervention of a quick thinking Afrikaans nurse, who got my blood flowing by making me run up and down the hospital stairs before taking another test, saw the infection detected and treated just in time. Another 24 hours and I believe I would have died. Grateful for my escape, I teamed up with the company of a friend of mine that produce and sell malaria protection to tell people about my experience and to give them a little education.

In 2004 I went to East London, South Africa, to meet Sturu Pasiya, the chairman of Mthatha Bush Bucks. I was still in the middle of a divorce and the feeling of limbo remained. I lived in a two-bedroom apartment complex in an East London suburb where the Gounbie River runs past into the sea. Gonubie is a unique place where you get four seasons in one day. The weather can change from one second to the next, exposed to the big, open Indian Ocean. It gave me a lot of time to think. What type of person am I? Why did my first marriage break down? Why did my new relationship with Karen not work out? What do I do with my life?

All the reflection ultimately ended up being good for me. I made some very good friends in East London, where I worked for a season. Their friendship helped ease me off the bottle, and I slowly got my life back to normal again, as they dragged me out to golf sessions and indulged me in good conversations and good meals. These friends – Abel and Romy Ann Reddy, who I had first met out in Zimbabwe; my divorce lawyer Mike Allam; and Shrek, a big Irish man – were a major reason for my turnaround and for that I am forever grateful.

In 2004 I would move to Manning Rangers, a club based in Durban. We had a game coming up in Cape Town and I decided to call Karen. We hadn't seen each other in six months. We went out for a meal to one of her favourite restaurants, the Cod Father. She told me she had decided to leave Africa and go to the UK to work as a locum and so, after a period where I missed her terribly, I decided to follow her all the way to Leeds, quitting my job in South Africa.

We bought a house in Wakefield. But I was still married to Debbie, who seemed determined to drag things out – making it a challenge for both of us to move on. It was not until the end of 2008 when I finally became a free man. Within a month, I was able to marry Karen in Cape Town. It was just before Christmas and the weather outside was touching forty degrees.

BACK IN THE UK, MY ENGAGEMENTS ON THE AFTER-DINNER speaking circuit meant regular questions about the match-fixing case. It was understandable from the public's point of view. In the end, I decided to tackle the issue head-on by starting discussions around the theme of a brown envelope. There would be quite a few laughs.

Other working opportunities would arrive. Karen had fallen pregnant when I went into *Hell's Kitchen*, the cookery programme. Ten weeks in, Karen found that the baby was healthy. There and then, I decided to leave the show.

Marco Pierre White, the famous chef, sat the participants down and said, 'One of you is going home.' I said, 'Marco I'd like to say something. It will be me going home tonight, irrespective of whether you were going to get me out or not, I'm going home tonight. If it's someone else, I'm giving someone else another chance, because they need this programme and exposure more than I do. There's someone out there that needs me more than you need me. That's my decision.'

Expecting a baby, we looked at which countries would be the best to raise a child and we chose Canada. We wanted to go somewhere where the schooling was good. Canada is a safe place. While my nomadic background meant I was used to moving around and found it no problem, Karen had a beautiful place in Hout Bay, Cape Town. We could have lived there but in cold analysis, we knew Hout Bay was close to some of the township. At night, you could hear gunshots. I had lived in Hout Bay while coaching Hellenic and one evening, intruders climbed over my fence, threatened me with a gun and took my laptop. We decided on Canada.

Fortune took us to Newfoundland, where I played a charity golf tournament and liked the place so much that I decided to visit the hospital the next day to see the head of the anaesthetics department. Recruitments for positions like that were hard in these quite remote areas. As I was sitting there, Karen rang. It felt like a sign we should try the area.

Newfoundland is half the size of the UK and has the population of Edinburgh. There is a lot of space and ten million moose.

Karen was heavily pregnant over in Canada and I was finishing up on the after-dinner circuit in the UK when she fell into labour. It's fair to say I'd had a lot to drink in Port Talbot when my phone rang just as I was about to take to the stage. The subsequent journey involved a swift sobering-up process through numerous cups of coffee, a police escort to the Welsh border, a sleep in Heathrow's Terminal Two car park, a flight across the Atlantic to Nova Scotia, another flight to Deer Lake, and a taxi ride to the hospital.

I got dressed quickly, walked in, held Karen's hand, and about two minutes later, Rotém arrived. I was so close to missing this moment. At 51, I was a father again. Typically, the sequence of events had been chaotic.

I WAS RELIEVED TO LEAVE SOUTH AFRICAN FOOTBALL, WHERE match-fixing was a problem. Before one game in a Rustenburg hotel, I remember hearing a knock on the door. Three men were looking at me and one said, 'Hello coach, how are you? We're the officials for tomorrow.'

'Yes?'

They said, 'Well, we're here for our envelope.'

I looked at him and spat out, 'Envelope? You can eff off!'

I closed the door. Then my number two got up and went out, and he returned into the hotel room saying, 'We'll be okay tomorrow.' With the authority from someone higher up than me at the club, he had given the match officials their envelope. I couldn't tell you how much a win costs in South Africa as I didn't see what was inside.

We played the game the next day and were leading 1–0, but ended up losing 2–1. I looked at my assistant after game and said, 'I thought you said it'll be okay?' My assistant turned round to me, 'The other team paid them more.'

✳

IN CANADA, WORK CAME UP AS A GOALKEEPER COACH AT OTTAWA Fury. In 2015 Paul Dalglish, Kenny's son, was appointed as our new head coach after my first sixteen months at Ottawa Fury. I was a little surprised they didn't ask me to have a go, as I had so much more experience than young Dalglish. All of a sudden I was having the son of an old Liverpool hero and my own old boss order us around.

I went back to Liverpool that year and visited the Dalglish's at Christmas. Marina, Kenny's wife, said to me 'I hear you're working with my son. Look after him while over there.' And Kenny turned round saying, 'Marina, Paul will be looking after Bruce.' Dry as hell.

It was great catching up with Kenny and Marina in Ottawa too when they came out to see their son and their grandchildren. They could walk down the street and nobody would recognise them.

It isn't easy to get recognition in Canada for the experience you have gained from English top-flight football and to find the possibilities to exert your influence and pass on your knowhow to the Canadian game. If nobody recognises Kenny

Dalglish, what chance do you have?

Canadian soccer won't improve much until they change their ways. Knowledge is power, I've always said that. My CV has been in at the Canadian Soccer Association for the national coach's position; my CV was in at Ottawa Fury before they became a professional side. I have been available for years, eagerly awaiting an opportunity to help Canadian Soccer develop, but it hasn't arrived.

Discipline and fairness underpinned my management and coaching. I adopted a three-strike rule: three strikes and out. If a player contradicted my instructions tactically or if he made a big mistake, he would have the opportunity to win back a strike by doing something positive. There is a difference between rules and expectations and I would prefer to say that players knew what my expectations were.

My first job in South Africa back in 1999 had been with Seven Stars, a club from Cape Town which I took from the relegation zone to a fourth-place finish. I saw what happened next as a missed opportunity because Mamelodi Sundowns of Pretoria were one of the biggest clubs in the country and they wanted me on a three-year contract, only to renege on an agreement and give the job instead to Clemens Westerhof, a very experienced Dutch coach. The next job offer, in 1999, I had was for Supersport in Pretoria. They were 15th in the League, going nowhere. I took them to 8th in half a season. The next season we climbed to 3rd in the League, and we played in the African Cup Winners' Cup all over Africa, in Libya and Mozambique. Instead, at Supersport, I hit a few problems – specifically after finding out one of our youngest star players was a little bit older than we thought and, having asked the authorities on his behalf to clarify his birth-date, discovered that the club was less willing to tell the truth than me. My relationship with the club deteriorated from there and like with the situation at Mamelodi Sundowns, it ended up in a court case that I won, this time for the equivalent of constructive dismissal.

Being in court as regularly as I was limited my options when it came to employment. With my knowledge and passion for football, I have no doubt I could have been so much further ahead in my managing career without these harmful experiences. Match fixing and subsequent court cases have robbed me of better opportunities. Those people making decisions at the club relate my name to negative things and conclude that I am not trustworthy and therefore not worth the chance because I would end up disappointing them. I still meet people who have stigmas about me. Then, at the end of the evening they might confess, 'Oh, you're not a bad chap.'

There would be other jobs at other clubs and gradually, my passions and focus would shift from management into coaching. This is where I see my future and a role where I feel perfectly suited to. As a former goalkeeper that has played at a high level, I appreciate that goalkeepers are individuals and therefore, training should consider the needs of the goalkeeper as well as the team in front of him – and the opposition. My general advice of all goalkeepers is, always concentrate on what the ball is doing from a shot rather than the player.

My dream job would be to coach Liverpool's goalkeepers, a department where there have been problems for several years, though maybe now those problems have seemingly been solved with the purchase of Alisson Becker for a huge fee. I would love to work there not only because of my emotional attachment to the club but also because I think I'd be able to have an impact by providing different experience and a different voice. I am not alone in wondering why the two goalkeepers before Alisson have struggled to meet the unique expectations of the club and made mistakes at vital times. When the same thing happens at the same place you analyse what links them and here, that person is the coach, John Achterberg, someone who is incredibly qualified when it comes to coaching badges but not necessarily when it comes to playing experience. Ultimately, there is a big difference between playing for Tranmere Rovers as he did and Liverpool and so, I wonder whether sometimes he is able to place himself in the position of the person he is trying to teach.

35

The Dream Team

IN 1985, BOBBY ROBSON CAME TO MEET ME. HE WAS THE ENGLAND manager and the World Cup was being held in Mexico the following year. I had a British passport for the first time. 'Do you want to play for England?' Mr Robson asked. 'I don't think I can,' I replied. He said, 'Well, we'll see.'

I had been disowned by Zimbabwe. My first autobiography had been released a few months before. The Zimbabwean government under Robert Mugabe had read it and they were unimpressed. I did not know this until I tried to renew my Zimbabwean passport in London.

It might sound outrageous but greeting me there that day was Comrade Mudede. My stick had captured him in the Honde Valley during the Bush War in 1976. He would later escape after the police Land Rover transporting him hit a small landmine which was strong enough to blow open the doors.

Nearly ten years later, Mudede was working as the Zimbabwean attaché in London. He called me inside his private office and said, 'Bruce, you're wanting your passport. But you have upset us.'

'What do you mean?'

From his desk, he pulled out a copy of my book, *More Than Somewhat*. Throughout the book, I had referred to the rebels as terrorists and guerrillas.

He had the relevant pages highlighted. He said, 'There are so many pages that we were disappointed with, because you used the term guerrillas and terrorists, but we weren't, we were freedom fighters. If you had changed all these words to freedom fighters and comrades, then we would have renewed your passport. So unfortunately you are not going to get your passport back.'

I said, 'Well, I'm sorry; that's what we were told to call you from the other side in the war; that was the way we were drummed.'

This was also part of Mugabe and his party ZANU-PF's way of pegging post-colonial power into the country after its first democratic election in 1980, where they forbade citizens to have two different passports and made them pledge loyalty to the new country. This was an attempt to force the small white population with British backgrounds to choose sides – and, indeed, to get rid of some.

Since then, I had been dependent on my South African passport to get into England and so this presented me with a problem. In essence I became a man with no country. I went back to Liverpool and told the club that I had no passport. Liverpool then went through the process of applying for my British passport, because I was already married to a British subject, and I'd been there for the required time.

At Bobby Robson's request, the FA went to FIFA and asked whether I could switch nationalities, considering Zimbabwe didn't want me and England did – now that I was effectively a displaced person. FIFA replied with an emphatic rejection. Had I been a cricketer or a rugby player, I don't think this would have been a problem. There have been countless cases before and since.

Maybe it was for the best in the end. As much as playing in a World Cup had been a big dream of mine – even though I was shut out of Zimbabwe and lost my passport; even though I was not able to play for my country during my peak years – Zimbabwe is my home and always will be.

Representing Zimbabwe made me very proud. I will never forget how I was welcomed home after signing for Vancouver Whitecaps, where I was only the reserve goalkeeper. The national-team manager John Rugg was there at the airport, along with Sunday Marimo, the captain. There were Rhodesian army friends and old teammates from my days at Salisbury Callies. There were many supporters too. They had followed my development in Canada, as if I had made a big international breakthrough.

PLAYING FOR ZIMBABWE PRESENTED PROBLEMS AND RISK. I WAS travelling further than anyone else to play for my country and this meant air fares and accomodation expenses. I was not a wealthy man before joining Liverpool but I was determined to play for Zimbabwe. This meant paying for travel and then claiming it back – even though I didn't really have the money. I lived off the charity of friends and relatives in order to make it happen.

Before one game much later against Cameroon, ZIFA had promised me $2,000 but then they refused to pay me. It was my decision to pull out of the national team on the spot.

The squad was shocked to hear this and the whole team threatened to leave if I wasn't paid within 24 hours. It didn't take long for the ZIFA president, John Madzima, and treasurer, Michael Mbomba, to meet me, and they gave me $200 for the next game coming up and more promises of more money. I realised the odds were small that I would ever get the refunds and the salary I was promised, but I admired the players and the coaches so much that I didn't want to let them and the supporters down.

It is fair to say that later, Liverpool did not like me playing for Zimbabwe. By flying to and from Africa, I was risking my future. Joe Fagan had a problem with it and it certainly built massive tension between me and Graeme Souness when he became manager. Quite simply, the people at Liverpool thought Zimbabwe was a distraction not worth focusing on. They wanted my attention to be absolutely on Liverpool and didn't like the idea of me flying halfway around the world by way of preparation for a First Division game.

An example of the attitude at Anfield centred around one game for Zimbabwe against Egypt.

I was desperate to help Zimbabwe reach the World Cup. In 1984, Liverpool were league champions and European champions. Zimbabwe were playing a qualifying game against Egypt, and little did I know this would be the last appearance for my country in eight years.

The international calendar in Africa didn't follow European patterns and clubs didn't always get much notice from the different associations involved about the release of players. A situation arose where Liverpool had a game against West Ham United one night and Zimbabwe had a game the following night in Egypt. Liverpool reluctantly allowed me to go to Cairo but only if I flew straight back afterwards. Upon arriving in Cairo just a few hours before the kick-off, having travelled there from Speke via Heathrow, the Egyptian immigration officials wouldn't let me through because of the Israeli stamp on my passport, which had been issued on our trip to the Middle East before the European Cup final in Rome a few months before. At the airport I was met by two Zimbabwean officials who told the immigration officers that no Grobbelaar meant no football match.

What followed in the hotel was the most bizarre team meeting I've ever been involved in. I arrived in a room where most of the players were sitting on the floor. As the only white player, I was given a chair. The president of ZIFA issued a welcoming speech where he then said, 'We will now have a vote to see whether Bruce should play. If any player present feels for any reason that Bruce should not be in the team, he will not play. Reluctantly I was eventually allowed in.'

I couldn't believe it. No hands were raised against me.

Following that episode, we were sent up to the eighth floor to visit the team's witch doctor. We were asked to strip naked and then the doctor rubbed some liquid on our faces, hands and feet.

Then we showered the liquid off and put our kits on while we were still wet. Next up was the treatment of the boots and my gloves. I hadn't had anything to eat for a long time, so I went and had my usual mushroom omelette while the witch doctor was working on my gloves. When I returned, I found out he had rubbed them with some kind of animal flesh, so they were very greasy, which made me wonder whose side the witch doctor really was on. I had to sneak away to clean them before they were usable again.

The black magic must still have worked because we played an incredible game. Egypt scored from a rebound after one of my many saves and though we lost 1–0, with our effort and quality we knew we would have a real chance to beat them at home to get a step closer to the World Cup.

I returned straight after the game as promised, and was on the training field the following day at Melwood. I had been promised I would get any expenses needed for the return game nearly a month later, and it was scheduled for a Sunday afternoon. I had already looked at flight options to get there, flying out immediately after our Saturday game against Sheffield Wednesday. But Fagan said no. We had a European Cup game on the Wednesday against Lech Poznan and he did not want any distractions.

I was crushed by disappointment, but still thought I could manage to sneak out there without anyone noticing, providing all the flights left on time.

My mind was on the important game coming up for Zimbabwe, and I made one of my daftest mistakes as a goalkeeper for Liverpool in the game against Sheffield Wednesday. I ran out of my penalty area to stop a ball from coming through and tried to make a short pass to Alan Kennedy but ended up giving the ball straight to Imre Varadi, who scored easily.

We lost the game thanks to my stupid mistake and I was really angry with myself as I met my friend Gordon Deardon, who was going to take me to the airport to secretly fly out to Harare.

I was only five minutes away from Speke when I realised what I was doing wasn't right towards the club that provided me with a living. I went to the airport and cancelled my flight, then went back to confess and apologise to Joe Fagan. He was calm, but told me if I had gone, I would never have played for Liverpool again. My time in Liverpool could have been over after only three seasons because of my determination to play for Zimbabwe.

Incredibly enough, one of the engines of the aircraft I should have flown on from Gatwick to Harare caught fire, so the flight was heavily delayed. This prompted a letter from ZIFA afterwards saying they were sorry the plane was unable to take off and that they regretted me being unable to travel.

Ultimately, in the return fixture against Egypt, Stix Mutizwa replaced me in goal. Zimbabwe took the lead but Egypt equalised from a free-kick from distance. I do not know if I would have been able to save that particular shot, but normally I would have been very disappointed not to stop a long-range effort. The World Cup dream once again was crushed.

I WONDER HOW MANY MORE GAMES I WOULD HAVE PLAYED IF my passport wasn't taken away from me between 1985 to 1992. Wikipedia says I played 32 games but there were also a lot of unofficial friendly matches, which takes me to a figure close to 50.

Zimbabwe lost me at my peak. Maybe they could have reached the World Cup if they had allowed me to play. In the end, they only invited me back in 1992, largely because of fears I would represent South Africa after the end of apartheid and end up playing against Zimbabwe. It also helped that Reinhard Fabisch had been appointed as the new head coach, and the German made it clear he wanted the best goalkeeper in his team.

Little did ZIFA know that FIFA's ruling was final; I couldn't play for any other country than the one I had already represented in an official FIFA game.

The irony was, while my career as the number one at Liverpool was threatened when Graeme Souness bought David James, I made my comeback at international level following an absence of eight years.

I desperately wanted to help Zimbabwe qualify for the World Cup in the USA.

Nevertheless, it took time to regain my passport and the process was not without its complications. The passport was ultimately delivered only hours before an historic game with South Africa in the Africa Cup of Nations. South Africa had a starting eleven which included black, white and mixed-race South Africans, while by having me in goal, an ex-soldier in a team of black freedom fighters, Zimbabwe showed some diversity in its selction as well. South Africa had players like Lucas Radebe and 'Doctor' Khumalo, while we had Peter Ndlovu and his brother Adam. To win 4–1 was incredible and this gave Zimbabwe some belief that qualification for the World Cup was possible.

We became known as the Dream Team during this qualification process and it's a name that endures nearly 25 years later, even though we did not end up reaching the US. In a key game against Cameroon, it felt like everything went against Zimbabwe and I still question why. For some reason, the match officals decided to rule out what would have been a decisive Zimbabwean goal for offside from a corner, even though Cameroon had two defenders standing on the posts.

DEBBIE AND I WERE SENT AN ETIQUETTE GUIDE ON HOW TO EAT A royal banquet. It included directions on how to handle soup spoons. I was back in Robert Mugabe's good books. In 1992, I was asked by formal invitation to visit Buckingham Palace to dine with the Queen on behalf of Zimbabwe, along with other successful sportspeople from our country. It was Mugabe's hope that my presence would secure respect and investment.

This, of course, was in the period where he had not yet emerged as the dictator which he later became, so I considered it my duty to help. We had encountered each other on a few occasions but his impression of me had been formed through the release of my first autobiography. By 1992, his attitude towards me had relaxed somewhat and when we met at a cricket match between Zimbabwe and India, he was actually quite humorous.

I'd returned to Zimbabwe to play an international match and it coinicided with the cricket, so on an afternoon off, I filled the time on the boundaries eating ice cream. Mugabe was in the posh seats with Alwyn Pichanick and Peter Chingoka, the president and vice-president of Zimbabwe Cricket Union.

I was in a mischievous mood, so I shouted out,

'Alwyn! Mr Pichanick!' He came and looked over the rail. 'You guys want some ice cream up there?' He said, 'Yes,' and I threw the whole box and it landed in Mugabe's lap. He stood up and looked over.

'Oh, it's only our football goalkeeper,' he said to Alwyn with a smile. 'You know, our football is very good in this country; all black, and then that one white man. And here with the cricket you've got all white men and just one African. We must make this cricket team all black with one white man.'

IN 1998 I BECAME CARETAKER PLAYER-COACH OF THE ZIMBABWE national team for five games, winning twice, losing twice and drawing once. The experience exposed me to the sort of corruption that happens in African football and when I tried to challenge what was happening, I soon found myself out of a job.

Leo Mugabe is the nephew of Robert Mugabe and he had emerged as the chairman of ZIFA. When I challenged him about the whereabouts of monies owed to certain players, he did not take kindly to the questions. For a short period, it resulted in my passport being taken away again, though the authorities would give it back when I started working as a coach in South Africa. There was a warped regional logic that said, 'We cannot allow his allegiances to switch to South Africa.'

Mugabe's attitude towards me would shift again. In 2007 he himself would make sure my passport didn't get renewed; after I had been a little too honest, he told me not to come back to Zimbabwe. I had been coaching for a few years in South Africa and was living in Hout Bay with Karen. I got up in the morning and was having a shower when the phone rang. Karen picked up the phone. 'Yes? Hello? Can I speak to Bruce, please, Bruce Grobbelaar?'

'Sorry, he's unavailable at the moment, can I take a message?'

'Young lady, may I speak to Bruce, please?'

'I've just told you, he's unavailable; may I take a message?'

'My name is Robert Mugabe...'

'Well, my name is Tina Turner, have a nice day!'

She put the phone down.

Two minutes later he rang back. 'Young lady, this is Robert Mugabe; my telephone number is...' and he started listing up his phone number and she froze, because 709 in Zimbabwe is the government. When I got out of the shower she said, 'I think we need bullet-proof windows now; I think that that was Robert Mugabe.'

I called him back.

'Your lady is very insubordinate; she doesn't know who she's talking to,' he said.

'Well, she's entitled to her opinion. What can I do for you?'

'Come on, Jungleman; you must come and coach the Warriors.'

'If you pay me in US dollars I will do it.'

'But we've got a problem with the foreign currency.'

And that's when I said the fatal words: 'Yes, because you're stealing it. Every bit of foreign currency coming into the country, you are taking.'

'You can't talk to me like that.'

I said, 'I am, and I will.'

'Young man, I don't like to be spoken to like this. You'd better not come back.' Then he put down the phone.

It would take eleven years for me to be able to go home.

36

Exiled

WHAT A BEAUTIFUL COUNTRY ZIMBABWE IS. HARARE IN SEPTEMBER and October is breathtaking, with jacaranda trees covered in purple flowers framing the roads. They had originally been planted by the *voortrekkers* heading north from Johannesburg to settle. Bulawayo is a different entity with its big, wide boulevards, enough for an oxen cart to turn a full circle. In the Eastern Highlands you have Nyangombe Falls, and Troutbeck where the river flows down and you can fish. Leopard Rock in the Vumba Mountains is a beautiful place with a golf course and spectacular views. Down in the south you get the semi-desert, an arid area where it is very cold at night but boiling hot during the day. Then in the north, the spectacular Victoria Falls is one of the great wonders of the world, where Dr David Livingstone said, 'It looks like the angels have come here to rest.' You also have the Zambezi Valley, which provides some of the best white-water rafting in the world upstream and crocodiles and hippos downstream.

Zimbabwe is a spectacular place, providing fantastic views. It is very green in the summertime but parts can go brown if it doesn't rain much.

The game has dwindled somewhat, but there are still elephants and all the big five. There are wild dogs and jackals but not many rhinos because of the poaching, and again because of the government. Hopefully rhinos may come back now, with a new government in place, if they set up a good breeding programme to save them.

Thirty-seven years of destructive governance by Robert Mugabe has taken its toll. Despite its natural beauty, he has transformed what was the breadbasket of Africa into one of the poorest countries in sub-Saharan Africa. It breaks my heart how he has plundered the land, but luckily there are still many resources within the country, so there is still hope.

Unfortunately a lot of African countries face the same problems. You have the filthy rich and the filthy poor. There isn't much of a middle class, which in my opinion provides the engine in a lot of economies. It is the middle class that fights back when things are not right. The poor in Africa do not have the strength and resources to fight back and your filthy rich just don't care. So it's left up to the middle class, your engine, to keep the economy running. They are the ones that pay the taxes. And unfortunately Zimbabwe is lacking that middle class.

According to the World Health Organisation, Zimbabwe is now one of the poorest countries on the planet, with one of the worst mortality rates. The AIDS epidemic hit the country hard and it is fourth on the list of countries that suffer most from HIV, with 30,000 people dying each year. Only the rich can afford retroviral tablets.

There have been many campaigns that have tried to educate youngsters in schools. But then the government under Mugabe claimed, 'The white man is trying to trick you – if you wear a condom, then our growth rate will go down and then the white people can come back and take over the country again.' Zimbabwe also suffers from malaria, particularly in the jungle and forested areas around its borders. I had suffered myself from the disease while at home in South Africa having been left in a hospital for three days without it being diagnosed. I am still convinced that had a doctor not realised what was happening to me on that third day, I would not be here now.

It explains why I am keen to raise awareness and prevent other people from contracting it. I have worked in programmes covering the whole of Southern Africa in countries like Mozambique, Malawi, Zambia and Botswana trying to encourage a greater understanding of how it can affect you. With me, it lay in wait for two weeks after I'd stopped taking my pills and then it hit me with headaches, nausea and flu-like symptoms. For a lot of people in Zimbabwe in particular, the battle against malaria continues on a daily basis. For any government, combating the disease should be a priority.

MUGABE AMASSED HUGE PERSONAL WEALTH WHILE ZIMBABWE suffered terribly. When he was finally ousted in 2017, the relief was enormous.

Hopefully, many more of the farms he seized will be returned to the people and become productive again, allowing the country to grow stronger. Shortly before this book was released Emmerson Mnangagwa was declared the winner of the latest election and became president. For Zimbabwe, it is crucial that democracy reigns.

I watched Mugabe's downfall from afar. His exit as president meant that finally, following eleven years' exile, I could return. All I needed was a passport. Fortunately, my friend Eddy Madziire is related to Mnangagwa. I spoke to Mnangagwa over the phone, and he said I could return, and with that he added, 'You will get your passport back.'

I tried to keep my expectations low before travelling to Zimbabwe. Prior to my return, I was talking to friends that had just been there. They warned me that Zimbabwe had fallen some distance since my last trip. And yet, I was still excited about seeing my home again. Most of all I was looking forward to the smell of Africa: that tropical, sun-heated, burnt smell; and the sound of the grasshoppers singing at night and the taste of an ice-cold Zambezi beer. I couldn't wait to see the sky at night again. The black sky is never as pretty as the star-packed skies in the bush in the southern part of Africa. It is like a carpet of diamonds. If you lie on your back by a campfire, you can look for shooting stars and you feel like such a small part of the eternity when the African night hangs over you.

I had mixed feelings on my way there, because I didn't know how I was going to be received; my older daughters were very worried about my safety and some of my best friends in South Africa even feared I would be arrested. This is Africa. Anything can happen.

I flew through Johannesburg in South Africa and I was greeted warmly there. It didn't take many minutes from when I picked up my luggage at the airport before some of the drivers in the arrival hall lit up with big smiles, giving me handshakes and saying, 'Welcome back, Jungleman!'

After seeing my cousin Archie and having offloaded some luggage with him, I flew in a small aircraft to Harare, and symbolically enough landed at Robert Gabriel Mugabe International Airport in the morning, after gliding over the green savannahs, with all its massive trees in the warm light from the sunrise.

Walking down the steps into Harare Airport after being away for eleven years was fantastic. I don't think I can ever describe it. I felt home. I got such a warm welcome everywhere. Passengers on the small aircraft from Johannesburg to

Harare recognised me straight away, as well as the ground staff. On the runway walking off the airplane everyone made a big fuss of meeting me, wanting pictures, hugs and handshakes. They said, 'You are home again! Have you returned to help us?'

On the Wednesday morning of 17 January 2018, my life in exile was over. At the passport control I gave the officer my South African passport and he told me to go and buy a visa.

'What visa?' I said.

'I'm Zimbabwean...'

I WAS SCHEDULED TO MEET THE NEW PRESIDENT AFTER ARRIVING back in Zimbabwe. I ended up being sent from one place to the next by different members of his hierarchy. There were phone calls and text messages. 'Go there, wait there, talk to him and him, he will help you.'

Several times, I was instructed to go to the old Sheraton Hotel, now called the Rainbow Towers, a tall glass-façade building, with a long row of flagpoles with various African flags. The main entrance has a red carpet and when you arrive, someone is always there to open the door for you. The hotel is huge and pompously decorated with marble floors and walls. There are golden ceilings and façade work, with a huge winding staircase in the centre of the spacious lobby that takes guests and politicians up and down from meetings.

In the bar, I met the driver of the new president's son. He was very complimentary, saying, 'Oh, you've got to come back, you've got to help us; we can't believe you're back and we're so glad to see you...' The driver then told me, 'The president had to go to Mozambique. He will see you in his home tonight and I will pick you up and take you to him when he is ready.'

This gave me an opportunity to take a trip down memory lane, visiting my old schools and the house we moved into when my mother could afford her own place. This was after my dad left her and before she remarried and moved to Bulawayo. Back then, this area was all white, and there were only white kids in school. Now, you couldn't see any white people.

David Livingstone Primary School opened in 1940. A main entrance with Roman columns in a semicircle greet you on arrival at the white-walled main school building, its name painted in light blue over the main entrance. At the foot of the columns a thick stripe of light blue brings some colour to the building. The school is behind a tall gate, guarded by security staff in uniforms. The school garden at the front is beautifully kept with low bushes and trees cut in round shapes along with red rose bushes in bloom and a few palm trees shooting up from the neatly trimmed lawn.

In my days, 400 students went here; now there are over 1,500 pupils and the space is limited with the chairs and desks being packed into each classroom to fit everyone in. Despite this being a state school, it doesn't get any funding from the government, instead relying on donations and parents' contributions.

I met the school's headmaster, his office full of folders and paperwork. I passed the cabinet in the hallway, displaying trophies won in athletics and netball and a couple of rugby cups. The ladies in the administration warmly greeted me before I walked to the field behind the school – a green patch of grass with football goals that means so much to me. On it the kids in school uniforms were having an athletics day. This was the field where I was discovered as a goalkeeper by Salisbury Callies. This was where it all started. Despite all the smacks I had during my years here for not studying hard enough, I still have such fond memories of this place and all the friendships in school and along the street leading up to the school; the street where I grew up and ran barefoot.

I walked the few metres up the road to my old home. Now my old three-storey home at number 99 has been painted in a peach colour and people have put barriers up to stop anyone from coming in through the verandas. The apartment block is framed by an earth-coloured painted brick wall with an iron fence with pointy spears on top. Inside the fence, the trees have grown tall. On each side of our block, there are other apartment blocks. None of my friends, who I would slide down the pipes outside the houses with, live in this area any more.

I WAS HOPING TO SEE THE PRESIDENT EARLY ENOUGH TO RESOLVE my passport problem with him in time for my return to South Africa the following morning. As the hours went by without me getting a meeting time, I decided to go to the passport and national ID centre to pursue the matter, as they had been sent all my information and details from the consulate in Canada. I had been told I would be able to pick up my passport in Harare.

There were long lines outside the office in the burning heat of the sun. I was taken through some really run-down, long and dark yellow corridors with no windows inside the maze of a place to see the boss himself, Mr Mudede, whom I'd once captured during the war – someone who had rejected my applictions before. Again, I appreciate this might sound far-fetched. On my way to his office, I passed piles of antique typewriters in corners and other junk and old files in areas that looked like prison halls. In the small waiting room outside the chief passport administrator's office was a completely worn-out, beige velvet sofa. The paint on the ceilings was coming off; the place was completely worn out.

When we got to Mudede's office, he was apparently too busy to see me, so I was shown into a colleague's office, and this lady said she couldn't find any files or paperwork from Canada. She asked me for my national ID and I told her I had sent it in with the paperwork from the embassy in Canada. She still insisted she couldn't help me without my national ID, so I had to walk from there empty-handed – the first disappointment after my return home. Getting my passport back was one of my most important goals, but I was still hoping the president himself would be able to pull some strings when we got to meet him.

The second disappointment came that same night. When the president eventually got back from Mozambique, it was so late that we were asked if we could rather meet in the morning. But we were also told to be ready if he got a slot that night, in which case the driver would come and pick us up and take us to his residence.

I had been on standby the whole day, boiling in my good suit. Eventually we got another phone call from the president's son saying his dad had had such a hectic schedule and needed to rest. They would let us know when we could meet him in the morning. Since we were due to fly out the next morning, we paid fees to change our flights to the 7 p.m. departure instead.

Appointments being moved around are the African way. It's how Africa works. Being head of a country is a powerful thing. With that comes money and money is power. In Africa, money is king. If you know that kind of mentality, that's what Africa is about and you have to live a life obeying these rules of waiting. You just don't know what's coming around the next corner.

My personality was shaped by the African system; by this need to be adapting and adjusting. I grew up in it. It's hard and frustrating, but that's how it is. People come from all walks of life and different countries to Africa and they actually get shocked by how the system works.

Growing up in Africa teaches you to become patient. If the head of the country says come now, you come now. If he's busy, well, you can't do anything about it. You just have to wait and see, wait for him to call. And that's exactly what I did.

A PICTURE OF PRESIDENT MNANGAGWA FRAMED IN GOLD WAS hanging over the portal to enter the security check. This was the closest I got to the man in charge. The following day, after postponing our flight back to South Africa, we had been on standby again all morning and afternoon, and eventually we had to give up and leave for the airport.

I had almost reached the gate when I looked at my phone. 'The President wants to see you tonight.' I had to apologise and tell them I had already left for South Africa. It was frustrating.

It was a classical AWA scenario: Africa Wins Again. That's when you are going to Africa for an appointment, and you've got an appointment, and you get let down because that person that you're going to see decides to do something else.

In Africa things happen when there is an opportunity, and unfortunately I didn't get that opportunity. I accept that the president has many responsibilities and that I am not his priority. He is trying to rally troops and to get the best for investors in the country.

Eventually, I would like to return to Zimbabwe and enter politics, focusing on sport and reconciliation. I would not be fazed by the responsibility. Growing up in Africa helped me handle the most difficult times in my life, and there have been many.

I am one of the most decorated football players in Liverpool's history but to reach Anfield, to survive there and thrive, to deal with the subsequent match-fixing allegations; I do not think any of this would have been possible without Africa's presence in my life.

37

Afterword

LOOKING BACK, THINKING ABOUT ALL THE DREAMS I WAS CARRYING as a kid I am happy with what I have conquered in life. I wanted to play for Liverpool and made that dream come true. I wanted to play for my country; I've played for the Dream Team. I wanted to manage my country; I've managed my country five times. But I still dream of taking Zimbabwe to a World Cup before I get too old – I would love a last dance with the Dream Team.

I've eaten with the poor, I've eaten with the working class and I've eaten with royals and many of the world's superstars and leaders; and hopefully I come across the same way to the lowest people as I do to the highest. That's not for me to judge.

The court cases I faced in the 1990s and early-2000s changed how I look at people. It takes a lot more for me to trust others now. I have always thought the best of people in the past unless they proved differently, and some of my closest friends say I have been a little naïve when it comes to trusting those I meet; that some have taken advantage of my generosity or fame. I do not let as many people into my closest circle anymore. It takes a lot for me to be willing to make new close friends. I know the friends that I can trust and those are the people that I will be friends with now.

Friends are like family to me. They say blood is thicker than water; maybe so, but my experience has been that friends can be stronger than family.

Playing for Liverpool and coming back to Liverpool brings me joy, and even through all the turmoil that I've been through, the Reds have been just as supportive as when I was playing. This was so important when I faced such an uneven fight with the newspapers and Crown Prosecution Service; but

I persevered and came out in the end. I landed the curve ball. Or made the most important save, if you like.

One thing that I have learned and which has become apparent to me whilst working on this book is that life isn't a linear journey, it meanders and often goes in circles. Since spending more time in the north west in 2018, I have reignited passionate relationships with friends that have lain dormant for nearly 40 years and it feels like I have completed a circle.

Football gave me my life and gave me my fame, a platform to be who I am – it gave me everything. Through the disappointments and the glory, I would never change anything, because no matter what life has given me, whatever life has tried to take away from me, I have no regrets.

It's your children that will tell you who you are; my three girls might have three different stories about who their father is. It will be up to them to assess what legacy I've created. It is not for me to say. My most important ambition onwards is to look after my kids; Tahli, Olivia and Rotém. Rotém needs her father a lot more than the other two because my eldest are independent and grown up, but they still need their dad. I live for today, but I've also got to live for all my three daughters' futures.

Some of us live in the future, always looking ahead for better days, others dwell in the past. I think I've been living most of my life in the present, especially since going into the army. When I was a youngster I looked at the future, what I was going to do in the future. From active service, I couldn't look to the future. I had to live in the moment of every day, as I didn't know if that day was going to be the last day I'd ever lived.

So that is how I've lived my life – in the moment and in the jungle. Because life is a jungle, a jungle of people, snakes, family, love, war, passion, kids, football clubs, friends, challenges and curve balls. When I came out of the army and became a footballer I could look a little bit to the future, because I got a contract that took me to that time. Within that timeframe I could plan, but I still had to live in the moment. You never know what will happen in life, so every day you go out and enjoy and every day is a bonus.

I believe that we don't have an automatic right here to be on earth. I also believe that there's someone there to look after us. Call it God or something else. I believe that he put the foundation down for how you're going to be on earth. You're only here on borrowed time; you're not going to take anything away with you. It's how you've been on earth, through your life that will determine where you're going to be in the next realm.

They can kill you but they can't kill your soul.

Everybody will be judged one day in his or her life, so it's how you lived your life on this fantastic planet that we live on that matters.

There's a fabulous saying that I heard – the world is a beautiful place; it's only people that mess it up.

I would like to thank everyone I have had the opportunity to come into contact with. I mean everyone: good, indifferent, nasty, ugly or bad. It wouldn't be a life without everyone who has touched my life in even the smallest of ways. Thanks to you all!

Bruce 'Jungleman' Grobbelaar, August 2018

Acknowledgments

FIRST OF ALL AS A GHOSTWRITER I HAVE TO SAY A BIG THANK YOU TO Bruce Grobbelaar for giving me the trust and the honour to capture your fascinating and rich life story. It has been a far from boring year to interview you and travel the world with you, a footballing gypsy and a great friend.

Travelling the world we have met so many of Bruce's friends, as he has good friends everywhere, and the hospitality and generosity have been great across the globe. Big thanks to Phil and Anh Drew in Ottawa including great after dinner questions and cooking lessons; Laurence and Gabriel Sher in Harare for updating us so much on life in Zimbabwe now; Abel Iglesias and Romy Anne Reddy in East London for great content contribution; and Anthony 'Archie' Archer in Johannesburg.

Thank you to the following who helped me stay healthier and sane during the hard work: Gill Branton, Jill Walker, Louise Pearce; my office mates Anthony O'Brien and Lee Chean from Beneficial Marketing; Tara Maguire and her YourYogaStudio, Andrea Cygler, Dennis Murphy, Carrianne Hayden and Gabriela Byrne.

Thank you to contributors to painting a full picture of England's most decorated goalkeeper: Ray Clemence, Ashley Fraser-Evans, Les Steel-Smith, Vernon Vern, Tage and Kamilla Herstad, Hotel TIA, Karen Phillips-Grobbelaar, Neil Hodgson, Silvester Maunganidze, Simon Mignolet, Nkonzo Tzizwe Chikosi, Michael John Allam, Seadon Pereira, Neil Jones, and Graham Duncan at CDP Printing, photographer Tony Woolliscroft (cover and press photos), Tony Morton for inputs, encouragements and transportation, Tahli Grobbelaar for providing pictures and interviews, Olivia Grobbelaar, Bernice Benton, Mary Evans, LFCHistory.net, Terance McPeake for the access of an impressive scrapbook collection, Bob Harris for writing *More than Somewhat* (1985) providing valuable input and capture of early days, Jack Gordon-Brown for editorial help and Megan Pollard at deCoubertin Books for promotion and events, Kate Highfield for wild hours of transcriptions, Simon Hart for proof reading, Leslie Priestley for cover design and typesetting, Jonathan Burd for the index, Christopher Wood for checking and providing facts and proof reading and for wonderful encouragement along the way. Collector Peter Mouat who generously shared the former unknown letter correspondence between Bob Paisley and the Department of Employment.

This book wouldn't have been the same without you all.

But most important – this book wouldn't have been what it is without the immense help of two of England's best sportswriters; Simon Hughes and James Corbett from deCoubertin Books, who have patiently lifted a Norwegian author's debut writing in a foreign language and my first autobiography. Massive gratitude to James Corbett who has also co-written the part about the match-fixing allegations and Bruce's time playing for the other clubs after Liverpool.

Finally a huge thank you to my husband Jostein Ansnes and our kids Elvira and Elias for their patience and support while I wrote away the family summer holiday of 2018 amongst many long days and months in front of the keyboard.

Ragnhild Lund Ansnes, August 2018

Index

www.decoubertin.co.uk